THE GENTLE WAYS OF THE

BEAUTIFUL WOMAN

THE GENTLE WAYS OF THE

BEAUTIFUL WOMAN

A Practical Guide to Spiritual Beauty

Three Bestselling Works Complete in One Volume

Disciplines of the Beautiful Woman

Disciplines of the Heart

Disciplines of the Home

ANNE ORTLUND

Inspirational Press • New York

First Inspirational Press edition published in 1998.

Inspirational Press
A division of BBS Publishing Corporation
386 Park Avenue South
New York, NY 10016

Inspirational Press is a registered trademark of BBS Publishing Corporation.

Published by arrangement with Word Publishing, Inc.

Library of Congress Catalog Card Number: 97-77407
ISBN: 0-88486-199-6

Printed in the United States of America.

CONTENTS

Disciplines
of the
Beautiful
Woman

To the three women I most admire
and who most influence me,
our two daughters and our daughter-in-law,
this book is affectionately dedicated:
Sherry Harrah
Margie McClure
Jani Ortlund

CONTENTS

A.

HOW THIS BOOK GOT STARTED

THE DOCTOR LEANED BACK. "There are lots of cysts in there," he said softly in an Alabama drawl. "You're gonna have to have surgery and get those out."

"Well," I said, "Something like ten years from now? I've got lots to do."

"Those cysts aren't gonna get any smaller," he said patiently.

I mentally shifted gears. "Okay, let's do it and I'll write a book." I could sense a delicious feeling coming over me.

"What does your schedule look like?" he asked.

We figured it out. Ray and I were leaving shortly for a Mediterranean cruise; after that I had a break from conference speaking because of Thanksgiving and Christmas.

"How about right after you get back?" he said.

"Give me a week," I said. "We always get our picture taken the first part of November for Christmas cards."

November 18, then.

So off we went across the Atlantic, with me blowing up balloons thirty times a day—that was to strengthen my lungs or something, I'm not sure what—in Israeli buses, aboard ship, in Grecian restaurants and Turkish spots of biblical interest. . . .

"Friends, this is where Paul heard the call, 'Come over to Macedonia and help us. . . .'"

Bang!

I left pieces of rubber all over the Middle East.

B.

FROM THE HOSPITAL

THIS IS NOVEMBER 20: two days past November 18, which was hysterectomy day for me. (For the last month, since surgery came into view, I've been wondering why "hysterectomy" and "hysterical" seem to have the same root word!)

Now at last my eyes are just beginning to focus; the mountains are beautiful out my window; my bed is rolled up into a sitting position, and I can once more put words on paper. A little. I'll pick at it.

Romans 12:1–2 is wonderful: "I present my body a living sacrifice." How silly to give God only my heart or my allegiance or whatever, and not my body! Certainly it is his to anesthetize, to roll into operating rooms, to poke with needles or fill with pills—to do all or none of these things, as he jolly-well pleases. He is my Lord. I am absolutely relaxed to let him do with my body what he wants.

The night before surgery, the last words I read were these: "May all God's mercies and peace be yours from God our Father and from Jesus Christ our Lord" (Rom 1:7, TLB). I thought about all God's mercies: his loving concern for me, his tenderly watching over me more efficiently even than doctors and machines and charts. I thought about his peace: the sense of well-being he gives, the cocoon-like feeling that his presence imparts. *Father, you're so wonderful. All things work together for good to those who love you.*

One of the disciplines of a godly woman must be the discipline of the mind. We are not free to let our emotions flip and flop all over the place. We are not free to fret and worry if we feel like it, to indulge ourselves in pouting and stewing. That doesn't mean that "blues" aren't permissible; they are. Many of the Psalms are David's laying out his feelings openly before the Lord—his "down" feelings as well as his "up" feelings—but putting them both into God's hands in completely surrendered faith. "Lord, I feel great today; I praise you"; or "Lord, I feel lousy today, but I praise you, anyway." Bad feelings aren't necessarily the result of sin; if I feel down, maybe I just ate something that didn't agree with me.

But *anxiety*—that's something else. Worry is disobedience. The disciplined mind makes no room for doubting God's plans for me. "What if———?" has no place in my thinking. The graph he has plotted for me can include automobile accidents, visits to the zoo, hot chocolate in front of the fire, hysterectomies—it's up to him.

A nurse has come in and given me a red and white Thing to blow into, something to protect my lungs from filling with fluid, so I'm holding it with my left hand and blowing while I write doggedly with my right. Now the nurse is discussing over my head the neighboring patient's needlepoint. I'll give up for now. . . .

. . . Quiet is a blessed gift. In this frantic world how we must cherish every moment of it, and carve it out for ourselves every chance we get. . . .

Before the interruption of the red and white Thing, Brother Lawrence was just about to come into my mind. He said we don't truly know peace in our hearts until pain is as welcome to us as lack of pain. Then the times when we feel no pain won't be marred by apprehension over the future when maybe we *will*. And pain is God's beautiful gift, anyway, to make us lean harder on him, when he knows we need it.

Or pain can simply be the means to that quiet we so long for. I had to laugh over a get-well card I received today:

> It sure isn't easy,
> Just "resting" in bed [Are you kidding? It's gorgeous!]
> When you'd much rather be
> "Up and doing" instead. [Who, me?]
> But relax, take it easy;
> Think of all that you'll do
> When you're up again, out again,
> Feeling like new.

I could say facetiously, "Thanks for reminding me; you just ruined my whole day." No, really, I'm living a very full life right here in bed, two days after surgery. I'm practicing the presence of God; I'm enjoying thoughts of him and all his goodness; and when I'm "up again, out again," I trust my life will be just as full as it is right now—full of him.

God, discipline my mind before you. "Thou wilt keep him in perfect peace, whose mind is stayed on thee: because he trusteth in thee" (Isa. 26:3, KJV). May I relax and cuddle my feminine self in the pink fluffy stuff which is your will for me and my unquestioning obedience to you.

Life has no other soft pillow but that! All else is steep precipices and darkness and sudden new violence. But in you, Lord—in your will, in your presence—*all is well.*

"Therefore my heart is glad, and my glory rejoiceth" and two days after surgery, "my flesh also shall rest in hope" (Ps. 16:9, KJV).

C.

SHIFT FROM ME TO YOU

THERE YOU ARE, a woman—how wonderful! How unique you are, not "made in Japan" but made in your mother's womb. A factory needs plenty of light; God was so smart he could make you perfectly in the dark.

That cowlick of yours, the length of your toes, your upper lip—he made all of you, and you are therefore very special and precious. (I'm unique, too. Children are amazed to see the crack right down the center of my tongue; I've never seen another tongue like it!)

The timing of your life is also unique. This is what Psalm 139 says: Not only are *you* one-of-a-kind, but so is your life. Your particular birth-to-death span was planned by God way beforehand.

Have you become aware of a developing pattern in your personal life? Is there something inside of you like a time-release capsule; every so often does something softly explode within you; are new gifts released, or new interests, or new opportunities?

I'm praying this book will trigger in you a new gentle explosion—or maybe total revolution. Much of this material I've given in women's conferences, and then letters like these come in the mail:

Your talk meant more to me than any I had ever heard. . . . Since that time there have been so many radical changes I can hardly believe it myself.

I really feel one of those books you plan to write should be a combination of your own life experiences and "how-to's."

Well, my life, too, has been a series of time-releases:

At age six, the first explosion. My father and mother surrendered their lives to Jesus Christ, which totally affected their lives and all their children's. At the time Dad was a young Army lieutenant stationed at Fort Benning, Georgia. For the next forty years, including Dad's career as a general, he and Mother taught Bible classes on all the posts where they were ever assigned. Now they've been a year in heaven, but I'm still teaching Bible classes and loving God's Word.

Length of effect of time-release capsule: forever!

At age ten, explosion number two: bang! Mr. Resta, my piano teacher and a great influence in my life, started me writing music.

Effect so far: around 250 songs and pieces, some published and used.

At age twelve: poof! Mr. Addleman, another wise, good man, began teaching me pipe organ.

Effect: an organ major, Bachelor of Music degree, an Associate degree from the American Guild of Organists, and a dozen years as organist on the "Old-Fashioned Revival Hour" radio program.

At age twenty: pow! The Navy arrived at my university, and I met Ray Ortlund. Seventeen days after our first date, on 29 August 1944, I wrote this:

> How glad I am I came your way
> And got acquainted with you, Ray!
> These last few weeks have held such joy;
> I've never known a Christian boy
> Like you before. The Lord's been good
> —of course, just as I knew He would!—
> In time of deepest need, to send
> The fellowship of such a friend. . . .

> *[It was World War II, and my only brother and closest companion, Captain Robert E. Sweet, U.S.A.F., had just been killed when his plane went down. Life was lonely at that moment, deeply lonely—but campus life went on.]*

> Our struggles over poli-sci
> (And even that's been fun with you!)
> The horseback ride—that lovely sky—
> The fun at Soltaus' barbecue,
> The picnic in the park, badminton
> Victories we never scored!—
> The concert at the Bowl, of course
> Our prayer group meetings with the Lord . . .
>   And then today you looked at me.—
>   And such a look! What did you see
>   Within my eyes that lit yours so
>   With such a sweet, disturbing glow?

Dear blue eyes, radiant Christian face,
It may be in the dear Lord's grace
That our two futures hold in store
Just that one look, and nothing more;
But oh, how sweet the memory
Of that one look will always be!
How glad I am I came your way
And got acquainted with you, Ray. . . .

Effect of time-release capsule: thirty-two years of close love, still increasing and bursting occasionally in new mini-releases.

At age thirty-four: The baby-raising period was over; Sherry, Margie, and Bud were eleven, ten, and nine; and I began to be invited to speak here and there.

Continuing effect: lots of conference-speaking.

At age forty-six: pow! A personal spiritual renewal at the Wheaton College revival where Ray was speaker. Since then the fullness has begun to overflow in book-writing.

What other capsules are yet inside of me? I can hardly wait to know! I'm ready, Lord!

What's inside of you, a wonderful, unique woman made by God for very special reasons? He never wastes anything!

And this is the woman's day. Whoever you are—young, old, married, single, mother or not, working woman, housewife—you were never taken more seriously by your world. This is *your* day. I write this book to help you see where you've come from and where you are, to cut away the unnecessary, to release one of God's time-capsules within you.

Several capsules?

1

YOUR FIRST DECISION,
AND WHAT FOLLOWS

THE GREAT MAJORITY of women in this world, not understanding that God has specific plans for their lives, would tell you that they just "take life as it comes." Because their lives have only a horizontal, humanistic dimension, they'd readily agree that they "just live one day at a time." Actually, that's what's known as drifting down the lazy ol' river, man, and it feels so good. . . .

Only it ends up at Niagara Falls.

Oh, my friend, I don't know you, but you're a little bit precious to me because you're reading my book (!), and you're very precious to God because he made you. Maybe these next words don't apply to you at all (I pray they don't!), but consider them, just in case, with all your heart.

Where are you in your life? Upstream, barely aware of the tugging current, thinking you're getting along all right on your own? Or maybe being carried rapidly along, occasionally realizing that you're not in control, but not knowing what to do about it? Or with the roar of disaster in your ears, unable to cope with your anguish and despair?

In any of these cases, listen so carefully. Niagara Falls is described in God's Word like this: "It is appointed for men to die once, and after this comes judgment" (Heb. 9:27).

But at any point in your life, including right now, God's hand is extended tenderly and strongly to lift you out of the canoe and onto solid ground. All you have to do is reach out to him! This is known in the Bible as "salvation," and whether it sounds old-fashioned or not, every living person needs to be saved.

The Apostle Peter told about it like this to some people who needed to be saved:

You no doubt know that Jesus of Nazareth was anointed by God with the Holy Spirit and with power, and he went around doing good and healing all who were possessed by demons, for God was with him.

And we apostles are witnesses of all he did throughout Israel and in Jerusalem, where he was murdered on a cross. But God brought him back to life again three days later. . . . And he sent us to preach the Good News everywhere and to testify that Jesus is ordained of God to be the Judge of all—living and dead. And all the prophets have written about him, saying that everyone who believes in him will have their sins forgiven through his Name (Acts 10:38–43, *TLB*).

One way or another, you have probably heard that story before, but right now take a fresh look at it. (Who knows, maybe your canoe trip is about over.) There are three elements to the story:

1. Jesus died on a cross and rose again the third day from the dead.

2. God has ordained him to be the future judge of all. (That's the Niagara Falls trip for those who don't heed his warning.)

3. Anyone who opens his eyes to the situation is free to reach for his hand: to believe in Jesus Christ and be forgiven of all sins, through the power of his wonderful name.

That's truly simple, isn't it? But if it's that simple, why does anyone hesitate? Because, my friend, it means giving up the canoe! The woman who reaches for Jesus Christ to save her has to disassociate her heart from that picnic lunch and the Saks-Fifth hand-knit sweater and her purse and binoculars and the portable TV—and many hesitate, gripped by paralysis!

But see the situation from a helicopter—from God's point of view, in the light of eternity. What shall it profit if you gain the whole canoe (for a short while) and lose your own soul—forever? While there's still time, reach out your hand to his.

I'm typing with tears in my eyes. Do stop reading, please; let him urge you, himself, and reach for him right now.

Let's presume (and I pray it's really true) that all of us now, I writing and you reading, are safely on the bank. Here's where "cream puff religion"—no strain, no pain—has deceived many, leading new Christians to believe that once they're out of the canoe onto land, they're in heaven! So a few months later when they still have problems, they're disillusioned.

Actually this is the time when we brush ourselves off, set our eyes on that distant City, and start walking. Cross country, woman. Realize what you were saved from, and know that that place is so fabulous it's worth hiking over hills, through thorns, through rivers up to our lip-stick, over cliffs—anything to get there. I pray I'll motivate you up to the point of delirious exhaustion, because that City is worth getting to.

Yes, this is a book about the *disciplines* of getting to Christian matu-rity. There's a great difference between opening our eyes to danger and being helped out of a canoe (just a simple, sensible act) and the subse-quent slogging over miles of life, one step at a time, one decision at a time in choosing our course, suffering anything, and arriving gloriously at our destination.

Now, the amazing thing is that if we're willing to do this we won't end up exhausted old frumps in muddy hiking boots. Through the tears, pain, and fatigue we'll grow into God's beautiful women. We'll arrive at the City with better posture, and looking zingier and lovelier, than when we began.

And the most wonderful part of all, the part that makes the whole process a worthy prelude to heaven, is the discovery that the hand that lifted us out of the canoe will never, never let go. By destination time we will know the warm clasp of those fingers very well, and it would be unthinkable not to be unceasingly conscious of his grip.

So we press on—and press on—and press on! Dear friend, there are so many in this world who are eager-beaver starters, and so few who are glorious finishers! The one thing I fear is that after I've encouraged other women toward Christ I'll stumble myself and fall on my face. I don't want to, oh, I really don't.

But when the Apostle Paul was an "old pro" as a Christian he wrote, "I haven't learned all I should even yet, but I keep working toward that day when I will finally be all that Christ saved me for and wants me to be. No, dear brothers, I am still not all I should be but I am bringing all my energies to bear on this one thing" (Phil. 3:12, 13, TLB).

I came to know the Lord in a Christian home as a little girl, was raised in a great combination of strictness and fun, somehow missed rebelliousness in the teen years, grew up hoping I'd marry a minister and did, raised Christian kids and taught Bible classes and dearly loved the whole local church scene. But after I'd been a pastor's wife maybe twenty years, I began to get thirstier and thirstier for more of God in my life.

I didn't understand what it was I wanted. One time when I'd read Ephesians 3:19, "That you might be filled up to all the fullness of God," I wrote in the margin of my Bible, "How can you put the ocean in a teacup?" What you haven't experienced, you never understand.

I would underline verses like "As the deer pants for water, so I long for You, O God. I thirst for God, the living God. Where can I find him to come and stand before him?" (Ps. 42:1, TLB). And "O God, my God! How I search for you! How I thirst for you in this parched and weary land where there is no water. How I long to find you!" (Ps. 63:1, TLB).

Pretty soon I was absolutely cotton-mouthed.

Ray felt the same—and he was the respected, faithful pastor of a large church. I remember him saying to me at the time, "Anne, you've got to pray for me! I'm so undisciplined! I've got to cut out extra meetings, prune and trim, and give myself more time to get deep in God's Word. I long to be closer to Christ, and I know it takes time. But I want more of Jesus!"

In that same period of time, which was building around our lives the way those wonderful beach waves build around your body before they crest, twenty-one-year-old Bud happened to be home from college. I was about to speak somewhere and I said, "What shall I say, Bud?"

He said, "Mother, tell them only Jesus satisfies—not a suburban house, not color TV, not a station wagon and a sexy wife. No trip satisfies, only the Lord."

Then he spread out his hands on the table before me and said, "That's what I want. The way the planets revolve around the sun, I want my life to revolve around him. I want him absolutely central."

I can remember looking out the window, and thinking how Sherry and Margie, our two collegian daughters, felt exactly the way Bud felt. And I remembered Isaiah 44: "I will give you abundant water for your thirst and for your parched fields. And I will pour out my Spirit and my blessings on your children. They shall thrive like watered grass, like willows on a river bank. 'I am the Lord's,' they'll proudly say" (Isa. 44:3–5, TLB).

It's six years later, the six best years yet for Ray and me. The Lord has truly overflowed in all our lives. The three older children are all in the ministry, and our little eleven-year-old adopted tadpole-son, Nels, is coming along fine in his own happy-go-lucky way.

What have I learned in these last six years? That Spirit-motivated *disciplines* facilitate the Christian walk. Oh, I'm not discounting all the warm feelings along the route, when I've sung Jesus-songs and held hands and the rest. But our sensuous age forgets that feelings come and feelings leave you, but the disciplines of life are what get you to where you want to go.

Do you feel as if your life is like a jammed closet, and you keep muttering now and then, "Some day I'm going to get organized"? Well, I'm not all the way there yet, but let me share with you what I've learned—woman to woman.

2

RESHAPING YOUR LIFE
TO THREE PRIORITIES

WHEN A SCULPTOR STARTS to shape a human form from a huge lump of clay, he doesn't detail the eyes and cheekbones first. He works with the large masses, attempts to get the head proportioned to the body, to set the direction of the trunk, and so on.

As you consider your whole lifestyle, you've got to think about what your top priorities are going to be, before you decide what time you're going to get up in the morning. Let's deal with the large mass of your life first, and I want to suggest to you three priorities that can't be circumvented,[1] though they may gouge and rudely disfigure your present life-form before you get things rearranged.

God first!

You're criticizing me. I can feel it: "Too vague, too theoretical." "HODE IT, HODE IT," as our Nels says. (That's a carryover from baby talk and it's now a family expression.) Wait a minute; don't prejudge.

"Seek first His kingdom and His righteousness, and all these [other] things shall be added to you" says the Bible (Matt. 6:33). We're to be seekers after Jesus, first. Everything else must flow out of the first. And really first! Top of the list in our lives! "The old saying of 'putting first things first' is not quite good enough. The New Testament makes it evident that the 'first' of which it speaks is a singular and not a plural; 'putting the first *thing* first' would be the only proper statement of the matter. . . . Anything else that might be taken out of 'all the rest' and set up as 'first' inevitably will result in doublemindedness rather than a single focus."[2]

---

[1] See Raymond C. Ortlund, *Lord, Make My Life a Miracle!* (Glendale, Cal.: Regal Books, 1975).

[2] Vernard Eller, *The Simple Life* (Grand Rapids, Mich.: Eerdmans Pub. Co., 1973), p. 21.

Don't think of yourself first as a wife or a single person or a mother or a worker in some field; you will some day stand before God all by yourself.

Says Proverbs 9:12, "If you are wise, you are wise for yourself, and if you scoff, you alone will bear it." Shed all relationships, all functions from your thinking, and consider yourself first as a woman. What will God have you be and do? He will not say at the Judgment, "I excuse you from this or that because your husband didn't cooperate," or "I understand that you didn't have time to know my Word because of your job. . . ." No one, nothing must keep you from putting God first in your life. You would have all eternity to be sorry.

We must all know intellectually and experientially that God is first. He must be our lives—in a class all by himself. Everything in our lives must converge at that one point: Christ. That's the only way we'll become integrated, focused, whole women. Jesus said, "Any kingdom divided against itself is laid waste; and any city or house divided against itself shall not stand" (Matt. 12:25). Are you divided against yourself?

The words of an anthem I wrote say it this way:

> How single, God, are You—how whole!
> One Source are You, one Way, one Goal.
> I tend to splinter all apart
> With fractured mind, divided heart;
> Oh, integrate my wand'ring maze
> To one highway of love and praise.
>
> O single, mast'ring Life of peace
> At Whose command the ragings cease,
> Keep calling to me "Peace, be still,"
> To redirect my scattered will.
> Keep gath'ring back my heart to You.
> Keep cent'ring all I am and do.
>
> O focused Spot of holy ground,
> Silence which is the Source of sound,
> I drop the clutter from my soul,
> Reorganized by Your control;
> Then single, whole, before Your throne,
> I give myself to You alone.[3]

I've been learning that functioning as a pastor's wife, as *Ray's* wife, or speaking, teaching, composing, writing, mothering—none of the good things in my life dare be a substitute for the best. God can have no competition in your heart, or in mine.

Are you saying, "I'm really afraid of total surrender; I've got so many dreams and plans, and I'm not sure what would happen to them if I give myself totally to God"?

The first Queen Elizabeth asked a man to go abroad for her on business.

"I sincerely wish I could, but I can't," said the man. "My business is very demanding. It would really suffer if I left."

"Sir," replied the Queen, "if you will attend to *my* business, I will take care of *your* business."

Work out the implications in your own life of putting God first. That's what this book is to help you do.

If we feel overworked and someone tells us to take a rest—that's temporary. If he tells us to go on a vacation, we'll come back afterward to the same old rat race. If he tells us to go to God, we've found a permanent solution. We'll be revolutionized. We'll go into our work rested, and remain that way.

"My presence shall go with you," God says, "and I will give you rest" (Exod. 33:14).

Let your heart go to God, then! Go to him, never to go elsewhere again. Settle into him; make him your home. John 15 calls it "abiding" in him—to nestle there, secure as in a strong, eternal fortress.

We were coming home after living for three months in Afghanistan, and in a Vienna hotel I put this idea into poetry:

> From here to there, and then from there to here
> The people of this planet circling roam,
> And I, as well—but, oh, one truth is clear:
> I live in God, and God Himself is Home.
>
> From hither and from thither comes the call,
> Perhaps to places near, perhaps abroad,
> But anywhere I am, and through it all
> My heart's at home—for Home is Sovereign God.
>
> To hurry here, and then to scurry there
> May be the thing that duty asks of me;
> But oh! my heart is tranquil anywhere,
> When God Himself is my Tranquility.

> Yes, in my heart of heart Shekinah dwells—
> The Glorious One, the Highest and the Best;
> And deep within, I hear cathedral bells
> That call me to devotion and to rest.[4]

Dear Christian sister, do we just know God? Or do we really *know* him? The Apostle Paul, a veteran super-Christian, wrote in Philippians 3:8–10, "I count all things to be loss in view of the surpassing value of knowing Christ Jesus my Lord, for whom I have suffered the loss of all things, and count them but rubbish in order . . . that I may know Him, and the power of His resurrection." What did he mean? Let me give you Ray's explanation taken from an unedited tape—just the rough, beautiful way Ray preaches, in pure Rayortlundese:

> "*. . . That I may know Him, and the power of His resurrection. . . .*" *Now, we* must *know facts about God, but then we must go on—go on, my friend, to the great discovery of God himself, God himself. You see, Paul was a veteran in the faith. He was in jail for Jesus' sake. And yet he pleads that he may know God.*
>
> *Friend, you were built to know God; and as you know him, and you get to know him as God himself, God himself—you come upon an ecstasy for which you were made. The facts about God are important. But God himself, to move into God is that for which you have been constructed.*
>
> "*Get to know God!*" *Paul cried out!*

In our first little church in rural Pennsylvania was a very old woman, the oldest person we had ever seen. Miss Ettie Neal was ninety-seven, and she was permanently in bed from a broken hip. The first time a church elder took her new blond twenty-six-year-old pastor to see her, she looked up and squeaked, "Oh, my! He's just a boy!" And truly, to her he was.

But every week Ray would go to visit Miss Ettie, and he would sit by her bed and take her bony hand in his (when she's 97 and the guy's 26, it's all right), and he would read the Bible and pray with her.

One day—now, think of this—Miss Ettie told Ray that when she was a little girl she'd gone to Washington, D.C., and had shaken hands with President Abraham Lincoln! Maybe some of you readers want to look

---

[4] © Copyright 1972 Anne Ortlund. Used by permission.

up my husband and shake the hand that shook the hand that shook the hand. . . .

Now, if someone from, say, Burma, said to me, "Do you know Abraham Lincoln?" I would say, "Certainly! He was one of our American presidents, at the time of our Civil War," and so on. But I don't know Abraham Lincoln as did Miss Ettie Neal.

And Miss Ettie didn't know Abraham Lincoln as did young Tad Lincoln, who could burst through his White House study doors any time, and climb up on those bony knees and be the recipient of his wisdom and love.

Do you see what I mean? We can know God, or we can come to *know God,* and it makes all the difference in the world. If you set yourself to really come to know him, you'll be a rare person indeed. This is what separates the winners from the fool-around-ers: setting your face toward truly making God the number one priority of your life.

How do we do this? Let me suggest four ways; his Spirit will teach you many more.

First, practice his presence. Jesus did! He said, "Do you not believe that I am in the Father, and the Father is in Me?" (John 14:10). Yes, Jesus was special; he was part of the Trinity; but he tells us also to abide in him! So we get our clues from Jesus: when we abide continually in the Father, the words that we speak won't be spoken on our own initiative; the Father within us will do the works.

Live your life consciously before him, moment by moment. Trust him to help you do it. Psalm 16:8 says, "I have set the Lord continually before me; because He is at my right hand, I will not be shaken."

Second, jealously guard a daily quiet time spent alone with God. Jesus did! He sent the multitudes away—and prayed (Matt. 14:23). When our three babies were age 2½, 1½, and brand new, I found my days were just one succession of bottles and diapers, and I got desperate for times with the Lord! Normally I sleep like a rock, but I said, "Lord, if you'll help me, I'll meet you from two to three A.M." I kept my tryst with him until the schedule lightened; I didn't die; and I'm not sorry I did it. Everybody has twenty-four hours. We can soak ourselves in prayer, in his Word, in himself, if we really want to.

Third, seek the Lord in occasional longer hunks of time. Jesus did! In Luke 6:12 he spent an entire night in prayer, because he felt the need—he, the Son of God! How much more do we need these extended times with God? Ray and I take one day a month, usually, to go out of town and pray, think, check our schedules, evaluate where we've been, see where we're going, discuss how we're doing as a wife, as a husband. The time is all too short!

And fourth, be diligent in your attendance of public worship.[5] Jesus was! Luke 4:16 says that *as was His custom,* He entered the synagogue on the Sabbath" (emphasis mine). Certainly the Son of God wasn't going to church "for what he would get out of it." Maybe it was often less than the best. He went because he pleased the Father in all things. Be committed to public worship of God every week whether you feel like it or not, whether the preaching is great or isn't! We go for what *God* gets out of it. He wants us to be there, not via television or radio, but personally with the Body of Christ (Heb. 10:25).

The second highest priority of your life must be commitment to this very Body. That's one reason why you must never fail to worship with them. Your physical family is precious, but they are temporary—for this world only. Your spiritual family is eternal. There is much we haven't learned yet about how to function as spiritual fathers and mothers, brothers and sisters, single aunts and uncles, and daughters and sons, and we're the poorer for it. This doesn't put down that precious, unique physical family of yours; it simply raises in your thinking the level of the spiritual family! A deep prayer life with, and accountability to, some close members of the spiritual family can help make your relationship with your physical family what it ought to be.

There's a lot of talk these days which pits the church against the family—a cruel thing to do, like trying to make two friends into enemies. This kind of talk makes the church the spanking boy every time, implying that it's "spiritual" to refuse to usher, sing in the choir or teach a Sunday School class, so that we can sit home with our families in front of the television with our feet up and munch corn chips.

There is dangerous, twisted thinking here. Let me tell you about my friend Bruce's family of schnauzers. We paid a visit when mamma schnauzer had her puppies. The whole family of them were in a play-pen in the kitchen. That enclosure was their whole world, and those tiny pups snuggled to their mother for warmth, food, love—everything they needed.

They had no idea that they were totally dependent on a larger family, a human family—Bruce and June and their children—who were (under God) the ultimate source of the provision of all their needs.

Do you have a physical family? Then snuggle close together and enjoy the warmth, food, and love hopefully provided there. But recognize that your true source of godly love, warmth, nourishment, and togetherness should come from the larger family, the eternal family. Look carefully at the emphasis of the New Testament epistles, God's

[5] See Anne Ortlund, *Up with Worship* (Glendale, Cal.: Regal Books, 1975).

directions for us in this church age. They tell us to use our gifts to nourish the Body of Christ, and draw our nourishment from the Body, so that all the adult singles, young people without Christian parents, and marrieds without Christian spouses will feel just as cared for and loved and nourished as anyone else in God's beautiful forever-family. And when we're loved and fed and prayed for there, our lacks and needs in our physical family relationships will be wonderfully met.

Paul knew what it was to hold the family of God the highest of all human relationships. He wrote to the Philippians, "It is only right for me to feel this way about you all, because I have you in my heart. . . . God is my witness, how I long for you all with the affection of Christ Jesus. And this I pray, that your love may abound still more and more" (Phil. 1:7–9).

"Oh, boy!" we think. "Those Philippians must have been so lovable, so adorable, so wonderful—not like the Christians in *my* church!" Then we get over to chapter four and find that Euodia and Syntyche were fighting. These were good women, who were both workers for the Lord, and Paul pled with the church to find some go-between to reconcile them and keep the church from splitting apart.

Yes, the early Christians were just like us latter Christians, with all the same temptations and weaknesses, and if we're going to love each other with a true "Priority Two" kind of love, it means struggling over a threshold of pain to get there.

Gilbert Tennent was pastor of a Presbyterian church in Philadelphia around 1750, and he had the fun of pastoring a church made up almost entirely of spiritual babies saved during the "Great Awakening," a spiritual revival that swept the American colonies in the middle of the century. One of his sermons was called "Brotherly Love Recommended by the Argument of the Love of God." (We'd never title a sermon that now, because it wouldn't fit on our bulletin boards.) But Tennent knew that the need of new Christians—all Christians—is to love each other. Here's what he told them, not in 1750 Philadelphia talk which we wouldn't understand too well, but a Ray Ortlund paraphrase—again rough, unedited, right off the tape:

> He urged his congregation to love each other, and love each other to the end. He said that when you begin to love each other, you come at a certain place—oh, hear me, my friends—you come at a certain place when you discover the real truth.
>
> And in every one of our lives there's a can of worms. Believe you me! There's a skeleton in the closet of every life here. And you see, we can be known, or we can be willing to know, up to that

point. That's it. That's safe—but that's superficial. But, he says,
you must love right in through that painful area, right in through
that painful point, love right on to the end. Refuse to let go,
though you know everything about that person. Refuse to let go.
He says fragile love will love up to a point—and that's not worth
anything. That's what most Christians experience. But there are
those who are willing to know and willing to be known, to the
point where they go crashing right on through that threshold of
pain, to where they really know and are known.

That, my friend—not a cup of coffee—is real Christian fellowship.
Whatever church God has guided you to, whoever your Christian family is, get your heart together with theirs! Guard your unity! Attend to
them, love them, care for them! Help them, strengthen them in God,
teach them, be taught by them. And every time you're confronted by an
area of painful difference, crash through!

Judy and I were in a small group of four together—meeting weekly,
praying over the phone several times a week, being committed to each
other at close range. Judy and I had a difference, and I guess we knew
that sometime it would have to surface: Judy speaks in tongues, and I
don't.

It came out one day while I was having lunch at her house, just the
two of us. It became a two-hour lunch, with voices raised and interruptions—there was probably more heat than light! Bible pages were
flipped and verses stabbed at, both of us trying to make our points.
Finally we were hugging each other and crying, reiterating our commitment to each other through it all. And since that luncheon, there's
been as much tension between Judy and me over our differing spiritual
gifts as between two sisters in a home where one has the gift of cooking
and the other prefers to sew.[6]

The third priority of our lives, after God and his people, must be the
needy people of our world. We musn't turn them off! A "God-bless-us-
four-no-more" kind of life will soon make us introverted and provincial.
The beautiful woman of Proverbs 31 "extends her hand to the poor;
and she stretches out her hands to the needy" (v. 20).

Most people admire philanthropy, missions, and witnessing—but
they leave them to the super people on whom they look with not a little
awe and reverence. That's ridiculous! There are people all around us in
deep trouble and desperately floundering, and they would welcome us

[6] For more on relationships with fellow believers, see chapter 13.

as angels if we lent them some money, told them about Jesus, or met whatever their need happens to be.

We know this, then why don't we act? Because if you're like me, I'm naturally—well, "chicken" is the word. I need a group of Christians to whom I'm regularly accountable, to whom I can lay out the needs of those around me, and who will be responsible for seeing that I act.

One day in the beauty parlor I sat down as usual under the hair dryer and was approached by a cute redhead.

"Hi," she said, "I'm Barbara. Your manicurist quit last week, and I'm taking over her patrons."

"Hello, Barbara," I said, and five minutes later she was sharing that her husband had left her, that she was afraid of being at home alone at night, that the children all thought it was her fault and not his—soon tears were falling all over my nail polish.

"Barbara," I said, "do you go to church?"

"No," she said. "And if I don't get my head together soon something terrible is going to happen."

"Would you go with me next Sunday?"

"Of course!"

I screwed up my courage. "Would you go to an adult Sunday School class, too?"

"Sure," she said, "I'll do anything!"

This was so easy, I decided to shoot the works.

"Barbara," I said, "if you really want the whole treatment, you need to do a third thing, too."

"Whatever you say," said Barbara.

"Well, you need to go to Sunday School, and you need to go to church, and then afterward you need to just hang around!"

Do you know all the wonderful things that can happen to the churchgoers who hang around afterward? The ones who bolt for the parking lot miss half the goodies. I'm thankful for my heritage of being raised by parents who were the last to leave the church, Sunday morning and Sunday evening! Even a newcomer can find her way into the hearts of the people if she'll hang around!

Through the weeks Barbara followed the one-two-three formula, and there was also an invisible foundation being laid under what was happening that she knew nothing about. Every week my group of sisters would ask, "What can we pray for, for Barbara? What's happening in your relationship with her? Are you having effective conversations with her about the Lord?" And then they'd pray—with me and for me.

Well, that kind of prodding from the rear is what any Christian needs who doesn't naturally have the gift of evangelism. And so it wasn't surprising that several months later, sitting beside me in church, Barbara confessed her faith in Jesus Christ as her Savior. (Ya-hoo! Three cheers! Fireworks in heaven!)

But do you see how the three priorities must be in that order, and then how they flow into each other? Priority One must come before Priority Two. Unless we are rich in God and in his Word, our spiritual lives will be thin and we will have nothing of eternal significance to contribute to our fellow Christians. And Priority Two must come before Priority Three. Unless we are close in with our fellow Christians, the chances are we'll have little or no success in effectively reaching our world around us—maybe even our own families—for Christ.

The three priorities are such a practical part of my life now that they even affect my daily list of things to do. Often I come to a point in the day when I have choices: what's most important of the things left to be done?

I check off Priority One: have I had my daily time with God? No? Then that's next; everything else can wait. At the very least, it calls me back to an awareness of him.

I check off Priority Two: which of the remaining items on the list affect my brothers and sisters in Christ? I do them next.

I check off Priority Three: What of these items concerns my work in this world, my witness to it? They come next.

If I'm guided in my "to do" list by these three priorities, then the important takes precedence over the urgent. That's so necessary! If we live always doing the urgent, we spend our time responding to alarm bells and racing to put out fires. Ten years later we'll feel totally impoverished, because over the long haul the seemingly urgent is seldom important.

Take a good look at your life. Whatever kind of woman you are— wife, mother, career woman, single parent—have you got your priorities in order? Are you building a life of eternal consequences?

If not, like a good sculptor, you need to do some strong, radical gouging and reshaping to start making the large mass of your remaining life what you—and God—want it to be.

3

YOUR ATTITUDE
TOWARD WORK

YOU WOULDN'T BELIEVE where I'm writing these words.

"Try me," you say.

All right. I'm sitting on a puffy plum and purple couch in a nook of the Royal Hawaiian Hotel in Honolulu. To my right is a huge brass bowl of pink double hibiscus and purple orchids in giant star-bursts— the total arrangement a breathtaking fifteen feet tall and twelve feet wide. In front of me, beyond the magenta Monarch Room, I see an outrigger canoe mounting the waves of Waikiki. The sounds: surf, giggling swimmers, birdsong, quiet talk.

Ray and Nels and I are here in Hawaii for a month. We've done the sight-seeing before; this time we're in one spot, being quiet—reading, resting, praying, writing, playing.

"What a life," you say.

Indeed. What a life! But this month in Hawaii comes after work to the point of physical exhaustion.

It's been six months since surgery. The first two months I really rested and slept! But somehow, in the four months following, I've been speaker for nine Bible conferences, taught twenty-five Bible classes and had some other single speaking dates, written ten hymns and anthems, worked on this book, counseled, run the home and entertained for Jesus' sake, gone to church meetings; I've mothered Nels, played with Ray, and traveled from Los Angeles to Washington, D.C., San Francisco, Chicago, Birmingham, and San Diego. Two weeks ago I had a checkup, and my weight had slid down two more pounds.

"You're abusing your body," said Dr. Stewart.

(I must say I'd never thought of it. What I'd done I've been Spirit-gifted to do, which made it joyous work.)

But God is so kind! At that point he'd arranged a month of dead stop in Hawaii. This first week we've slept ten or more hours a day, and the pounds are going back on. . . .

I think of Paul's life:

"Are they servants of Christ?" he wrote of others, "I more so; in far more labors, in far more imprisonments, beaten times without number, often in danger of death" (2 Cor. 11:23).

"Where was Paul's Hawaii?" I ask myself. And he comforted the Hebrews, "You have not yet resisted to the point of shedding blood" (Heb. 12:4)—as Paul himself had.

Never do we see in the Bible the notion of "Now, be careful; don't overdo; take it easy." Somehow you and I do that very easily without being told.

But God puts a high level of value on work—all work, and especially eternal work: "Therefore, my beloved brethren, be steadfast, immovable, always abounding in the work of the Lord, knowing that your toil is not in vain in the Lord" (1 Cor. 15:58).

Payday is coming! What is the labor of this little life by comparison? Remember the example of Epaphroditus! Paul wrote about him to the Philippians: "Receive him in the Lord with all joy, and hold men like him in high regard; because he came close to death for the work of Christ, risking his life to complete what was deficient in your service to me" (Phil. 2:29–30).

There is no hint here that Paul ever rebuked him or tried to get him to slow down; there's nothing but commendation!

Obviously he was doing high-quality work; I want to make sure that my so-called Christian work isn't just shuffling papers, more or less. But to spend your precious years connecting people with God, influencing them toward heaven by every means we can think of—for this, my friend, don't mind getting totally, gloriously exhausted. We have only a few short years to earn our rewards, and then all eternity to enjoy them.

Let's think about so-called secular work.

You may be a single working woman—like Lydia, a dealer in expensive fabrics (Acts 16:14–15). Or you may be a working wife—like Priscilla, who made tents with her husband (Acts 18:2–3). Or you may preside over the running of a home—like Mary, John Mark's mother (Acts 12:12). All three became spiritually powerful women, and all three were certainly in God's will in their chosen vocations.

But I hope you work, one way or another, and God has plenty to say about work. There are twenty-eight Proverbs on the glory or the benefits of hard work! Interestingly enough, many couple it with having money; some don't. But consider these:

> Lazy men are soon poor; hard workers get rich (Prov. 10:4, TLB).

Work hard and become a leader; be lazy and never succeed (Prov. 12:24, TLB).

Lazy people want much but get little, while the diligent are prospering (Prov. 13:4, TLB).

If you won't plow in the cold, you won't eat in the harvest (Prov. 20:4, TLB).

The lazy man is full of excuses. "I can't go to work," he says. "If I go outside I might meet a lion in the street and be killed!" (Prov. 22:13, TLB).

Here's one that Solomon didn't write down, but could have: "The industrious spider gets a large web."

Hard work never hurt anybody. It's only a bad attitude toward work that causes the gears to grind, the tensions to mount. That's why our work done in God's will should only bring physical fatigue—from which rest will bounce us back—but not emotional or spiritual fatigue.

The world's supposedly oldest person, a Russian Caucasian man whose unproved age was 168, died recently. This fellow, Sirali Mislimdv, attributed his long life to constant work, mountain air, and moderate eating! According to the *Los Angeles Times* he chopped wood regularly, and on his last birthday worked all day in his garden, besides taking his usual half-mile walk.

The point is to see that work is God's plan for you. If you're exhausted emotionally and/or spiritually, check these points:

1. Have you rearranged your life to make God first—living in his presence and allowing plenty of time for worship, thanksgiving, his Word, and asking him about things?

2. Have you settled into the best church available, and made your fellow believers second in your life? Are you especially loving a few of them at such close range, in a "small group," so that you can exchange your joys and burdens and needs, get counsel from them, and be held accountable to them?

3. Have you a plan for reaching those around you for Christ? Are you giving yourself away to the physical and spiritual needs of others?

These three priorities, in this order, will probably give you all the spiritual and emotional stamina you need. But if you say "yes" to these three and your job still exhausts you, you may be in the wrong job.

Work is God's plan for us, so we must find the work that best suits our gifts. We will probably shift in our lives from one type of work to another; that's good. Circumstances may cause this, or maybe those time-capsules going off inside, opening up new interests and gifts.

But don't necessarily connect work and money! If you live on an inheritance or are supported by a husband, you still need to work without pay. The world is so needy! Give yourself away. Or maybe you have no income, and you still feel called to work without salary. Fine!

The source of your money is never your job. If it were and you lost your job, you might have a nervous collapse. No, the source of your money is God. He owns it all; he distributes it as he pleases; and he has promised over and over to take care of the physical needs of every one of his children.

I know a fellow who felt that God was calling him to go to seminary full time to be trained for the ministry. But he has a wife and two small children. He didn't see how he could go to school full time and minister to his family and work at a job as well; neither did he feel his wife should leave the children and go to work. School and family were higher priorities than a job, so he simply trusted God as his source of supply and started in to school. Through a continuous series of unexpected supplies, he's finished his first year of seminary with his needs cared for, and no debts.

God is always our source! Now, from tending the garden of Eden on, people have always been given important, meaningful things to do in life. These things are his will for us, and they may or may not cover our physical needs in reimbursement. Never mind. We're still to do them with all our hearts. Even Jesus said, "My food is to do the will of Him Who sent Me" (John 4:34)—and his own needs in turn were met.

But the life of faith demands that we *do his will first*—before we concern ourselves with supply. That is, before we concern ourselves with supply of money, physical energy, time, or any other need. In the Christian life it's not "seeing is believing"; it's "believing is seeing." *First* seek "His kingdom, and His righteousness," and *after that* "all these things shall be added to you" (Matt. 6:33).

In July of 1975 I got a real test of my willingness to do his will and expect him to supply time for me. What I'm talking about is not saying "yes" to every good thing that comes along; the overwilling person soon becomes the goat! Sometimes I've been that—although my more natural tendency is to be lazy. But this time God seemed to have legitimately called me to do more things than I had time to do.

I was up to my ears in writing, speaking, church work, counseling, composing, mothering, being available to Ray—and our church went into the "Evangelism Explosion" program.

"Anne," Ray said to me, "I'd really like you to get in on the ground floor of this to make sure it fits our church philosophy."

E.E. is a wonderful program, but it's a lot of hours every week of memorizing, visitation, and so on. I began to feel that the top of my head was ready to pop, but Ray had asked me—my loving, caring Ray—so I said yes. I wasn't sure how I'd manage it.

With the first week of the program came the news that our church organist was resigning. Whenever I'm needed I always fill in—and practicing for services is an extra seven hours a week, minimum. Suddenly I thought my head was going to pop for sure.

But almost immediately a lady emerged out of nowhere who said to me, "Anne, I would think that you must be a very busy person. I'd count it a privilege if you'd let me finance a part-time maid for you. How many hours could you use one?"

By the following week—and ever since—a dear woman, conscientious and capable, has worked for me four half-days a week—shopping, running errands, cleaning and cooking, washing and ironing. She prays for me as she does it; she knows she's contributing to ministry; she brings me cups of tea or an encouraging word. The house shines, and my work load is exactly matched to my capacity. "Come to Me," says Jesus, "all who are weary and heavy laden, and I will give you rest. Take My yoke upon you and learn from Me, for I am gentle and humble in heart; and you shall find rest for your souls. For My yoke is easy, and My load is light" (Matt. 11:28–30).

Don't think the moral of this story is that every woman who serves Christ gets a trip to Hawaii and a maid. I only know that when we work in obedience to him, saying yes unreservedly before we see how, he will make it right. He will make it up to us in a thousand secret, delightful ways.

And we will learn to rest as we work. We will feel exhilarated, challenged, pushed along by the work he has given us to do.

Some have called this "The Age of the Great Goof-Off," when people want more and more money for less and less work. Dear Christian woman, see the glory of productivity. May part of the way you represent Christ in this world be your reputation for hard work!

"Walk in a manner worthy of the Lord," says Colossians 1:10, "to please Him in all respects, bearing fruit in every good work and increasing in the knowledge of God."

4

YOUR LOOKS

GOD FORBID that anybody but my husband should see me the way I look when I first get out of bed. (He loves me very much.) Some women are just naturally gorgeous. Our daughter-in-law Jani is as beautiful when she steps out of the Pacific Ocean surf as when she steps out of her house for an evening date. Nels says it's because she's part Indian.

But me? For one thing, I haven't any eyes. I mean they just don't seem to be there until a little eye shadow makes them emerge into view.

Maybe it's because of my own particular handicaps, but my advice to all is: when you first become conscious in the morning, get decent. I know some people say have your devotions first, but don't you sort of feel sorry for God when daily he has to face all those millions of hair curlers and old robes? What if *you* were the Almighty, and got prayed to with words spoken through all those unbrushed teeth? It seems to me like the ultimate test of grace.

I look over the day's calendar briefly, next warm up a little and then stair-climb (the world's fastest way to keep in shape, I guess), then shower and put on my face while I'm beginning to talk to God. (I'm just starting to get alert.) Hair next and clothes, and then I'm ready for breakfast, meeting God, and all the day's agenda.

Am I affected by the visual more than most people? Maybe you're like me: you feel better about it all when your person is groomed and your bedroom is groomed, so you do both as quickly as possible. Babies and small children can interrupt, so you don't have a nervous breakdown if you have to go to Plan B, but you know that over the course of your lifetime this is the way it will normally be: first you, then your bed; and then the stage is set to meet God and the beautiful new day.

How little God talks to us in his Word about care of the body! So I don't want to overdo it, either. I suppose all of us women would like to

do what Esther did. She got to spend a whole year of her life beautify-
ing herself: six months with creams and oils and then six months with
perfumes and cosmetics. Zowee! And this was God's plan for her—to
sweep King Ahasuerus off his feet and rescue her people the Jews.

Still, it's certainly God's plan for you and me that we both influence
and rescue! How are your elbows, knees, heels? Are you creaming your
shoulders, face, chest, arms, and hands, the parts of you that probably
get the most sun? How are your hips, thighs, tummy? Do you need to
get into that jogging suit and run? How is your hair? Does it have a
good cut, and is it clean and healthy? What kind of program are you on
to stretch, bend, and stay supple; to stand tall; to be a good advertise-
ment of God's wonderful care of his children?

The first Psalm describes how we should be:

> He will be like a tree firmly planted by streams of water
> [having a hidden source of continual nourishment],
> Which yields its fruit in its season
> [ready constantly to give out to others],
> And its leaf does not wither
> [no sagging, no drying up, ever];
> And in whatever he does, he prospers.

The ninety-second Psalm carries the thought further:

> They will still yield fruit in old age
> [There's no spiritual menopause, friends!];
> They shall be full of sap and very green
> [young-minded, bendable, pliable, vigorous],
> To declare that the Lord is upright.

That's the reason to look good! God's children, when compared with
the children of darkness, should declare without a word that God is
good. Daniel did it. He and his friends were in a hostile, pagan land.
They said, "Look, let us take care of our bodies by our God's standards,
and then you judge for yourselves." "And at the end of ten days their
appearance seemed better" (Dan. 1:15). Hooray for Jehovah!

Once I was studying Proverbs 31, the description of a "worthy
woman," and it struck me in a new light. I noticed that twenty-two
verses describe this woman's kindness, godliness, hard work, loving relationships—and only one verse out of the twenty-two describes how she
looked. But she looked simply great! Verse twenty-two says, "She makes

coverings for herself; her clothing is fine linen and purple." Purple was the fabric of the wealthy.

Seeing this kind of proportion in Proverbs 31—one verse out of twenty-two describes her good looks—I prayed, "Father, I want to give 1/22 of my time to making myself as outwardly beautiful as I can; and I want to give all the rest of my time, 21/22 of my life, to becoming wise, kind, godly, hard-working, and the rest."

I don't mean that this should be a pattern for any other woman; this is simply the pact that I made personally with the Lord. What it means is that out of every twenty-four hours I give a little over one hour to my looks.

Most of that hour is first thing in the morning. I exercise; I shower; I put on my face, do my hair, and dress. Later in the day I may quickly repair my face and re-dress. At bedtime I exercise again, shower, and slather on body cream. (Before Laney the maid, I allowed only forty-five minutes a day and didn't exercise at night; that left me time to keep the clothes washed, ironed, dry cleaned, and mended. Ray has always polished the shoes on Saturday nights.)

This leaves me just time to get my hair and nails done weekly—and practically no time for shopping. Then that's when God takes over in miracles for me. (Giving God your time is like giving him your money. Give him so much that unless he comes through for you, you can't manage. Then watch your life become a miracle life.)

I'm almost never in stores. A while back I needed two new street-length dresses for church and speaking, and I had about twenty minutes of time.

"Please, Lord, help me," I said, and headed for a Pasadena store that sells purple, if you know what I mean. On the rack inside the door were two dresses, my size, my style, my color, both originally $120 apiece and reduced several times to $45 each! I slipped into them, slipped out, paid my money and left the clerk open-mouthed. And I've felt so comfortable and so right in them ever since!

If I'm out of time and out of money both, someone may give me my need. God will always keep me clothed! And I have the fun of passing on good-looking things to my Christian sisters, too. Love in the Body! It's what life is all about.

But there's another side to this coin. I have promised God to give 1/22 of my time to my looks; if I gave less than that I'd get seedy fast. Before God, as the Old Testament priests sacrificed daily and always kept fire on the altar, I offer him that "one hour plus" of caring for the body. It's for you, Lord.

Concerning that morning ritual: almost all the time goes for exercising, showering, and doing my face and hair. I need something over five minutes to actually dress. You ask how so fast? *Because I have so few clothes to choose from.*

This is part of my religion! I keep my closet stripped down:

4 dressy, street-length outfits

4 long casual outfits

6 day pants

5 day dresses

2 sandal dresses

3 at-home outfits

3 evening and party outfits.

Now, this may be an entirely different kind of wardrobe than you need. Wardrobe should be determined by ministry. Do you know what I mean? Not ministry in the narrow sense of being part of the clergy, but ministry in the broad sense of being put by God into your piece of the world, to live for him and bring your own kind of people around you to know him. I know a beautiful couple at the beach whose only wardrobe is jeans. They love people to Jesus in their jeans and bring them to church in their jeans. Your lifestyle for him will determine your wardrobe.

Then everything in the closet should be ready to grab. Hanging there means it's ready. When something is dirty, it gets washed or cleaned; when it's ripped, it gets mended. When something becomes unnecessary or just so-so, give it away.

The world is so needy! All around the globe are women who have so little! And yet they are just as feminine as we are, with the same longings to be pretty. I have bent down and stooped into a thatched hut deep in the jungles of South America and seen a cotton print dress hanging inside, the joy of that little primitive, pudding-bag-shaped woman. Someone she will never see had parted with it, and through missionaries bearing the love of Jesus, it came to her.

Oh, women! It is just wicked to cram and stuff our closets and drawers with things we seldom wear or don't need to wear! Continually get rid of them! Maybe you'll give your nicest to your best friend; it may look better on her than on you! But keep giving and giving! Keep stripped down! In your wardrobe as well as in the rest of your life, "eliminate and concentrate."

Now, when I buy a dress or a pants outfit or whatever, I don't just buy that alone. I make sure at the time I have everything it needs: shoes, bag, jewelry, underthings, scarf, whatever. I stand before a full-length mirror when it's new and check the whole effect. I jot that complete outfit in my notebook: everything is listed to complete the ensemble. Then it's ready to go. I never have to dawdle over "Does this blouse go with this skirt?" "What beads would look good with this neckline?" I know the whole outfit, and I can fall into it fast and get on to life's more important considerations.

This may sound expensive—but I have one more guiding principle to share. Everyone has a skin color which makes a certain family of colors exactly right for her. Maybe you're a pink, baby blue, lavender, mint green, navy woman. Maybe you're a black, white, red, kelly green, sharp yellow person.

I'm a brown girl: my Bible is brown, my notebook is brown, and all the shoes and handbags I own range from chocolate through the browns to creamy white. Then when I buy a dress (avocado or orange or turquoise or gold or whatever), I probably already have all the accessories I need to go with it. Traveling is easy; I already coordinate. And I can more easily stay stripped down to the minimum.

Here is a little extra hint, a fast and easy one. Every night dump your purse onto your bed. Throw out the gum wrappers, file the receipts or whatever. Then return the minimum contents.

You've noticed my using the words "eliminate and concentrate." I think they're two words that are a key to good living.

You want to manage your time? You eliminate clutter and concentrate on your goals. You want to disciple? You eliminate crowds and concentrate on a few people.

You want to keep a sharp wardrobe, before the Lord Jesus? Eliminate the unnecessary, concentrate on a few "right" outfits in one color scheme.

My goal here is to look really "together," really "kept," in the least possible time; to look "quality" on the least possible money; for 1/22 of my time and concentration to be a woman "clothed in fine linen and purple," and to use 21/22 of my concentration and time to be like this:

> The heart of her husband trusts in her. . . .
> Strength and dignity are her clothing,
> And she smiles at the future.
> She opens her mouth in wisdom,

And the teaching of kindness is on her tongue.
She looks well to the ways of her household,
And does not eat the bread of idleness. . . .
Charm is deceitful, and beauty is vain,
But a woman who fears the Lord, she shall be praised.

Sometimes before I speak to groups I pray, "O dear Lord! Cause my heart for you to be twenty-one times more obvious to these women than how I look. Keep the proportions of my life like the woman in Proverbs!"

And I've been praying, "Father, if it's all the same to you, please let this chapter on looks be only 1/22 the length of this book!"

5

YOUR GOALS

"I HAVE A DREAM," said Martin Luther King. Everyone has to have a dream, to get any place. My dream for right now is to get this book written and blow the mind of every woman living in the Western world. What's yours?

A dream is a precious, exciting thing that carries you forward from day to day; a goal down the way that keeps you on the straight road to get there, looking neither to the right nor to the left; a purpose just for you alone, exhilarating enough to give you momentum for a long time to come.

Every woman has some nebulous thing, enough to make her choose what she chooses. It influences whether she marries or doesn't; gets a job or not; whether she's messy, elegant, too fat, zealously intellectual, sexy, overcautious, organized, deeply spiritual, full of fears—you name it. Something guides us all inside.

Let me put it another way. As I mentioned, last November we were cruising the Mediterranean—160 of us on our hired ship. In the morning all 160 of us would wake up, eat our meals, enjoy each other, go to bed at night, and wake up to another morning. All would seem the same: our shoes were in the same place in the closet; we looked the same to each other. But all was not the same. All 160 of us were in a new place each morning, a different spot in the Mediterranean than we'd ever been before.

So we live our lives. We go through the motions of a day and go to bed at night and wake up to another morning, and we may feel as if we're in the same place. But we're not. We'll never again be where we were yesterday. And we've moved into brand-new, fresh territory.

When we were traveling that Mediterranean, the captain long before had laid out the itinerary. He knew where we were to go each day of the trip, and how to get there. He knew what provisions to take on board before each leg of the journey. He planned ahead, in order not to get caught.

Then, along the way, all kinds of contrary winds and cross currents were trying to take us off-course. The captain had to be continually refocusing, redirecting, recentering us on our destination. Otherwise we wouldn't have ended up in the right place at all.

This is what life-planning is all about. Under that wonderful umbrella of "if God wills," we need to decide where we suspect he'd like us to go. We need to see what provisions are necessary for each leg of the journey, and get them. Then we need to say "no," "no," "no," daily all the rest of our lives to everything that would get us off-course, and keep returning and returning to our personal charts to make sure we're getting there!

Jesus came with the life goal "to seek and to save that which was lost" (Luke 19:10). This gave great pressure and urgency to his decision-making. At one point he even said, "I must journey on today and tomorrow and the next day; for it cannot be that a prophet should perish outside of Jerusalem" (Luke 13:3).

The Apostle Paul knew where he was going; he wrote, "Therefore I run in such a way, as not without aim. . . ." (1 Cor. 9:26). Similarly, Solomon wrote,

> Let your eyes look directly ahead,
> And let your gaze be fixed straight in front of you.
> Watch the path of your feet,
> And all your ways will be established.
> Do not turn to the right nor to the left;
> Turn your foot from evil.
>
> (Prov. 4:25–27)

And again he wrote, "The plans of the diligent lead surely to advantage" (Prov. 21:5).

The first section of my personal notebook is my "goals" section, and I've discovered that my life goals do more than point me in a direction to go; they give me my identity! When you make goals, you discover how you're different from other people; you find out who you are in this world.

I don't open up to you the "goals" section of my notebook easily. When I wrote them—about six years ago—I sincerely thought that they were strictly between God and me, and would always be.

The struggle goes like this: I read that Paul was willing to call himself an open "epistle, . . . read of all men" (2 Cor. 3:2, KJV). I see that he commended the Corinthians for being "followers of the Lord, and of me" (1 Cor. 11:1).

"But, Lord," I say, "I'm no Apostle Paul."

One half of me says that the Word must continually be made flesh—lived out in the lives of people—in order to be authentic.

The other half of me trembles at exposure, at being examined, criticized—and misunderstood.

One half of me says, "Lord, I'm no shining example, but on the other hand, you know I'm no fraud. False modesty would keep me from saying, 'Look, people, following God works!' Fakery would cover your glory at work in one lowly handmaiden. I'm willing to be used, however you want me to be. Be it unto me according to your Word."

The other half of me fears appearing brash, overeager for the spotlight, obnoxious—posing and bowing when nobody's looking or applauding!

Cover me, O Holy Spirit of God; thine be the Kingdom and the power and the glory.

I was starting to tell you about my goals. At the top of the "life goals" page of my notebook I have written "Iguassu Falls" and "Jeremiah 29:11." They go together in my mind!

Jeremiah 29:11 says, " 'I know the plans that I have for you,' declares the Lord, 'plans for welfare and not for calamity to give you a future and a hope.' "

Iguassu Falls, a series of immense waterfalls bordered by Brazil, Paraguay, and Argentina, is where four of us went last August for "rest and recuperation" after ministering as a team in Bolivia. It is glorious, indescribable. We walked for most of an hour facing almost continuous falls. At the end was the inevitable—a souvenir shop, faced with glass and positioned terribly close to a roaring, majestic cascade. But the clerk sat inside as in a little closed box. The glass wall was so dirty, she could see nothing except the trinkets immediately around her.

"Lord," I prayed, "I don't want to spend my life like that! Clean my windows! Give me a long-range view of your glory!"

"I know the plans that I have for you," he was saying to me, "plans for welfare and not for calamity, to give you a future and a hope."

On my "goals" page, under "Iguassu Falls" and "Jeremiah 29:11," I've written "life purposes" and "life goals." They're what I hope to be, what I hope to do, by the time I die. Most are measurable! Why should we have just vague dreams of turning out to "be a good Christian"? But my "life purposes," my "be" goals, may not be all that measurable:

Inwardly, to see self decrease and God increase, as my unpleasant characteristics are crucified and a meek and quiet spirit becomes an altar of worship to give God pleasure.

Outwardly, to leave a mark on others contemporary to me and following me, through my life and my talents, which will point them to God.

You know, the longer I live, the more I realize that all that's important in this life is God, and people, and connecting the former with the latter. I'm willing to shed a lot of things to strive after the Important. Aren't you, really?

There's a comforting verse after these purposes jotted down once as I was praying over them:

> The Lord will accomplish what concerns me;
> Thy loving kindness, O Lord, is everlasting;
> Do not forsake the works of Thy hands.
>
> (Ps. 138:8)

He won't, he won't! You and I are reliant on his mercies.

Following the "life purposes" (what I hope to be), I've written my "life goals" (what I hope to do). I know the words don't make that distinction clear, but allow me some shortcomings. "Give me some slack," as Bud says.

There are six goals, and since I wrote them they haven't changed, although the first one ought to:

1. To bring glory to God in specific ways of pleasing him which I don't yet know how to measure. (Show me, help me, Lord.)

2. To bring glory to Ray as his wife, being a credit to him and making him proud of me, as well as satisfying him personally.

3. To see all four children spiritually settled and fruitful. (Three down and one to go on that one. But eleven-year-old Nels is coming along.)

4. To write three books, each of which will aid the Body of Christ and help us retire without penny-pinching. (Oops! Well, you're getting to know the "whole me." This book is number three of that goal.)[1]

---

[1] Number one was *Up with Worship* (Glendale, Cal.: Regal Books, 1975); number two, coauthored with Ray, was *The Best Half of Life* (Glendale, Cal.: Regal Books, 1976).

5. To write five really successful songs which will greatly bless the church. (I feel I'm only one down and four to go, there. Only "Macedonia" is in world-wide use and in most new hardcover hymnals. There are hundreds more waiting to be discovered!)

6. To serve God together with Ray until we're at least eighty-five—seeing Acts 1:8 fulfilled abundantly.

I hasten to add what follows, Jeremiah 10:23–24:

> I know, O Lord, that a man's way is not in himself;
> Nor is it in a man who walks to direct his steps.
> Correct me, O Lord, but with justice;
> Not with Thy anger, lest Thou bring me to nothing.

I don't deserve a single day, but I must say I want to be like that woman of Proverbs 31:25; she "smiles at the future." "Little old ladies" have been kicked around so long that I'd love to be a way-show-er, an old woman with God's glory on her head who would help change the image.

And I'd love to do it with Ray at my side—an old couple madly in love with the Lord and each other! Why not? I've written beside this, Psalm 61:6: "Thou wilt prolong [my] life; [my] years will be as many generations." But I'm glancing upward: "Only if that's what you had in mind, Lord. . . ."

Acts 1:8, included in that last goal, is a promise God gave Ray years ago—a breathtaking one, to be sure: "You shall receive power when the Holy Spirit has come upon you; and you shall be My witness . . . even to the remotest part of the earth."

He was a young blond preacher at the time who hadn't ministered too far away, but whose heart was totally God's, and the Lord has been wonderfully fulfilling that verse in his life ever since. In meditations on this, I have jotted down Psalm 67:1–2:

> God be gracious to us and bless us,
> And cause His face to shine upon us—
> That Thy way may be known on the earth,
> Thy salvation among all nations.

Keep doing it, Lord! To the dirty places, the very hot and cold places, the places of oppression and discouragement, bring Ray—and me, too, when you will—to cause your way to be known!

What are your life dreams and goals? Have you been at conferences and retreats or had other special moments when you dreamed dreams and saw visions? In your highest moments, what has God said to you?

Get away for a day with him. Recapture those visions, or get fresh new ones. Be courageous to make them specific and large—and all for his glory! And

> May He grant you your heart's desires,
> And fulfill all your counsel!
> We will sing for joy over your victory,
> And in the name of our God we will set up our banners.
> May the Lord fulfill all your petitions

(Ps. 20:4–5).

Page two of my "goals" section records my current one-year goals. You need to do that, too. If you're young and you figure you've got another fifty years to live, you could fool around for forty-nine years, figuring then you could scramble like mad to get everything done.

But only God knows how long you have, and he isn't going to tell. So this next year is a piece of your life, and if you can see a chunk of your life goals come to pass in this coming year, you could begin to say, "Hey, I think I'm going to make it! I think I'm going to be one of the winners!" As Ray says,

> It's hard
> By the yard,
> But a cinch
> By the inch!

The psalmist says it better: "So teach us to number our days, that we may present to Thee a heart of wisdom" (Ps. 90:12).

My aims this year come out of my life goals, of course, but they're divided into the three priorities.[2] I see now what I didn't see when I wrote life goals six years ago, that grouping goals under the three priorities helps me become a balanced, whole person—reaching in correct proportions upward to God and outward to my fellow Christians and to the needy world.

First, I've written Psalms 23:3 and 25:12 from *The Living Bible*; they're great eliminate-and-concentrate verses! "He helps me do what

[2] See chapter 2, "Reshaping Your Life to Three Priorities."

honors him the most." And, "Where is the man who fears the Lord? God will teach him how to choose the best."

Under Priority One:
1. To use ACTS every quiet time. (That's a helpful formula for prayer: Adoration, Confession, Thanksgiving, and Supplication. I desperately need more ACT and less S-S-S-!)
2. To become a woman of prayer, moment by moment; not "stewing" but praying; turning every situation into an opportunity for talking continually with God. (This is a very measurable goal for me. I can make eloquent speeches straightening out my husband, the Board of Trustees, etc.—speeches nobody ever hears, rehearsed when I'm ironing, or when I ought to be sleeping. I can sound so convincing, and every word hits its mark, and when I'm done I'm nothing but frustrated! "Not stewing but praying" is a slogan in my heart this year, to "cast my burdens on the Lord.")
3. To read the *New American Standard Bible* through. (I'm on target: Proverbs finished today, July 5.)
4. To increase my prayer life by:
   a. Praying over goals three times weekly;
   b. Praying over members of each small group[3] three times weekly. (The first year I made one-year goals I found not many got realized. Then it dawned on me that there's nothing magic about writing goals down on a piece of paper! It was only as I brought them back to God over and over that they began to be the true basis of my living and planning and doing.)

Under Priority Two:
1. To support and satisfy Ray in every way possible. (A good marriage, even when you're as much in love as we are, is an unrelenting discipline, to be shored up by constant prayer.)
2. To have prayer and Bible study daily with Nels (I'm not doing too well here. I notice the recent dates on our times together: June 8, 13, 14, 17, 18, 21, 24, 27, July 3 . . . Lord, help me!)
3. To function as a loving, praying sister in Christ to Beulah, Betty, Doris, Peg, Fran, Joan—others, too—the members of my current small groups.

[3] See chapter 9, "Your Closest Relationships."

Under Priority Three:
1. (This one's exciting, and every woman should have something similar.) To lead 6 people to know Christ; to lead 4 to be committed to morning and evening church; to lead 4 to be committed to adult Sunday School; to lead 4 to be committed to small groups; to lead 4 into church membership. (After all, I'm only doing people a favor! And if I say I long to make a mark on people for God, why shouldn't these marks be specific and measurable?)
2. To finish well two books: *The Best Half of Life* (done) and ———— (whatever the title of this will be; the baby doesn't have a name yet).

Well, your goals will be very different from mine — but wonderful! God makes no two flowers or snowflakes or women alike.

But then, you probably need to break down your year goals into something smaller: a quarter? a month? or just a week? When Ray and I go away for our monthly "think days," we evaluate how our year's goals are going and consider what should happen in the next month. Some people I know make out a specific calendar a week at a time, with weekly goals listed. I fear getting to be a "paper person," who is so busy planning there's not much time to realize the plans. Yet, if at any stage of life you feel you're "flying by the seat of your pants," taking each day as it comes without having anticipated it, planned for it, shaped it, and prayed over it, then take time off and get back to poring over your goals. Then you will control your days, instead of letting them control you.

We'll talk about the daily process in the next chapter. It's wonderful, though, how living by goals makes each day — indeed, each hour! — so precious and important. And daily duties get eliminated, streamlined, or become very important in the light of your whole life! Praise God, what fun!

Alexander Whyte, the day before he died, wrote these words: "A life spent in the service of God and communion with Him is the most comfortable and pleasant life that anyone can live in this world."[4]

---

[4] Quoted by William Paul in Keswick "Daily Readings" calendar, 21 February 1976.

6

YOUR DAILY SCHEDULING

OUR FRIEND JACK LA LANNE came bouncing onto the television screen one morning, muscles rippling as usual, and said, pointing his finger at me, "You have twenty-four hours every day to do whatever you want. And you are the sum total of how you use those hours."

I told him, "I know it's true, Jack. You yourself are the visible proof of what you've been doing with your time, and I want to be proof of mine."

Dear fellow-human in this world, our minutes and hours and days are so precious! But they will be largely wasted unless they flow out of predetermined goals and strategies.

"Most people don't think in terms of minutes," says Alan Lakein, president of the only company in America devoted exclusively to time-management. "They waste all the minutes. Nor do they think in terms of their whole life. They operate in the mid-range of hours or days. So they start over again every week, and spend another chunk unrelated to their lifetime goals. They are doing a random walk through life, moving without getting anywhere."[1]

The Los Angeles Herald Examiner had an interesting article recently entitled "Timely Tips for Managing Your Minutes."[2] Most of it was made up of interviews with famous people on how they manage their time.

Executive Fred Harris lives a ten-minute walk from his work in downtown New York. (When Ray's secretary Lorrayne shifted from World Vision to Lake Avenue Congregational Church, she moved from her apartment five minutes from World Vision to an apartment five minutes from the church, although the two are only 30 minutes apart. Some women would have been tempted not to go through the

[1] Jane O'Reilly, "How to Get Control of Your Time (and Your Life)," *New York Magazine*, 17 January 1972.
[2] Ron Scherer, 14 December 1975.

hassle of moving, but in the succeeding years Lorrayne has saved at least sixty minutes every day.)

Christine Beshar and her husband are both lawyers, and they know how to delegate responsibility. Their seventeen-year-old daughter has her own checking account and does most of the food shopping, and two nights a week the children cook dinner.

Laurie Woodruff stacks simultaneous activities: he reads a novel and dries his hair while eating his lunch. (I do the same; for instance, I don't shave my legs, I cream the hair off so I can be studying at the same time.) Barbara Walters echoes, "Like most busy people I do three things at once." Then she adds this cute sentence: "Women must balance their time more than men because they don't have wives."

The point of all this is not to feel driven—although people not under God's authority may well feel that way! The point is to get done as efficiently as possible the necessary mechanics of life, so that you can give yourself to what you really want to do—like getting to know God better, and fulfilling your gifts, and bringing others to know him.

So how are you going to control your time? It probably won't be hard for you to sit down and make a list of bad habits and obvious time leaks.

There is also the trick of never handling a piece of paper twice. Paper shuffling can be a great waster of time! Read your mail with a red pencil; then you'll only reread key items when you answer it. Or act on it immediately and throw it away.

Read a newspaper as you would a page of a history book: read what will be important to the unfolding of world or local history, and skip all the rest.

And keep up to date two things: a calendar and a notebook. The calendar stays at your desk. The notebook is small enough to go with you wherever you go. The calendar is beside the telephone, and appointments get written into it as soon as you make them.

Then the appointments get transferred to your notebook, and if you turn out to be like me, you'll live out of your notebook![3] The first section of my notebook is calendar pages, a page for every day. Here I plot my life: my appointments, the working out of my goals, times for rest, and times proportioned to be with people I love, so that none are missed over a span of time.

The "to do" aspect of my notebook calendar pages is crucial. In the "B.N." years ("Before Notebook"), I wrote lists on scraps of paper—"to do" lists, shopping lists. And then, where did I put that scrap? Or I

[3] See chapter 9.

thought of something I had to do next week, next month, and I just thought, "I'll try to remember."

But now my notebook never leaves me. (I hear former Congresswoman Shirley Chisholm carries a pocket calendar and does the same thing.) Anywhere I am and I think, "Oh, I mustn't forget to do so-and-so," I not only write it in my notebook, but I write it on the day when it should be done. Then it's out of my head and into my notebook. This includes shopping items, things I need to tell people—every reminder I need for living.

I keep about three months' worth of pages ahead in my notebook. I put an arrow by the most important items, to give them first attention. I cross them off as I do them. At the end of a day I rewrite on a future day any that didn't get done—and I throw the old day's page away.

The calendar pages get filled with everything from the crazy to the humdrum to the exotic. Look for a vacuum cleaner. Twice a month, deposit paycheck, write and mail bills. Remind Nels to clean the hamster's cage. 7:30 P.M.: deacons here for dessert. 11:30 A.M.: Fly Northwest Orient to Honolulu. Pray over possible disciples for fall. Three nights in a row, warm oil in my ears! For six weeks the top of every day said "George"; at one of our couples' meetings I'd promised to pray for George every day until a certain deadline.

Last winter sometime, I was driving along in Pasadena and I suddenly thought, "When was the house last checked for termites?" At the stop light I pulled my notebook to me on the car seat and wrote "Termites?" on April 16. (Naturally you can't fork out an unknown sum until after income tax time.) So when April 16 finally came, there was my reminder. The termite people said it had been five years, and yes, we needed a little work.

Beautiful system! Let me list several benefits. First, the pressures are off me to remember things. (Ray says I'm more organized now. I'm really not; my *notebook* is organized, and I do whatever it tells me to.)

Second, my weeks and months are evenly scheduled. My notebook regulates the flow! For instance, I've written in on a day early in November to order Christmas cards. I mark out a few days after Thanksgiving to address the envelopes. Last year when a possible appointment loomed for the first week in December, I'd already written that it was the best time for Christmas shopping, so I didn't take the appointment. I can predict my pace and therefore regulate my pace.

Third, I can see at a glance whether my life is *important* enough! If I make a notebook of my days and the pages are too empty or the lists filled with trivia, I can quickly see that I'm not being a good steward of

God's precious time. Or that I'm not using my gifts, although this is seldom my particular problem.

(Do I come across too smug and sure of myself? You don't know how I can agonize behind the scenes. For instance, I just left this manuscript for a couple of days and then came back to it, approaching it with this lovely, pink-edged image of it in my mind as a spiritual book to draw women everywhere to God; and the first thing I read when I picked it up was "I don't shave my legs, I cream the hair off. . . ."

"Dear God," I gasped, "I must be out of my mind! If you don't help me, this thing will be nothing but repulsive trivia, and I'll be the laughingstock of everyone."

So please be kind enough to sympathize a little with my "backside" feelings.)

Fourth—and this definitely was my problem—my notebook keeps me from time-wasting and the resultant uneven bunching. I don't dare let the days "come as they will." First I'd procrastinate; then I'd be pressured by deadlines.

And fifth, my notebook forces me to put first things first. Oh, dear, important woman in this world, life is so precious and so brief! Perhaps by the time you read this, I'll be gone. That's why God is urging me along to get this book written, so that hundreds of thousands, perhaps millions, of women will get some "handles" on life, to grab hold of quickly and get reshaped, reoriented to life's highest and best. While there's time!

Your life didn't start too well? Let it finish well! That's far better than the reverse.

Eric Hoffer said this wonderful thing:

> The genuine creator creates something that has a life of its own, something that can exist and function without him. This is true not only of the writer, artist, and scientist, but of creators in other fields.
>
> A creative organizer creates an organization that can function well without him. When a genuine leader has done his work his followers will say, "we have done it ourselves," and feel that they can do great things without a great leader.
>
> With the noncreative it is the other way around: in whatever they do, they arrange things so that they themselves become indispensable.[4]

[4] *Reader's Digest*, August 1971. Eric Hoffer is a San Francisco longshoreman and philosopher whose books include *The True Believer* and *First Things, Last Things*.

I say this honestly: God can take me any time. But I pray this book will become a true friend of yours, to steer you and guide you to God, to an integrated life, and to putting first things first.

Start now. Here is a list of things you can do when you're tempted to dawdle—or watch TV indiscriminately:

1. Exercise.

2. Memorize Scripture.

3. Look over your coming calendar, and prepare what to wear.

4. Give yourself a pedicure.

5. Write a list of your blessings.

6. Walk around your house critically: adjust, rearrange, throw out, give away.

7. Cook ahead for the freezer.

8. Cream yourself all over.

9. Read part of an important book.

10. Clean out your cosmetics drawer.

11. Write a letter to an old friend.

12. Do your nails.

13. Weed your garden.

14. Bring your recipe file up to date.

15. Encourage a Christian friend by telephone, someone you don't usually call.

16. Put all those old photos into albums.

17. Take a walk in the park.

18. Nap on a slant board, or with your feet up.

19. Have a prolonged time talking with God: partly on your knees, partly standing with hands raised, partly on your face before him on the floor.

20. Polish the silver.

21. Write a poem (don't be silly; everybody does).

22. Write your pastor an encouraging note.

7

YOUR GROWING LIFE

I'M SITTING BESIDE the yacht basin in Honolulu harbor, and stretched out in front of me are hundreds of yachts bobbing in their slips.

I'm looking at sleek white cabins and fun-colored sails. But when one of these boats puts out to sea, everybody aboard had better be thankful for what I can't see, as well—the keel. Without a good-sized keel the boat would quickly capsize and everybody would be gulping sea water.

The importance of the invisible! This is true of any life as well. If all of our life is visible to others, from the time we get up in the morning until we fall into bed at night, then we'll be as unsteady as a ship with no keel. Indeed, the more of us is invisible, hidden from the world in quiet, in study, in planning, and in prayer, the more effective our visible life will be.

Everybody knows stories of someone who says, "If I have a normal day, I can get by with one hour of planning and quiet with God. But if I have a very busy day, I need at least two or more."

I have to get away from the house for these quiet times. Of course for years I couldn't, when the big children were little. But I could have, sooner than I thought of it; as soon as little Buddy was in kindergarten, I could have slipped away from the house.

In the house I see too much to do! Don't you? I'm having a great time in the Book of Jeremiah and suddenly I think, "Did I take the synthetics out of the dryer?" Or the phone rings. Or somebody's at the door.

When Nels is breakfasted and put off to school, then I go to a quiet corner of a restaurant where I know no one, and there I have breakfast, plan, read, and pray (I write out my prayers).

Or in pretty weather I just park the car somewhere where I'm anonymous, and sit in the car.

Or I go to a secluded couch in the nook of a hotel.

For everyone, God will give a spot. But if you're stuck at home for now, vow not to answer the phone or the doorbell. Turn your chair to the corner of the room if you must. Shut out the world! Jesus called it "entering into your closet" (Matt. 6:6). For you, that may be the bathroom. But the quality of your life will be determined by the amount of time you spend alone with God in reading, praying, and planning.

What makes a wedding an exquisite occasion? Every detail has been thought out and planned, maybe for months. What makes an exquisite life? Everything is thought out and prayed over, behind the scenes, well in advance. Then you're truly ready to live—ready with what to wear, where to go, what to do, what to say, whom to be with, and so on.

Ray's morning quiet time includes praying over his schedule for that day. With date book in hand, he prays over each of his appointments; he prays for the interruptions, the unexpected telephone calls, any unpleasant surprises. As the day goes along he's not easily ruffled, because he says he's already "got it covered." So it is with the godly man in Psalm 112:7: "He will not fear evil tidings; his heart is steadfast, trusting in the Lord." A mother of small children gets a dozen unpleasant surprises a day! She needs time to settle her heart with God and be a growing Christian.

The keel determines the stability of a ship. Our invisible times of quiet determine the stability of our lives.

What are your papers, your magazines, your books? They tell volumes about whether you're a dawdler, like a sheep nibbling on any tuft of grass that comes along, or whether you're going after what's important to you. They represent a quiet part of your life—part of your ship's keel. They should be a reflection of the depths of you.

You have a special interest; what is it? Housekeeping? Ham radio? Dog training? High-diving? Collect books on whatever turns you on; subscribe to a magazine on the subject; find a pen pal with the same interest; clip and file articles. Get to really know what you know!

Eliminate and concentrate! Throw the rest of the clutter away; better yet, recycle the paper stuff and give the old unread books to a library or the Salvation Army. But begin to build a personal library which is truly meaningful to you.

My friend Ginny's first husband was a lawyer whose off-duty interest was the exploration of space. By the time he died, he had collected so many books on the subject that California Institute of Technology, their recipient, called them the world's finest library on the subject and built a building just to house them!

You probably won't do that, but your collection of whatever it is will be a meaningful contribution to somebody someday. Furthermore, it may become a new career for you, a way to earn money after the children are grown, or a job you'll switch to after this one. Who knows?

Most important, every Christian needs to become a specialist in God! Many of your magazines, books, and papers need to feed your spirit. These lives of ours are to get us ready for eternity, you know! So we must "be diligent [or study, as the King James Version says] to present [ourselves] approved to God as [workmen] who [do] not need to be ashamed, handling accurately the word of truth" (2 Tim. 2:15). We need to be knowledgeable women—knowledgeable in doctrine and in Christian world affairs. This world globe has a timetable with it; we need to be alert, discerning the times and living with care.

Submerge as much of your day as you can, to make it your invisible keel, by eliminating less important things. You need time to look into the face of God, time to read and study his Word systematically, time to think and plan for your life, time to praise, time to intercede, time to get wisdom for handling people and for making decisions.

If you're in the years of early housekeeping and small children, you need time for what Pat King calls "backward planning" for each day, time to sit at your kitchen table early in the day and work out the day backwards:

> Let's say the goal this particular Monday morning is order by noon. . . .
>   "The kitchen is the biggest mess of all—it should take an hour. So . . . I must start the kitchen at eleven. The bathroom will take 20 minutes, so I should start it at 10:40. It's going to take fifteen minutes to put away everything in the front room. . . ."[1]

So she hustles through the morning with one eye on the clock, and disciplines herself to stay on schedule. It must work; she has ten children and looks beautiful! And it's true that if you don't have that period of time to think it all through first, you'll forget things, duplicate, backtrack, and spin your wheels.

If you're working outside the home, there is much to pray over and plan for, to balance job and home management and make the precious hours count. And the most healing, productive task you have is just to sit before God, adoring him, communicating with him, enjoying him. That you can't rush!

Part of my personal notebook is for Bible study. Recently, watching a televised Billy Graham Crusade in Lubbock, Texas, I heard the remarkable testimony of the quarterback of the University of Oklahoma's football team. Out of his mouth poured beautiful Scriptures. Then he said

[1] Pat King, *How Do You Find the Time?* (Edmonds, Wash.: Aglow Publications, 1975), p. 79.

it had been his habit since junior high school to study his Bible each day with notebook and pencil in hand. No wonder his mouth and his heart are full of God's truth!

I don't know where I've been all my life, but I didn't start systematically writing during my Bible readings until recently. For preparing to teach Bible classes, yes. But that was for someone else's heart, not mine!

And I must say that over the years I must have forgotten most of the wonderful truths that grabbed me at the moment, because I didn't write them down.

There's value in marking our Bibles, of course; daily I jot down thoughts and cross references in the margins. But I didn't realize, when I started making systematic notes, all the rich material I'd be adding to my store, ready to give out!

If you say you don't know how to study the Bible, don't worry. Just start in! That's why God has given his Holy Spirit to you, to teach you. Amazing what 1 John 2:27 says: "You have no need for any one to teach you; but . . . His anointing teaches you about all things."

Ray's first love and greatest gift, I guess, is preaching God's Word. It's certainly his passion to study the Scriptures correctly and feed his flock a balanced diet of truth. But in all his years he's never sat under expository Bible preaching; seminary helped in many practical ways, but not in learning the Bible; and he's never been to a Bible school.

So where did he learn all he knows—everything which for seventeen years has been broadcast weekly halfway around the world, and taught millions? He's learned it just the way you and I can—from digging on his own. From asking good teachers for suggestions on study books. From reading the book itself, and its marginal notes and cross references. From tracking down word studies in concordances. From praying over it. I know this, because for many years he has let me get out of town with him one day a week and study with him. What a privilege!

And you know what? Whether you're a long-time Bible student or a novice, the Holy Spirit is your personal teacher, and he will grade the material for you! Each time you read it, he'll make it right just for your level of understanding at that time. He's wonderful!

So set aside time each day; have your notebook and pencil ready. Begin with one book or one section, probably something in the New Testament if it's new to you. Note the key thoughts, key words; how the passage fits what's before and after; what you don't understand, to ask somebody; how it can help your life that very day. Dig in!

For the last five years I've read the Bible through each year. (More than once I've sat in our church watch night service on December 31, sneaking in the last few pages of Revelation to get under the wire.) This is quick reading: five pages a day will do it.

You see, there are many ways to study. To study, for instance, a mountain, you can get down on your hands and knees with a magnifying glass and see what kind of worms and bugs it has, whether the soil is sandy or rocky, what kind of plants grow on it. Or you can go up in a helicopter and study the mountain's topography—where its watershed is, its timberline, and so on.

Study your Bible both ways! Sometimes on your hands and knees, examining one verse or one word in detail. Sometimes sweeping through it to see the peaks and valleys. You'll see entirely different things, each way.

What do you do with all this accumulating material? Have a simple file system with a folder marked for each book from Genesis to Revelation. When you finish studying a book or section, drop your notes into the right folder. Gradually you'll acquire a great deal of material, amassed by you personally, on the Book which God wants you to know better than any other. You'll be more and more ready to pass it on to others, which is what he's put you on earth to do. You'll begin to be engrossed in that which is the truly and eternally Important!

Betty is my neighbor across the street. She and Dick both accepted Christ year before last, and they've been two of the fastest growing "spiritual babies" Ray and I have ever had. Recently I discovered why.

Lately Betty's been redoing their large, gracious home, one of Pasadena's loveliest, and she invited me upstairs to see what the decorator had done with her private room for special interests. One section compartmentalized her sewing; another organized her entertaining notebooks, her recipes and menus, her guest lists. . . . And here was her Bible study file. Everything I've taught Betty every Wednesday morning for almost two years, all the notes she'd taken, were filed away in beautiful order, ready to be restudied or to be passed along.

No wonder, then, that recently when Kay, next-door to me, expressed an interest in studying the Bible, Betty was ready to take on her own first disciple, every Friday morning. Kay, the new spiritual baby, is thrilled; Betty, the parent, is thrilled; and I, the spiritual grandparent, am delirious with joy.

Betty's diligent life behind the scenes, the keel of her ship, has made her steady and knowledgeable. This is how 2 Timothy 2:1–2 works out in any woman's life: "Be strong in the grace that is in Christ Jesus, and the things which you have heard from me. . . . these entrust to faithful [people], who will be able to teach others also."

8

YOUR LIFE BEHIND
THE SCENES

WHERE IS THE REAL YOU? It's deep inside of you, where your thinking and deciding really take place. Your life, as Ray says, is like a wheel, with the hub the true center of who you really are. The rim is all the places where your life touches this world, where there's apt to be plenty of friction, heat and dust.

But in the center is the true you. If you have made God your highest priority of all, he is there. You are learning to abide in him, and he in you. There is calm, there is peace. He is your refuge, to which you continually run. He is organization, and living in him you sense control and plan. He is spirit—your living and breathing, your laughter and tears—and all of it becomes holy because his spirit is holy. Wonderful! Alleluia!

If this is true, your mental and emotional life should reflect his presence, whether there's nobody around but you, or kids everywhere: "Whatever is true, . . . honorable, . . . right, . . . pure, . . . lovely, . . . of good repute [or attractive], . . . let your mind dwell on these things" (Phil. 4:8). (Yes, God says this even to mothers, and he never asks anything of you that he doesn't also give all the ability necessary to carry out.)

And also, if this is true (that God is at your life's center) then your immediate surroundings ought also to reflect him. Your immediate surroundings—your drawers and closets, your bedside table, your desk—are the filmiest clothing of your most personal, private life. Even if you have ten children, those areas should be yours alone, and they should reflect the order and peace of your inner life with God.

The smaller your family, the more the circumference of your immediate surroundings expands. If you're the unmarried president of a bank, you may have a whole penthouse to yourself. If you have many children, you may not have much of the house to call your own. If you share a college dorm room with two other girls, you have one third of a room. Whatever is yours, let it reflect the beauty of a woman whose heart is with God.

If you say you don't have enough drawers and closet space for everything, you own too many things. Give away, pare down, and let your intimate rooms and drawers and closets look serene and controlled—*kept*, like you.

I must say that all through the years, my chief delight has not been to wax or scrub. Raising four children didn't make house cleaning any easier, either. But I've always figured if I could make a room look *pretty*, pride would force me to keep it passably vacuumed and dusted! What has disciplined me is the philosophy that you can't see a daisy in a bud vase if there's a sock in the middle of the floor.

So even when Ray was a student at Princeton Seminary and we were in a tiny student apartment with three babies, the children's play area was either a gated-off space with all their toys, or out-of-doors. Some parts of the little apartment were for adults only.

And the picking up goes on forever, doesn't it! Dirty clothes must go into the hamper just as fast as dirty thoughts in our minds must be done away with. Both are unworthy of lying around, untended to, in the life of a child of God!

What's on your bedside table? Maybe a lamp, an intimate picture or two framed with love, and if you live in a kind climate or can afford it, one flower. Sort out everything else—throw it away, give it away, put it away. Have you a drawer in your bedside table? Put in your bedtime reading materials. No drawer? Put them in a pretty basket under your table. A few areas like this are sacrosanct, off-limits to the children.

My most luxurious feeling comes from seeing a fresh flower in a bud vase where I brush my teeth; it makes me happier there than in the living room! It gives me the feeling of truly "living from the inside out," of having my most intimate life with God beautiful and orderly, whether the outer circumference always is or not. If I'm living with him there, I'm in the eye of the storm, and the outer areas of life can't touch the real me.

Next closest to God in my life is my husband. For you it may be a husband or, because of sheer proximity, a roommate. Honor that person by looking nice as much as you can. This life isn't really "behind the scenes"; this is "living from the inside out." Instead of being a fake with a mask on, your public life will reflect your private life. And your private life will have beauty and order. Why are so many people polite to strangers, and shrews with those closest to them? The closer people get to you, if you're "abiding in God," the more enjoyable you should be. Your husband or roommate isn't really blessed by your belching, picking your toes, throwing your dirty underwear around. . . . Read Song of Solomon again to soak up the atmosphere of God's idea of a beautiful woman: her perfume, her washed feet, her total femininity.

One time Ray got to pay a visit to some of the world's leading race horses, worth hundreds of thousands of dollars. Their stalls were completely padded, to guard against any infection from little scratches and bumps.

How much more should God's woman, so needed in this world and precious to God, guard her inner chambers! Don't let cheap music blare or vulgar television shows ruin the atmosphere. Don't yell at the kids. When you can help it, don't bruise or become bruised by those close-in people around you.

You say, "But when do I get to be the real me? When do I get to express myself?" This is the very thing I'm talking about!

A generation ago, worldliness was smoking, dancing, drinking, lipstick, and playing cards. Today, worldliness is substituting for Christianity a pseudo-psychological, me-pampering, feelings-oriented religion that says, "If it feels good, do it." Many Christians haven't read enough Scripture to catch the real possibility of holy living. The "real you" that I'm talking about should be "in God," practicing his presence, living in holiness. Of course you should express yourself! When Jesus is the control-center of your heart and life, you'll express yourself in blessing, not cursing—and it will be the "real you." You won't be bottled-up and inhibited, trying to hold in that temper and keep shut the lid to Pandora's box. You will truly put away "all bitterness and wrath and anger and clamor and slander, . . . along with all malice." And you'll "be kind to one another, tender-hearted, forgiving each other, just as God in Christ also has forgiven you" (Eph. 4:31–32)! Once in a while you'll include a loving rebuke just as you expect to be lovingly rebuked in return (Gal. 6:1–2).

Beauty in relationships, beauty in physical surroundings, in your private life! Amen, Lord! So be it! And when cursing instead of blessing slips out of your mouth, James 3 says that's not the normal; that's the abnormal, the unhealthy. Say you're sorry right away, to God and your loved one, and get back again to the health and fun and beauty of blessing each other.

Relationships within the private life are forever shifting and changing. They need constant vigilance in prayer and a thousand, thousand hugs, kisses, pats, "I love you's" and "I'm sorry's." If you live alone and don't get in on this kind of stretching and growth, get all the deeper inside part of the total Christian family—the Body of Christ—to expose yourself to all this. It will keep you from isolation, which is deadly.

Now back to physical surroundings. Bathroom counters (like kitchen counters) can be disaster areas. Keep yours almost totally bare; if you haven't space in cupboards or drawers for your make-up, put it all in a pretty basket. You'll clean the counter oftener if you only have a basket to pick up! But if your cosmetics are in drawers, it may be time for reorganization: hair items here, face needs here, body creams here. The items you haven't used for a while, give away or throw away. Do the same to the medicine chest.

Now for your clothes. Maybe you want to go all the way and repaper your closet, paint matching shelves, border the shoe boxes with paper and ribbon; you know how far you have a desire to go—or dare to, if you share it with someone!

But everything in your closets and dressers needs reexamination. If you haven't worn it in a year, why haven't you? Because you've gained or lost weight? That's another whole area you need to lay out before the Lord, and probably before a doctor, submit to what you're told to do, and get yourself to the proper weight. There are so many books on the subject of weight-control, I won't add words to this one to discuss it. Certainly it's a key factor in being a beautiful woman for God. And I'm just as serious about the worrier who's too thin because of a tied-up stomach!

Both problems are not too big for God. He wants you to be one of the winners, and he can help you get to and keep the weight that is right for you. Then all the clothes you have will be one size, the right size, and all else should be given away.

Before you ever check out your present clothes, sit down in front of a large mirror with plenty of good daylight and hold colors under your face. What makes you look especially pretty? If the autumn colors do it, you're a brown gal like me, and you've found the key to your wardrobe. If black and white make you dazzle, they're your foundation. If the pastels are your cup of tea, navy could be your basic accessory color.

By the color test, you may see clothing right now in your closet you need to give away—or eventually. I know it takes time and money to change over to a coordinated wardrobe.

Once past the color test, next try on every one of your pieces of clothing, with shoes, bag, and jewelry, in front of a full-length mirror. First question: does the clothing call attention to itself, or does it make a great background for you? You have the choice of being thought of as a clotheshorse, or as a beautiful woman! Then, how are the seams, the zipper, the buttons, the hemlines? Notice the bust darts, the fit of the shoulders.

How about the total fit, the necklines. Are they modest? You don't want to be just a classy woman; you want to be *God's* classy woman. Look critically.

Does the outfit do the most for you? If you're hippy you don't need a gathered skirt or huge hip pockets. Unless you're willowy-slender, watch the layers.

The shoes should usually match or be darker than the skirt; if the skirt is a print, they should match the darkest color. Do the shoes and bag have the right "feel" for the clothes? Spectators demand a sporty outfit. A silky dress may need patent pumps. Is the need for chunky jewelry, dainty jewelry, or maybe, refreshingly, none at all? Check the total look, the focal points; "eliminate and concentrate!"

Check your underwear. Do you have the right underpinnings for each outfit? Then throw away what's lived its total life. Check your panty hose, and put the ones with runs in a separate box to go with pants.

Make a list of each complete outfit, and give away everything else you don't need. Somebody else does!

Probably your drawers need organizers. Your closet needs a place for belts, for bags, for shoes, for hats. Have you a spare closet or a container for out-of-season clothes? Also, keep an evening outfit, a play outfit, or whatever ready for a sudden occasion.

Are you using all your closet space? How about storage boxes on the top shelf, more rods and hooks? You ought to buy shoe trees. And if you can afford it, buy padded hangers and give all those wire ones back to the cleaners.

Are your dresser, your closet, your armoire or whatever—all your dressing needs—close together so you can dress in one spot with everything within reach? Maybe the bedroom needs rearranging.

(Important note: if you live with a husband, be sure his conveniences are met first, that he has the largest closet, the most convenient space. All through the years this silently testifies that you care for him, that you're concerned about his needs first.)

Now, step back and look. Is there a full-length mirror? Is there a place for everything, and everything in its place?

Now wander through the rest of your apartment or home. You're moving out from the center, and after the center is right, the rest is an extension of that. By "right" I don't mean expensive, but I mean two things: organized and pretty.

Is there simply too much of everything? Too much furniture, too many things? Give away, throw away, and call the Salvation Army.

Are the colors right? You may like coordinated flow, or you may like planned potpourri. But if you need to paint or slipcover, do it.

What needs organizing? Alphabetize your addresses or recipes or whatever. Group your games. File your old photos. Systematize your sewing equipment. What haven't you touched or used in six months or a year? Unless they're books or treasures, give them away.

What needs hiding? When you clear all the unused stuff out of your kitchen cupboards you'll have room to put in the toaster, the mixer, the coffee pot. You still haven't room? Then clothe them in matching jackets. Maybe your sewing area needs a pretty screen in front of it.

See if your kitchen counters can be almost bare; then add one thing just because it looks good: a bowl of fruit, a happy plant, glass canisters of raw things.

To give your home or apartment at least an illusion of beauty, let the most obvious eye-catchers in each room be beautiful, not utilitarian.

You see not the ironing board, but a rose.

Right?

9

YOUR CLOSEST RELATIONSHIPS

I LET YOU SEE my "life purposes" in chapter five. The second one was "Outwardly, to leave a mark on others contemporary to me and following me, through my life and my talents, which will point them to God."

"To leave a mark on others"! A Hollywood partygoer I read about doesn't expect to. She says, "The whole idea of life is living with enjoyment, as much enjoyment as you can from a very imperfect world. If you fail to look at your life that way, you can go right through it with absolutely a zero at the end—I mean, when you disappear, so what? You haven't left a footprint, a mark, or anything at all."

Poor, poor dear! Dressed to the teeth, coifed and jeweled, all dressed up for life, and nowhere to go! Contrast that with fitting your life into God's plans for you. Then only he himself knows how deep, how wide will be your mark on eternity!

One day a fellow approached Jesus, scuffed his toe in the dirt, couldn't think of a great conversation-opener and so he said, "Sir, where are you staying around here?" Jesus spent hours with him and revealed to him the fact that he was the long-awaited Messiah (John 1:35-41).

The fellow turned out to be Andrew, who went and got his brother Simon and introduced him to Jesus.

The result for Andrew and Simon? Seeing thousands converted in one day, writing letters which became part of God's sacred Word, and becoming two of the foundation stones of the eternal Church (Eph. 2:20)—not to mention having their names written upon the final Heavenly City of God (Rev. 21:14).

How's that for making a mark, when all you did was approach Jesus and ask an ordinary question?

When you link up with him, you have gotten to where the action is, and only God himself will determine what the eternal effects will be.

And he commands us to be diligent and deliberate about making our lasting marks on others. That's our script in his play. He spells it out in Matthew 28:18–20: "All authority has been given to me. . . . Go therefore and make disciples of all the nations, . . . teaching them to observe all that I commanded you; and lo, I am with you always."

"Make disciples"? Jesus said this to his own disciples, so naturally they knew what he meant. "I've been with you at close range for three years. I chose you out of the multitudes and have poured my truth into you. Now I'm leaving, so you turn around and each choose a few, and teach them everything I've taught you."

Soon came Pentecost! Pow! Explosion! Fireworks! 120 believers had 3,000 new converts to assimilate. How would they do it? No problem, with Jesus' last words ringing in their ears. Each veteran took on an average of 25 spiritual babies, absorbing them into his life at close range. He taught them everything he'd learned from Jesus ("the apostles' teaching," Acts 2:42); they fellowshiped; they ate meals together; he took them along to worship services.[1]

Where did all this take place? In two locations: in the temple, where there would be room for all, and in homes, where obviously they met in small groups (Acts 2:46). How often? Daily. And this new Body lifestyle, sketched out for us in Acts 2, was so successful that soon the 3,000 grew to 5,000 (Acts 4:4).

Discipling is what we're for, in this world! We're not for adoration and worship of God only, although that's number one. If that were all we're for, God could take us straight to heaven, where our worship would be undistracted.

No, the reason he leaves us here a while is so that we can make a mark on others before we go. We lived for several months in a country which punishes its citizens with death if they become Christians. One night we were taken secretly to have a private dinner with a young man of that land who loves Jesus with all his heart.

How handsome he was, and what an attractive personality he had! He sat on the floor across from us and said, "I can never have a girl friend. I don't even think about a wife. I know before too long they'll get me.

"But, oh," he said, and leaned across so earnestly, "my burning desire is to replace myself with several other Christians before I go!"

The Hollywood partygoer didn't know what life is all about, but that young fellow did.

---

[1] "Prayer," in Acts 2:42, is actually in the Greek "the prayers," identical to Acts 3:1, "the prayers" conducted at stated hours in the temple.

Recently I read this comment on 1 Corinthians 15:58: "Be steadfast, . . . knowing that your labor is not in vain in the Lord":

A solid bar, five inches thick, actually bent under the pressure of my hand! I couldn't have believed it, but a remarkable precision instrument convinced me!

This set me thinking. Am I . . . exerting "pressure" on the scene around me—a pressure measurable not by ordinary means, but real? My very little strength may seem not worth trying to exert. But not all that happens is visible to human eyes.[2]

I have a section in my notebook called "disciples." At the top of the first page I wrote two years ago, "Father, please: one hundred disciples in my lifetime?" And in parentheses I put "four a year for twenty-five years?" That seemed a reasonable request. I was fifty at the time; that would be from fifty to seventy-five, and I'd still have a remainder of ten years to goof off while still ministering with Ray!

I've had twenty-three disciples these last six years, but they were scanty at first and have increased to about eight a year, so I would think, God willing, I can affect hundreds at close range before I die. And besides, if anyone is still asking me, I'm not going to say "no" after I'm seventy-five!

At the top of my "disciples" page are several Scriptures I've jotted down while praying over this aspect of my life. One is John 17:19: "For their sakes I sanctify Myself, that they themselves also may be sanctified in truth." I dedicate myself to this; I set myself apart from lesser pursuits.

Also I've written 2 Corinthians 12:15a: "I will most gladly spend and be expended for your souls."

How precious is this attitude of Paul's—and doubtless of thousands of other Christians through the centuries! I want it to be my attitude, too.

I've kept a list of the twenty-three women I've counted as disciples. With some I've taken the initiative; especially when I've led them to know the Lord myself, then I say, "Hey, how would you like to get together once a week for some Bible study and prayer?" Some have come to me and asked, "Would you pray about discipling me for a while?"

On my notebook list of disciples I enter the date we first got together, and the date we terminated.

[2] F. W. Schwartz, Keswick "Daily Readings" calendar, 6 May 1976.

The first two were failures. Probably it was my fault; I just didn't know how to disciple well enough. I introduced them both to Christ, and I still believe their conversions were genuine. One met with me weekly for seven months and the other for nine months. Both drifted away because of being distracted over husbands with problems.

But I see from John 6:66 that Jesus himself lost some disciples, so apparently that doesn't make me a failure! I've found that if some fall away, there are always others near at hand ready to pick up the ball and run with it! So we're not to lose heart, but just learn from our mistakes and keep on with God's business.

The other twenty-one are all in good shape. In the early years of discipling (1970–1974) I never thought of cutoff dates; we met until there was a mutual agreement that the woman was ready to turn around, form her own group, and disciple as she had been discipled.

More recently we're apt to say, "Let's meet for six months," "over the summer," "from September to June"—something like that. A cutoff date makes it easier to start; you don't feel you're getting caught in a lifetime thing, like proposing marriage. Then instead of eventually petering out, you may decide to extend your time together. Or else, more likely, you end strongly and then multiply by dividing!

Year before last eight of us met together from September to June, and in June we made a date for a luncheon the next October when we would report what had happened to us since. The eight had grown to fifty-one!

I had a beautiful letter recently from a woman in the Washington, D.C., area after I had spoken there, saying, "My question is, just what do you *do* when you disciple women?" Well, dear friend, let me give you here all the guidelines I can, although that's a little like asking "What do you *do* when you raise children?" You follow a few basic rules, but then you find your own style and spend your life at it. You know that what you *are* in your life in Christ will have a greater effect than what you say or do.

Basic guidelines? Well, let's answer the question first of how you get together. You don't divide up a church membership by the alphabet or by neighborhoods and post the groups on a bulletin board. Your chemistry may not mix! This is something that becomes dreary and ponderous if it's administrated and watchdogged from above.

No, it must spring from the grass roots. People motivated by the desire to live obedient, biblical life styles just say to people they feel would be responsive, "What do you say we get together for a few months?"

But how do you find a leader? Well, obviously, if this is a true discipling situation (which we all need to be involved in), the leader is automatic. The discipling process needs to be a continual flow through every believer's life: you must be continually learning from someone who knows more than you do, and then (don't be the dead end!) you must be continually passing on what you know to someone who knows less. You say you don't know much? If all you know is John 3:16, get together with a nonchurch neighbor, have a cup of coffee, and tell her about it. Then if she says, "Hey, this was great; let's do it again next week," you've got one week to learn something new to tell her. Discipling is a wonderfully stretching experience!

But besides discipling groups, there's another kind of discipling, in which peers meet before the Lord. You might call it a "supportive fellowship." This is such a wonderful experience, you probably need both kinds of groups in your life. Here those who want to, take turns leading, and the idea is "where you're strong and I'm weak, you help me. Where I'm strong and you're weak, I'll help you. We'll all learn about Jesus from each other."

How often do you meet? Well, you meet together regularly, probably weekly, although I know many teen-agers and businessmen who also check in by telephone daily. Have the feeling, though, that this is not a meeting, it's a relationship. That means you're on call twenty-four hours a day, seven days a week.

How many meet? Occasionally God has guided me to a one-on-one relationship, but usually it's a better use of time to say that whatever you're sharing with one could be shared with perhaps four. At Lake Avenue Congregational Church, where we have hundreds of small groups, we've found by trial and error that groups can be four to eight. With more than eight you can begin to get anonymous; there's not time for the quiet ones to share their lives.

The meeting time must be systematic and structured so that it doesn't turn into a coffee klatsch. Four people will probably need 1–1½ hours weekly together; I'm in a group of four that needs 2–2½. Our group of eight last year found we needed two full hours without food; even then we barely made it.

But begin and end right on time, and follow an agenda so that everything gets included that you want to include.

This is not a Bible study, but it must include God's Word—enough of it for your life situations to spring out of it. No book studies, no filling in blanks! It's not primarily for information. Your adult Sunday School classes and other Bible classes provide that.

This is not a prayer meeting, but it must include prayer. Sometimes more, sometimes less. Vary the pattern, vary the format for freshness.

This is not a worship service, but it must include worship. Every time you gather in Jesus' name you must spend part of your time focusing on him alone. You can worship him in prayer. You can sing to him, or read together the words of worship hymns. Pray psalms to him. Talk of his attributes. Use your sanctified ingenuity!

This is not a sensitivity group, but it must include sharing. Don't let the sharing swallow up the whole time! Not often should it come first; we all are too prone to forget time when we talk about ourselves. Still, sharing is a crucial part, and needs special consideration.

Some people are afraid to get into small groups because they fear getting trapped into a confession session. Boy, so do I! Is it "airing dirty linen"? Count me out! And yet with our hundreds of small groups in our church over many years, I have yet, even once, to ever hear this mentioned as a problem.

You see, when you meet *in Jesus' name,* he is in the midst! And his Holy Spirit is a gentleman! When he is in charge, everything will be seemly and proper. Your group is not to be problem-centered, but Christ-centered!

The first few weeks or months you probably will stick pretty closely to worship, to the Scriptures, to prayer, to more surface issues of your lives. Fine. Don't worry. Don't force anything. The layers come off gradually, in an atmosphere of holy love and growing acceptance.

Plenty of things will never be exposed. There are things in my past I wouldn't tell anybody; why should I? God has forgiven and forgotten them. The point of a small group is to lift, to encourage, to edify, to "strengthen one another in God," as Jonathan did David.

The last essential ingredient of a group is accountability for, and responsibility to, each other. Setting and sharing goals helps here. If you know your sister's highest dreams and longings, you know her better, and you know how to pray for her. And when she knows yours, you have put yourself on the line to be accountable. As a functioning sister she should say to you from time to time, "How are you doing? How is your quiet time coming? Have you been able to witness to Gladys, your neighbor?" Submission in the Body of Christ includes vulnerability, but that's what moves us all along faster in our spiritual progress.

One more question: do you mix the sexes? Not for discipling. Titus 2:3–5 spells out, for instance, that "older women [I would think spiritually older, most often] are to . . . encourage the young women to love their husbands, to love their children, to be sensible, pure, workers at home, kind, being subject to their own husbands, that the word of God may not be dishonored." (You see what I mean? This type of thing isn't a Bible class, though you need that elsewhere; it's giving and getting help in life situations.)

You may not want to mix the sexes in a supportive fellowship, either. Our men tell us that when they meet as brothers and want to learn from each other how to love and lead their wives, they'd feel pretty inhibited if the wife were sitting there in the group. The opposite is also certainly true. Women have women-situations, and they need to be alone to dig deep into them. But I try to mix single and married women in my groups; both need the other and are so much the richer for it!

Couples' groups serve a different purpose, and they're wonderful. Ray and I give every Thursday night to four other couples, and how precious they are to us! We've gone through deep waters together— fasted for each other's children, prayed through financial temptations. All the couples, at some time or other, have taken planes home early from out of town to be together, and the men have frequently gone without dinner, when business ran late, in order to be there. We've even phoned each other on Thursday nights from different states, three couples on one end of the line and two couples on the other, though normally we're right in Pasadena when Thursday comes.

That's commitment! It speaks louder than words.

When I had the hysterectomy a few months ago I missed the Thursday I was in the hospital, but the following one I was home. So they met in our living room (I had to insist; they thought it would be too hard on me). I put on my best nightie and robe, and it was one of the sweetest times we've ever had. God is so good!

We had a sad letter recently from a couple of missionary "dropouts." They are dear friends of ours and wonderful people. The letter began, "We're home!" and went on to explain:

> There seemed to be no spiritual side to our work or our lives. We were living in spiritual isolation—no fellowship with other Christians, local or missionaries. The lack of the spiritual side to the work made the name "missionary" uncomfortable. The lack of spiritual fellowship with other Christians made it impossible.
>
> All in all, coming home seemed the best thing to do, and here we are.

I think in their place we would have come home, too. God didn't make any of us to be Lone Rangers, riding off into the sunset jangling our silver bullets. He constructed us so that we're lonely unless we have firm, deep fellowship with him and with other believers. Not even God himself is a loner; he's a Trinity, and he commands us to get deep into him and into each other.

Dear Christian friend, when your life is all over, what will it all have been about? For what will you be judged? I used to read 1 Corinthians 3 and think that all the stuff about wood-hay-stubble versus gold-silver-precious stones referred to the quality of life we'd lived, and how we'll be judged for that. Then I woke up to the context of that passage. Paul has been talking about himself and Apollos, another discipler, and he says in verse 9, "[Apollos and I] are God's fellow-workers; you [Christians] are . . . God's building."

Then he begins to show that once the foundation of Christ has been laid, men build upon that foundation the super-structure of the church, the temple of God. Each person they add to the church is one more stone in the building. But they'll be judged for the quality of the stones that they add—"the quality of each man's work," the quality of Christians they add to the church of God!

At the end, fire judges it all. The wood, hay, stubble—some Christians' work during their lives—will burn up, but they themselves will be saved, just barely making it into heaven, the smell of fire on their clothes (v. 15). But those who discipled carefully and well, who built quality Christians into the church—these will receive a reward.

And that's how a Christian's life will be judged—by the quality of his (or her) "ministry."

Lord, how precious to me are the names on my "disciples" page! You say the test of fire shows whether or not they remain. Oh, keep me faithfully loving and teaching and sympathizing and empathizing and interceding, that my work may remain. . . .

I have to tell you one more story. Number sixteen on my list is "Nels Ortlund," the only male! Beside his name is May 27, 1975, and no terminating date.

I can't tell you how much fun this little eleven-year-old son of ours is. He's going to be some kind of tiger when he's grown—and that's the kind of children we love to raise. Aggressive? This little fellow is there first with the most.

At his last annual medical checkup the nurse was doing the preliminaries—weighing, measuring, asking questions.

"How is he sleeping?" she said.

Nels piped up, "I sleep very well." She wrote that down.

"How's his appetite, Mrs. Ortlund?"

"I eat everything," said Nels. She wrote that down.

"Mrs. Ortlund," she asked me, "how are his bowels?"

Nels was in there again first, trying to be helpful: "A, *e, i, o, u,*" he said. . . .

The nurse was still barely under control when she left the room five minutes later.

Well, that wasn't the story I started to tell you.

The evening of last May 26 Nels had been a very bad boy. He was so naughty I spanked him, and Ray spanked him, and I cried, and Ray cried, and Nels cried. It was the crisis of his ten-year-old life! When he was finally in bed and we shut the door, we could still hear him sniffling out loud, "God, I don't know why I was so dumb. I'll never do that again; I'll never, never!"

The next day he came to me and said, "Mother, you disciple all those ladies; will you disciple me?" What a tender moment! The two of us bought him a notebook like mine. We decided to meet daily at breakfast. (Ray is always out on business or prayer breakfasts.) And we'd start out reading about Daniel—a real "he-man" teen-ager who dared to stand alone for God, who prayed every day, and who took care of his body and ate the right foods and so on.

I shared with him my goals, for him to pray over and help me, and he made four for me to help him with. By his birthday, October 15, he wanted

1. His temper cooled down

2. To get acquainted with new friends at summer camp

3. To know Daniel thoroughly by then

4. To eat some green vegetable and some fruit every day (He called that his "Daniel diet.")

He's been doing great ever since!

And it has made me realize the vast difference between seeing our children just as our children and seeing them as our disciples—our obvious, number one, built-in disciples. If they're just our children, then our only concerns are the concerns of any worldly mother: to feed and clothe them, get them into the right schools, well married, etc. But if they're also our disciples, then, more than anyone else, within those twenty or so precious years we have them, we're to teach them everything Jesus has taught us.

We don't deserve the children we have. We did a lot of things wrong. But here's a letter from Margie, our second daughter, written ten years ago when she was away in college. It still brings tears to my eyes, and if we had a fire it would be one of those things I'd grab first:

Dearest parents,

I felt compelled this afternoon to write this after a big wave came over me of love and gratitude for you both, mingled with a twinge of homesickness. I felt a little bogged down with soon-coming decisions that will have to be made, and my first impulse was to talk to you, and get your advice. Then I felt frustrated that I couldn't. And then I felt so grateful that that *was* my first impulse. And you've made that to be true. Because of your wise patience and obvious love and understanding, it is very natural for me to turn to you. That's unusual for a college girl, sadly so. I couldn't be more blessed to have you as parents. I can feel confident that I will always be happy, content, and will have a happy home, because this is my heritage and all that I know. I have models to follow: one is for a wife and mother in you, dear Mother; another is for a husband—I know what I want when I see the type of man you are, Daddy; and the third in a home, for I've never been confronted with a happier and more exciting one. My heart wells with thanksgiving to God for His goodness to me. And you're a big hunk of that goodness!

So thank you for being so wonderful and open to me in my childishness, inconsistencies, and stupidity. (But I'm learning!)

Much love,
Margie

The sequel to this is that now she's married to a wonderful pastor, and is the happy mother of three.

No, we don't deserve them. But we're to teach them everything Jesus has taught us. "And lo," says Jesus as we do it, "*I am with you always*" (Matt. 28:20, emphasis mine).

10

YOUR PUBLIC LIFE

THERE ARE TWO KINDS of personalities in this world, and you are one of the two. People can tell which, as soon as you walk into a room: your attitude says either "Here I am," or "There you are."

Which kind are you?

Let's back up and recap the book so far. At the center of your life must be God in Jesus Christ. There the ultimate issues are settled, and you can start living from the inside out.

Your person is part of the center, too; your body is the flesh that clothes his Presence. Fantastic thought! So your looks are important, before him, and representing him.

Your long-term goals set the course of where you want to go, under his plans. Your short-term goals keep redirecting you to stay on course, and your daily scheduling is the discipline to get you there, with God's glory and rewards when it's over. Goals and scheduling take time— quiet time—and are part of your life behind the scenes.

Moving out from that central core of you, you push aside a filmy gauze curtain to your immediate surroundings, which you share with no one or a very few: your bedroom, bath, closets . . . we'll conclude with desk and notebook.

Within that concentric circle are people—perhaps a husband, perhaps a roommate, perhaps children . . . and others. There are enough marriage books and human relationship books. There are enough child-raising books. This book is mostly to help you deal with the one thing you will be all your adult life: yourself as a woman.

As a woman your eternity-oriented task is to affect others, to move them to God through the Savior, Jesus Christ. Your temporary task, for the years you have them, is to affect the members of your physical family, by whatever means you can, to be "born again" into God's eternal family and to grow within that family to spiritual maturity. Your lifelong task, at least from conversion on, whether married or single, is to influence everyone you can, by whatever means you can, to the same ends—to help them become temple material of gold, silver, and precious stones.

The ways you'll do this are as varied as God's creative powers allow, which are infinite. He never stamps out cookie-cutter Christians.

Now we're moving out from the middle to the edges of your life. But where are the edges? Lines and shades blur. The more God-integrated and focused your central core is, the more powerful is the push outward, until (only God knows) your public life may become public indeed. At least it will be as far as eternity is concerned.

When you read the chapter title "Your Public Life," you may have thought you have no public life at all. But you certainly do. Beyond your most intimately known circle of people, what lives do you touch? Who knows you? Many at your church, and perhaps in other organizations. The grocer, the bank teller, the postman, your neighbors—are you not just touching their lives, but influencing them for Jesus?

> Only one life; 'twill soon be past;
> Only what's done for Christ will last!

Walk out that door of your home to your job, or whatever your world may be, saying, "There you are! There are all you precious people, with feeling and needs. Who of you is ready today to be pressured to God, gently or strongly, as he leads me?"

Let me tell you a visual way I see this happen. I know a Hawaiian woman who strings a number of leis early each Sunday morning, not for anyone in particular! Then she comes to church praying, "Lord, who needs my leis today? A newcomer? Someone discouraged? Lead me to the right people."

That's emerging into public life saying, "There you are!"

Your public life should flow out of your private life. How important your outward direction is! You represent Christ. Hold your head up, as Psalm 3:3 tells you to. Plan your shampoos so that you don't go to the grocery store in rollers. Switch purses—it's worth the time—so that you coordinate when you go out. Compliment the friend you're meeting for lunch by looking like God's woman. Gideon was known by his appearance and clothing to be a leader among men (Judg. 8:18); so should you!

Look quality—and think quality. It will tell on your face if you obey Philippians 4:8, letting your mind dwell on that which is true, honorable, right, pure, lovely, and so on! It will help that lovely woman you long to be grow as you practice God's presence in public, keeping a running conversation going with him: "Lord, bless that man walking toward me; Father, help me to be a wise, careful driver; God, I love you. . . ." Discipline yourself to bring "every thought captive to the obedience of Christ" (2 Cor. 10:5).

Look quality, think quality—talk quality. It frightens me, how many of the New Testament references to woman have to do with the problems of her tongue! There are plenty of books on all sides of the women's liberation movement, but let me just remind both you and me that it was Eve who sinned first and not Adam (1 Tim. 2:14), so let's conduct ourselves with care, and caution.

Have you a boss over you at your work? Give him the deference the Scriptures command (1 Pet. 13–20).

Have you people who work under you? In your most feminine way, "boss well." God will give you all the resources you need to be wise, to be firm, to handle people with authority, and yet like Teddy Roosevelt to speak softly!

(Incidentally, regarding the tongue, have you noticed that because some areas of humor are off-limits to Christians, a few of them think what's really racy is bathroom jokes? As Casey Stengel used to say, "Include me out.")

Look quality, think quality, talk quality—and expose yourself to quality. In your entertainment and social life, watch what feeds your mind. Our computer-expert friends talk about GIGO—"Garbage In, Garbage Out." I don't know how you feel about it, but of the few PG movies I've seen, most were such garbage that I'm sorry I exposed my mind and heart to them. Don't get insensitive; don't get used to garbage. What goes in will come out; pretty soon we'll smell.

Once in a while you may get caught in something not of your own choosing. Well, you can't stop birds from lighting on your head, but you can keep them from making a nest in your hair.

One way of keeping your public life wholesome is by seeing that your larger circle of friends, as well as your intimate circle, are godly people.

Ray and I went to a fantastic dinner party one evening. Dave and Jackie, the host and hostess, live in an elegant home, so we dressed appropriately. We had been briefed that the rule for the occasion was that all the conversation must praise God. The whole evening was both hilarious and spectacular, but what I remember most was sitting on our high-backed chairs in that baronial dining room as Jackie described the first week of her life as a Christian—a week of straight Bible reading, chain smoking, and tears. We laughed, we cried, we were lifted.

The Bible has a lot to say about how to treat the larger circle of our Christian family. 1 Timothy 5:1–2 says it well in *The Living Bible*: "Never speak sharply to an older man, but plead with him respectfully just as though he were your own father. Talk to the younger men as you would to much loved brothers. Treat the older women as mothers, and the girls as your sisters, thinking only pure thoughts about them" (written to a fellow). And again, *The Living Bible* in 1 Peter 3:8: "You should be like one big happy family, full of sympathy toward each other, loving one another with tender hearts and humble minds."

There's no flirting here. The relationships may be precious indeed between spiritual brothers and sisters, even to greeting one another "with a holy kiss" (2 Cor. 13:12)—in this case a peck on the cheek— but God's Holy Spirit guides always what is affirming and encouraging in Christ without going any further. Love in the Body of Christ is sensitive love. On the one hand, if you're a wife, it "is not jealous," or easily "provoked" (1 Cor. 13:4–5). On the other hand, if you're the nonwife, it "does not act unbecomingly" (1 Cor. 13:5).

In the matter of marital status we have to be absolutely loose, satisfied with what we are. Are you bound to a husband? Don't seek to be released. Are you single? Don't seek a husband (1 Cor. 7:27). These are hard things to say in a corrupt society which pressures us women either to marry, or, more recently, to be swinging singles. Often the married ones long for freedom, and the singles fight the "swinging" image and long for a husband. Paul talks long and deeply about this in 1 Corinthians 7; read it carefully. He seems to say, in essence:

1. In troubled times, you're really better off being single—free to please only God.

2. If you do marry, you haven't sinned; but be warned: it's not easy to have the necessary double allegiance of pleasing both God and a husband.

3. Because time is so short, and the present form of this world is passing away: if you have a husband, love him and obey him, but—easy does it. Live for eternity. Live for God. Don't be possessed, don't be entangled, until you're only a wife, nothing more.

Concerning sex he says, "If you're married, enjoy sex regularly, faithfully! Your body belongs to your husband." And "If you're not married, God will either give you control or give you a husband!"

I point you to these Scriptures as a wife who is deeply, joyfully in love. Why shouldn't I be? I'm spoiled to death with such a treasure of a blond, beautiful, godly husband, and I know with total certainty that I'm his sweetheart, and he is mine. Still, both of us have to be loose enough in our possession of each other that the loss of one of us wouldn't destroy the other.

"For me, to live is Christ," not Ray. Into God's hands I commend my spirit, and my life, and all I am. He can give, he can take away, his name will still be "Blessed." God will keep in perfect peace the mind which is stayed on him, himself.

The last thing to say about your public life is: make it very public! You've already made the decision to disciple chosen ones behind the scenes, and you've proportioned your lifestyle to give them a meaningful chunk of your time.

So don't cling to them in public as well. Reach out! Socialize. Stretch out your heart to know many who are different from you—richer, poorer, or whatever. Make your circle of this broader, necessarily shallower love as large as possible.

Be sure that you have nothing against any other believer, that all the lines of communication are open and clear (Matt. 5:23–24). Then once that's settled, be a "baby-kissing politician"! Touch is wonderful; reach when you pass people to grab a hand, touch a shoulder.

On this earth you will probably never know them all, but affect all the lives you can. "Behold how those Christians love one another," they said in the first century. And of the ones who aren't believers—your warmth, your smile may open doors which will draw them in.

"There you are," you say to your public world. "God loves you, and I love you. What can I do for you today?"

And from that well-tended, precious center of you, the circle will enlarge . . . and enlarge . . . and enlarge.

11

YOUR DESK

I'VE SAVED for close to the end of this book your desk and your note-book. They're the two means of putting you all together, tying you up in a package with a pink ribbon. (Salmon? Black and white?)

The philosophies of life have to be right, first. Then you're ready to house the tools needed to carry out the philosophies.

My particular desk is like me: it's still in process. I dream of a lovely one, with built-in shelves and cupboards on the adjoining wall—the total look both efficient and feminine, but leaning slightly more to the feminine. Well, one of these days! It's not on the financial agenda yet.

In the meantime, I have a door laid over two-drawer filing cabinets. It's in a light, airy corner of our pale blue and green, fifteen-by-thirty-foot master bedroom, and the door (let's say desk top) and chair are painted pale blue, matching the woodwork. The chair arms are a shade too high for the desk top, and from being shoved under, some paint has come off each arm. Well, as I say, I'm not yet what I'm going to be, either.

Over the desk hangs a large photograph of Ray, taken by and framed in exquisite blue velvet by our artistic, loving son, Bud. Ray and Bud had been attending the Lausanne Congress on Evangelism in Switzerland, and one afternoon sat beside Lake Lucerne praying together. As they finished prayer Ray turned his face away to look over the lake— and Bud snapped the picture.

Under the picture is a pale blue plaque of Psalm 34:3, the words Ray used when he proposed to me: "O magnify the Lord with me, and let us exalt His Name together!"

On the desk are pale blue appointment books and matching telephone, and a few other sentimental treasures.

A "Week-at-a-Glance" notebook is central, containing social appointments and telephone numbers. It lies open to the day. As soon as appointments are made by phone they go into my "Week-at-a-Glance."

Then if they're within the next three months, they're transcribed to the "to do" section of the notebook that goes everywhere with me.

White wicker desk organizers hold note paper, business envelopes, post cards, and stamps. A small bookrack holds several Bibles, a dictionary, and a few books I'm reading at the moment. A white onyx dish from my friend Myrtle holds paper clips and rubber bands. Blue velvet containers from my sister Margie hold pens and pencils, Scotch tape, scissors—you know—and letters to be answered. The large matching lamps are special, because they've been with us since our early-poor days when they flanked the living room sofa.

The left bottom file drawer holds original manuscripts of all the books Ray and I have written so far, plus file folders of material for future books, into which we continually drop new quotations and ideas.

The left top file drawer holds financial information: a folder for bills, another for receipts, another for bank books and information. It holds boxes of extra blank checks, and it holds a three-by-five-inch index card file box of Christmas card addresses. Then there's room for supplies of typing paper, scribbling tablets, and music manuscript paper.

There's a large brown leather notebook initialed in gold in which I do my writing; it was a gift from our loving choir when I substituted at the organ for a while.

In the bottom right drawer I've filed all correspondence with music publishers and SESAC, my composers' affiliation; all copyright certificates; and copies of all my published and unpublished music works. That one is stuffed to overflowing! Either I quit writing music or reorganize for more file space.

So far, you probably relate to drawer two, but not to one or three. Never mind, you have your own special interests. I didn't even mention that for years I've torn pictures I loved out of decorating magazines, and they're also filed away, under "bathrooms," "bedrooms," "breakfast rooms," et cetera—for ideas when we redecorate, or just for occasional perusing while in a warm tub.

But drawer four—to this one you must relate. This top right drawer I set up after reading Ernest Dimnet's *The Art of Thinking*, which for me was a terrific motivator.

The first section of the drawer is file folders from A to Z just to put things in, so I'll know where they are! Since Dimnet, I never—well, hardly ever—set anything I must do something about soon, or someday, on a vacant spot somewhere. (Then, when "soon" or "someday" comes, under which pile of accumulation did I put that whatzit?) No, I think of the word with which I'd most likely associate it, and I drop it into the alphabetical file. If I need to be reminded about it, I jot that onto the right calendar day in my notebook. And when I want it I can put my finger right on it.

C holds concert tickets, mail order catalogs.

D holds unused Disneyland tickets!

G holds all those little guarantee slips for the household appliances and other things with dated guarantees.

I holds our insurance information.

L holds our "Let's Dine Out" cards.

S holds the correspondence on my future speaking dates and Nels's school information.

Well, you get the idea!

Behind that alphabetical file is another A to Z series of folders. These are my own Bible studies or sermon notes or ideas on any subjects I want to file and pursue. I find I've stashed away, for instance, things on the Bible, on family, on the Holy Spirit, on marriage and, among other things, on "self-image." (I think it's often being taught erroneously, and I toss into the folder Scriptures I find on that subject, to study one of these days.)

Behind that file is another series of folders marked from Genesis to Revelation. Anything anyone teaches me from one of the books of Scripture, or anything I study on my own, I drop into the file. But the accumulation of Bible truths grows; I've got lots of things I can pass along when I have an opportunity.

I think of all the years and years I studied or read the Bible without writing anything down. I must have forgotten tons of wonderful stuff. The Lord was patient to keep teaching me anything new.

I was talking about this to 400 women at a conference recently, trying to explain how my filing system works.

"Suppose Ray's been preaching a series on Christ our Wisdom from the Book of Proverbs," I said. "When the series is done, I drop all my notes into the Proverbs file. There they are, in my own words, the way I understood it, ready to pass on to others.

"Or suppose I've studied the creation in Genesis; I drop all my notes into the Genesis file. Or, say, the miracles of the Gospel of John—I drop them all into the John."

I began to feel the place rock and reel.

"File!" I shouted. "The John file!"

Sometimes the Lord has to scrape my talks off the floor, the walls, and the ceiling, and put them back together again.

Remember, Jesus said to you and me in Matthew 28:19–20, "Go therefore and make disciples, . . . teaching them to observe all that I commanded you." Perhaps you'll someday be a gifted, important Bible teacher in front of huge classes; perhaps you won't. But if you take Matthew 28:19–20 seriously, you need some system for accumulating what Jesus is telling you, so that you can make disciples, at least one-on-one over cups of coffee, and teach them what you've learned.

There's your desk, large or small, my friend. Put it together to work for you. Make it your servant, to respond with what you want immediately, at the touch of a finger. Make it sleek and uncluttered. Make it pretty and feminine.

Mostly, make it a tool to help you live a life of obedience to God and effectiveness with people.

12

YOUR NOTEBOOK

LAST YEAR I SPOKE to a luscious-looking crowd of 150 women gathered for a one-day mini-retreat at the La Canada Country Club. I talked to them in the afternoon about what a notebook could do for their lives.

The next day, noticing I was nearly out of filler paper for my own, I dropped into the local stationer's store.

"I don't have any," said the manager. "I don't know what's happened. We've had a run on it like you wouldn't believe, just yesterday and this morning. And not just paper, but the binders, dividers, calendar pages—everything." He scratched his head.

"Well," I grinned, "you just ought to plan better."

And the letters keep coming in:

"Because of you, I now carry a notebook. . . ."

"Your suggestions for a notebook . . . have been such a blessing to me. . . ."

"I began a notebook . . . and don't see how I ever got along without it! I have many different sections now, such as songs, books and tapes lent and borrowed. . . ."

"Thanks for the much needed shot in the arm. . . ."

Wherever I go, beautiful, motivated women bounce up to me hugging their notebooks. The brunettes have black ones, the redheads carry brown, the blondes have navy. They've heard me speak somewhere.

I can't believe it, either. I, too, scratch my head.

When I first bought a notebook and organized it into sections, no one had suggested it to me. I didn't do it because it was going to be some great new beginning in my life. I can't even remember actually getting it.

Over the ensuing months I began leaning on my notebook more and more for daily living, seeing what it could do. Fortunately it was brown and just Bible-size, so it was easy to get the habit of going out the door with Bible, notebook, and purse.

After several years of literally living out of it, hesitantly, very hesitantly, I shared it one time at a women's conference. Whammo! It went off like a bombshell. Scores told me they were going home to buy notebooks. I shared it at other conferences, and the feedback began. I'd hear the words "It's changed my life."

Even so, I was fearful of speaking about it. Opening up my notebook was opening up *me*. Why wouldn't they think I was on an ego trip? Why would they be built up in the faith by hearing about my Bible studies with Nels, the building of my wardrobe, my occasional struggles over merging my heart with Ray's or over finances, the pouring of my life into disciples, my goals, my devotions?

Well, I've already shared with you my reticence about this. In early conferences I always said, "Now, this part of my speaking is so personal, I'd prefer no taping." But as the blessing grew and I realized my life on the altar was being used, I threw caution out the window and let it all be taped. And here I am, putting it in a book.

So my notebook is 7″ × 9″, three-ringed, and holds paper 5½″ × 8½″. That's a comfortable size to rest with my Bible on my left arm, with my purse hanging from a strap. For all of us women, that's simple. We've typed whole pages while talking and cradling a phone on our shoulder, or cooked three-course dinners with a baby on one hip.

Now, as I tell you what's in my notebook, remember that yours won't be identical. I'll just share mine to give you ideas, and your notebook will become a reflection of your own individual life.

The first section of my notebook is my calendar pages, torn out as each day ends, so that when I flip open my notebook I'm looking at "today." These days in Hawaii are gloriously empty, but today includes a thing or two: wire congratulations to Joan and Marv on their twenty-fifth anniversary. More stamps for post cards. Ho, hum!

(Actually, the schedule of this month has been: up at 8:30; leave house at 9:30; brunch out with Ray and Nels; to the beach where Nels plays, Ray plays, prays, studies and writes, and I sit in the shade and have devotions and then write. End of afternoon home to change clothes, out to a great dinner and occasional entertainment, usually home to early bed. One day a week we break the routine and sightsee or cavort together all day.)

The first day after return home says 8:45 hair tint (after a month, I'll need it), deposit paycheck, write and mail bills, electric blanket ready to pick up at laundry, etc.—a quick slip back into routine.

The important thing about your "to do" section is to have your notebook forever with you. When you think of something you need to do, a shopping item to buy, jot it down immediately *on the day when you intend to do it, or buy it.* If someone asks you for a date, you'll always know if you're available or not.

"I'd love to have a copy of that song," says a lady at church. In my notebook I jot down on the following Sunday's page to bring her one.

I leave off shoes for repair. "They'll be ready Friday," the man says. I flip open to Friday and write "shoes." I clip the claim check to the page.

If you keep your notebook with you, to write everything and then read everything, you'll never forget anything again! That's a promise.

(I don't see how any woman who's had a hysterectomy could ever live without the "to do" section of a notebook. Some pages of the month say "One pill." Some say "Two pills." Some say "No pill." I don't know what would happen if I ever got them mixed up. I don't dare ask. Maybe I'd grow a beard.)

One woman wrote recently, "To say the least, I can't tell you how much I've received, as so much of it has become such a part of my life I can't remember when I wasn't carrying around my notebook, jotting my whole life down everywhere I go."

What are the jobs you hate? Write them in on different days; spread them out! But put them in your notebook: clean the oven, face a sister about a ticklish issue. It will overcome your habit of procrastination and give you a great sense of quiet accomplishment.

Write in your time with God every single day, when it realistically fits your schedule that day. It may be at a different time every day, but it will be there because you deliberately planned for it and saw to it that it happened. It is priority number one in your life, no matter what else goes on!

One characteristic of a good driver is that he always looks ahead half a block or so; he anticipates. So with a good *liver* (what a word!); you live glancing ahead half a week or more to know where you're going.

Then each evening take a good look at the following day. Decide what you'll wear: hang it out, or jot it down. (Shoes polished? Everything ready?) Chart your course from first to last item, particularly if it's an errand day. It will save you time and gas. Number the items from first to least importance; if some don't get done you can rewrite them on a future day. What do you need to take with you? Pile them together in a handy spot: the book back to the library, the china cup to be mended. Pray over the events of the day, the people you'll see. You'll sleep easier, and the next morning you won't spin your wheels getting going.

As the day advances cross off the items. At the end of the day rewrite what you didn't get done, thank the Lord for it all, and throw the page away.

The first divider in my notebook says "goals" on it. I shared them with you in chapter five, and now I'll tell you what I prayed on paper after I wrote the goals. (You'll have to believe me; I never dreamed when I wrote these words that anyone but God would see them!)

Father, I want to pour my life increasingly into You, into people, and into work. [Those are the "three priorities," as you recognize.] Oh, may I be so submerged in Yourself, in Your Word and in prayer that my personality will be oiled by the Holy Spirit.

I want to be sweet, gracious, thoughtful, hospitable—working hard behind the scenes without seeming pressured.

I want to relax and play with Ray when he needs me; give us fun dates together; make me fun to be with. For Nels, too, Lord.

Make my hair, figure, make-up, and clothes right, Lord, so they'll be proud of me.

Help me to write music for You, Lord—songs, hymns, and anthems that will meet the needs of the Body.

Help me to complete our house, inside and out, without being consumed by it.

Thanks, Father, thanks!

I don't know what your dreams and visions are. I only know that God has them for you, so you need to get away, if you don't know, and commune with him and find out. Be specific; make your goals as measurable as you can, so you'll know if you're making them or not! This is absolutely crucial before you strike out on your own in some new direction not of God's leading.

And don't clean out your closet before you make goals. Remember, the sculptor deals with the large mass first. Details come later.

At the back of this notebook section are other miscellaneous goals. House goals: as God wills, complete my desk area, repaint the downstairs, re-cover living room furniture, etc. Financial goals: finish paying back our life insurance loan, increase our savings accounts. I notice jotted in between things,

> Take from our lives the strain and stress,
> And let our ordered lives confess
> The beauties of Thy peace.[1]

---

[1] John Greenleaf Whittier. "Dear Lord and Father of Mankind."

Well, your notebook is just your personal thing! Put in it whatever you please.

Another page, my wardrobe: a list of my current outfits, with accessories, jewelry, etc. Another page, my exercise goals: in my stair climbing I've worked up gradually from ten round trips to 72 each morning and 60 each evening.

You'll probably have plenty of other projects and interesting side trips in life to record with your goals. They'll be as varied and as wonderful as all God's beautiful women in this world!

My next notebook section is for Bible study. Pasted onto the first page is a chronological outline of the books of the Old and New Testaments, so I can remember what goes where. Then comes the study I happen to be doing at the moment, principles of leadership. I started with the lives of Moses and Aaron, reading from Exodus 2, and so far I've gotten to Judges 9:55, just jotting down beside each reference principles as I see them. Pretty soon I'll quit that and drop them into the Bible study file in my desk, under L for "Leadership"!

You may be a long-time Bible scholar or a brand-new beginner, but you can begin writing something as you study each day. He'll help you; he'll put an idea in your head, and another idea months from now, and by ten years—dozens and dozens! How rich your storehouse will be, and it will all be yours! Get going in the study of God's Word!

The next section of my notebook is called "disciples," with the list I told you about in chapter nine. The list is in ink, and at the bottom of the page in light pencil are those who've asked recently if they can join me for a while. So I've written in my "to do" section, on August 3, "Pray over disciples for fall." Well, Jesus did that, too, in Luke 6:12–16.

Also in the "disciples" section is a page of the thirty-nine members of a Wednesday morning Bible class I teach. They come from all churches, Protestant and Catholic, as well as from no church. What a dear, eager group they are! Recently we had a big splashy dinner together, adding husbands, boy friends, and friends, and there were eighty of us at Betty's house across the street. Then Dr. Ralph Byron, chief surgeon of the City of Hope and one of our Sunday School teachers at church, sketched the story of his life and how he'd met Jesus, for the benefit of lots of the guests who haven't yet. To use Ralph's favorite word, it was a sensational evening.

The next three notebook sections are titled "Nels," "neighbors," and "couples," and you can guess why. In Nels's section, we record each time we're together, what Scripture we read, one summarizing comment by him, and any other pertinent information. Some pretty astute words come out of his eleven-year-old mind, like the latest entry:

"It takes a while to learn a lesson, but there's no stopping God from getting through to you."

(When I think of Nels I always have to put in a little extra. He's our favorite entertainment in these years of our lives. Recently Nels experienced his first major illness, a few weeks of infectious mononucleosis. The first week he was really sick, with a burning throat and a neck like mumps.

We went in to see the doctor for a gamma globulin shot. Oh, how they can hurt! Nels lay on his tummy as the shot went into his hip, and he never made a sound, but his face was contorted into the look of strong crying, and tears were streaming down his big-boy cheeks.

As he lay there trying to get his breath back, his eyes lighted on a Dr. Seuss book on the floor, *There's a Wocket in My Pocket.*

"There's some heat," Nels finally said, "in my seat.")

The "neighbors" are Beulah next-door on our south side, whose heart God opened two Januarys ago (we started meeting together weekly); Betty across the street, who accepted Christ and joined us in October of that year; and Doris, down the block, whom we prayed in shortly after. On page 1 are their names and birthdays (love has to be practical and thoughtful, right?), and then a prayer I wrote to God on behalf of each of them, expressing the visions and goals God had given me for each of their lives. Clipped to the back of the page are some sentimental treasures: written expressions of love from them, prayer requests that recall God's wonderful answers. Then each page notes our meeting date, at whose home, what we studied, what the prayer requests were, etc.

Recently one of the three made group goals for us, which the rest of us ratified:

1. Greater accountability
2. Check list for prayers and how answered
3. Outreach
   a. List names of people we know that need God's Word
   b. Work together, or as individuals, to reach them
4. Two weekends a year together
5. Attend one of Anne's conferences per year
6. Check our progress every three months
7. Wednesdays adhere to a time schedule. Homework often.

A lot of these goals indicate they're hungry to stretch and grow and that includes shaping up *me,* their leader. Good; that's just the kind of shove from behind I need, and I love them for it.

	Betty	Beulah	Doris	Comments
Suffering together				
Rejoicing together				
Bearing one another's burdens				
Restoring one another				
Praying together				
Teaching, admonishing				
Refreshing one another				
Encouraging one another				
Forgiving one another				
Confessing to one another				
Being truthful with one another				
Stimulating one another to good deeds				
Giving to one another				

One page of this "neighbors" section of our notebooks is worth duplicating for this book, for you to copy if you like. It lists every way the New Testament mentions that members of the Body of Christ can communicate with other members. These are often repeated, but they boil down to thirteen ways, which we listed in a column. Then, as the months go by, each of us can see in how many scriptural ways we're communicating with each of the other three. I can see where I'm weak, and pray for new ways to help and encourage my dear sisters, as they help and encourage me. What we came up with is on page 89.

The "couples" section of my notebook, concerning Ray's and my Thursday night group with four other husbands and wives, has the same format. These sections become the records of our spiritual pilgrimages together, and they are precious indeed. As I look back six months and read what each one was praying for at that time, I marvel at how God has met our needs, answered our requests, and moved us along. He is magnificent! Children have been turned to Christ, large business ventures have been prayed into being; it's been some year together.

When I talk about putting lives together in small groups at conferences, afterward I get letters like this:

> When you spoke at the Women's Retreat at Mount Hermon, He used you in my life to awaken and burden me for a closer daily walk with Christ, by means of a small group. How anxious I was! And what a blessing it's been! I'm really learning to adore my Lord, praise Him, and give thanks. Accountability, and knowing I have five sisters who love me and are always available has made the way so much easier these past few months. I know God doesn't want us to go it alone.

No, dear woman whoever you are, he doesn't want me to, either. I've fallen on my face enough times by now to see how closely tied I must be to a few close-in brothers and sisters!

Another letter received recently says:

> I want to share with you how successful the notebook idea has been in my life, and that I have initiated a five-gal prayer-and-share group, after much prayer myself. We all have read Ray's book,[2] and started our notebooks together, and what a closeness

[2] Raymond C. Ortlund, *Lord, Make My Life a Miracle* (Glendale, Cal.: Regal Books, 1975).

we already have and specific answers to prayer and such loving care for one another.

Already another group has formed through one of my friends, as I've shared the notebook idea with so many. . . . Something so simple has certainly got my life together so much more, and so many of my friends God has allowed me to influence for Him in this way.

Something funny before I close. My sister was waiting in her doctor's office recently and noticed an attractive lady across from her with a notebook and Bible just so busy and engrossed in her writing and reading. The nurse looked into the waiting room and called who would be next: Anne Ortlund! my sister . . . just couldn't believe it; the teacher actually practices what she preaches!

The next notebook section every Christian should have! I titled it "sermons," but it's for every time I hear teaching or preaching. Then my pen is ready, and I start writing notes as copiously and completely as I can. Particularly, I note all Scripture references. Every few weeks I transfer my note pages to the Bible study file in my desk, and at a moment's notice (almost) I've got material to pass on to others. It was somebody else's thoughts, but when I write it down for myself I understand it, and it becomes mine to pass on.

I think about our daughter Sherry, and what a wealth of scriptural knowledge she has. Last year when she was twenty-eight a few college girls came to her and asked if she would disciple them—since she was a "godly older woman"! "Think of it, Mother," she complained to me in shocked tones. But she gave them a wonderful year.

How was all this knowledge of the Word of God acquired? Perhaps a major reason is that Sherry has taken notes on all sermons since she was in junior high school.

And what a joy for a preacher to have people in front of him taking notes! Otherwise, how can he tell if they're planning next week's menus or next year's vacation, or what? In fact, it encourages the whole Body of Christ in worship together.

The last section of my notebook, "prayers," is the best of all. How could it have taken me forty-two years of living the Christian life before I ever started writing my prayers? I had absolutely no idea what it was going to do for me.

Before, if you'd asked me what I'd prayed about three days earlier, or maybe an hour earlier, unless it was something crucial, I'd have no idea.

When I started writing prayers I just let the words flow on paper the way they had done out of my mouth, putting down both the important and the seemingly inconsequential. After a few months when I started looking back over what I'd first prayed, I was staggered to discover how seriously God had taken my prayers! A sentence or two, just sort of thrown in, had sometimes started the wheels of heaven turning until the requests had ever-enlarging ramifications and affected ever-enlarging numbers of people! I was learning such a lesson of the power of prayer, it utterly shook me.

A letter from a woman confirmed another feeling of mine about writing down prayers. She said, "Recently when I wrote down for the first time on paper 'I love You, Father,' it had never been more meaningful. It's a completely different feeling from list-making."

The first thing I ever happened to write (as I say, I just fell into this) was "I offer You my joy as a personal sacrifice. Whether I feel like it or not, before You continually I will rejoice."

It felt so good, I kept going: "Bless Ray: show him how to direct cantankerous people [there really are not many; what a wonderful flock! But in every group of people you have a few]—what to say and do, how responsible to feel. Give him guidance in Your perfect, highest will for his life. Keep him growing."

I went on to pray for Nels: "Give him a sense of responsibility. Help him to bring home Spelling Unit 24 today. [In the margin I wrote later, "Thank You, Father!" He did.] Help Ray and me to give him enough attention, not just playing with him but talking to him, listening to him, and teaching."

Well, if you could peruse as I do the pages of more than two years' worth of prayers, you would catch me in every mood of my life:

Praise You, Lord! This beautiful Sunday morning is Happy Day at Lake Avenue Church—worship day, fellowship day. May there be crowds flowing onto the campus all day to honor You together.

Father, give me a heart that gives really joyously. Help me to join Ray in giving recklessly! Make us ever more sensitive to the material needs of those about us. Father, is it asking too much that after we've done this, and as we continue to give, You might pour back to us enough to fix the house, too?

[Concerning Ray] Father, You are helping put our hearts together. It's not easy. Thank You that we love each other so hard that hurts really hurt.

Father, I adore You, lay my life before you; how I love You!

O God! Have You left us to wander on our own?

Dear Lord, I need music! I feel so dry.

Father, it's a cold Thursday, a study day. Ray and I are study-
ing in front of the fire. How wonderful! Lord, fill us with You
today.

Lord, how the human element must be sanctified! O God, the
cross, the cross! Help me to hide there again and again!

Father, I come to You about money. We're in a squeeze right
now.

Dear Lord! It's so good to write to You again. I ran out of
paper in South America.

Oh, Father, Hosea 12:6 is too much: "Always be expecting
much from him, your God" (TLB).

Dear Lord, George and Joan need a buyer for their property.

Thank You, omnipotent God of all, for being my Friend.

Father, I love You so much.

Whatever it is, I spread out my heart before him. (Sometimes I laugh later at the dumb things I asked him for, which he was wise enough not to give me. I'm glad he has the final signature or veto. When I was a little girl I couldn't understand why sometimes my mother said "no," like the time when I heard that if your initials spelled a word you'd always have good luck. For several weeks I begged Mother to change my name from Elizabeth Anne Sweet to Elizabeth Anne *Ramona* Sweet, so that my initials would spell *ears*.)

Maybe you wondered at the first of the chapter why the "to do" idea can't be a tiny notebook to slip in your purse, why a whole notebook has to be toted around. Because the whole notebook is to be used continually, not just the calendar section.

You're waiting for an appointment to show up; use the time by browsing through the names of those in your small groups. Pray for them so continuously in the odd moments of your day that they become part of your bones.

You're on lunch break from work, and you have ten extra minutes. Flip to the "prayers" section, and just write to your heavenly Father whatever's on your mind. Tell him all about it.

You're dressed to go out, and you have five extra minutes. Peruse your "sermons" or "Bible study" sections, to refresh your mind about what you're learning.

You're stopped at a stop light! Flip open to the "goals" section; whatever goal hits your eye, you have something to mull over and pray about as you start up again on the green light, something you really long to be, or do.

As your notebook is filled with that which is most meaningful in every area of your total life, and as you learn to use it continuously through each day, you'll:

1. Stay on target in your living;

2. Become more prayerful;

3. Be more deeply impressed by God's truths;

4. Keep your mind filled with the pure, the beautiful;

5. Not forget what you're supposed to do!

When I was a girl growing up riding horses on Army posts, I learned that no jumping horse ever really wants to jump. No matter how pedigreed he is, if possible he'll turn aside at the last minute and let the rider go over the jump alone! So there's a crucial moment when spurs, knees, and hands tell the horse, "You're going to jump, and you're going to jump *now*."

All through the years I had fleeting thoughts of wonderful things to be or do. Or I had moments of actual conviction that I really ought to be this or do that. But somehow I let the moment pass.

I think of all the years I've believed in a daily quiet time, practiced a daily quiet time, taught others the value of a daily quiet time. But when a particular morning comes along with a long list of things to do, I'm just as tempted as anyone else to let it slip—just this one morning.

Then I need a sudden pressure—the equivalent of spurs, knees, and hands—that says, "You're going to meet the Lord first, and you're going to meet him *now*."

That pressure is my notebook.

13

YOUR REACTION TO
WHAT YOU'VE READ

"THANKS FOR THE BOOK," you're saying, "but it's too much. I couldn't do all that."

Why? Let's talk about it. You may have legitimate reasons, or maybe not.

"Well," you say, "I've just never been an organized person."

Dear feminine friend, neither was I. Ask Ray. But as life's pressures and responsibilities began to get to me, I groped around for solutions. Shaping up to the three priorities has been the most basic help—learning to live with God first, from the inside out. The tools to accomplish this—my notebook, desk, closet—came along as a result.

Actually, I'm still not organized. But my notebook is, and I live by my notebook!

"But here I sit," you say, "with a girdle in the middle of the floor, dishes in the sink, and unanswered mail strewn on the bed. Where do I start?"

Start with God. Shut your eyes to the mess, or go for a walk. Humbly surrender your heart to his control. If you haven't before, let Jesus Christ his Son totally forgive you and wash away all your inner mess—of which the outer mess is just a reflection. Get washed clean, "squeaky-clean," holy and pure as only God can make you. Invite him to live at the very center of you, the control center.

(No, don't struggle intellectually over the legitimacy of conversion, as if it were a simplistic answer. God's order is first crisis, then process. Surrender to his crisis!)

You've done that? Then bite off bits and pieces of this book. Allow time to think through what week you'll work on this, what month you'll shape up that. I'm doing the same thing! He's not through with me, either.

"No," you say. "You don't see my problem. If I lived alone, I'd be free to do all these things, but there are other human beings within my walls. . . ."

You're right. And Philippians 2:1–16 talks about submitting and adjusting and being patient to reach goals the lowly way.

Your problem is probably temporary. Babies aren't organized, but they aren't babies long. Do the best you can. Children aren't usually organized; well, they leave you soon. Balance your goals for orderliness with a sense of humor. A husband isn't always organized, but statistics show you may not always have him to put up with. Adjust—and have yourself a great romance in these tender years. Roommates can be a problem. So you can change roommates, or decide the problems can be overcome.

But remember, for all your adult life you'll be a woman. And how you live your life as a woman, all by yourself before God, is what makes the real you. Nothing on the exterior can touch or change that precious inner sanctuary—your heart, his dwelling place—unless you let it. And God, who loves you very much, has tailor made all your outer life— your circumstances, your relationships—to pressure you into becoming that beautiful woman he's planned for you to be.

How much of his planning will you accept? You have a powerful God, and your expectations for yourself should be enormous!

Let me tell you a story that illustrates the difference high expectation can make. Do you remember the widow in 2 Kings 4 who had a big debt to pay, and got the news that her creditor was going to take her two sons to be slaves as payment of the debt?

The poor woman was beside herself, and she cried to Elisha, the man of God. His answer was, "Go borrow from your neighbors every container for oil that you can get. Don't borrow just a few. Really get out there and round them up!"

The woman borrowed containers from her neighbors. She poured and she poured, drawing from her scanty little supply. She poured, and when all the containers were full, she said to her son, "Bring me another one."

"That's all we have," he said—and with that the oil stopped.

Now, the oil poured so far was enough to sell and completely pay her debt, and keep her and her sons for life, as well.

Talk about a godsend!

But it was up to the woman how literally she took Elisha's instructions to get lots of containers. If she had taken his words even more seriously, she could have tramped over the countryside and rounded up thousands of pots! The oil would have filled them all, and the rest of her life she could have fed the other poor, donated huge sums to the temple, lived in a larger house, given her sons every educational advantage. . . .

Her expectation-level of God's ability to provide determined the quality of her lifestyle, forever afterward.

Lift up your eyes. Your heavenly Father waits to bless you in inconceivable ways to make your life what you never dreamed it could be.

How many containers will you put out?

14

WHAT IS A BEAUTIFUL WOMAN?

HOW CAN A SET-UP of goals, a daily schedule, a notebook, etc., turn an ordinary woman into a beautiful one?

Well, what is a beautiful woman? Only once does the Bible say it just like that: "beautiful woman." The words referred to Sarah, Abraham's wife, in Genesis 12:11, and literally they mean "a woman of beautiful appearance." We know that she was still alluring to men at the age of ninety; she was some woman, physically! And yet she laughed at God's words in disbelief and then lied, denying it. And she was jealous of her maid. So physical beauty can't be everything.

In fact, when Proverbs 31 describes an admirable woman, her good qualities seem to be in opposition to physical beauty: "Charm is deceitful, and beauty is vain, but a woman who fears the Lord, she shall be praised" (Prov. 31:30). (Like the two fellows who were talking about their girl friends, and one said, "My girl has a great personality." And the other said, "Yeah, my girl's ugly, too.")

But the New Testament seems to put it all together by suggesting that the godly woman gives an *illusion* of outward beauty:

> *Let not your adornment be external only—braiding the hair, and wearing gold jewelry, and putting on dresses; but let it be the hidden person of the heart, with the imperishable quality of a gentle and quiet spirit, which is precious in the sight of God. For in this way in former times the holy women also, who hoped in God, used to adorn themselves (1 Pet. 3:3–5).*

Notice the word "adorn," which implies outer appearance.

Now, it's interesting that some Christians have stressed the submission of wives as if there was nothing else of significance in the Bible; but the fact remains that here in this section we find it used as the measurable test of a woman's gentle and quiet spirit: ". . . in this way in former times holy women . . . used to adorn themselves, *being submissive to their own husbands.*"

Whether we like it or not, these are the words of Scripture, in black and white; there follows a verse which redeems Sarah, with all her problems of disbelief and jealousy: she "obeyed Abraham, calling him lord," and for this reason she qualified as a beautiful woman.

"Never mind the features and figure you were born with," says 1 Peter. "What will adorn you with an illusion of beauty is a meek and quiet spirit, which is precious in the sight of God."

In other words, the beautiful woman is disciplined, chaste, discreet, deferring, gracious, controlled, "together." This kind of woman God considers godly, which means she's got his qualities, and she's close to his heart. This is *"his* kind of woman"—his kind of beautiful woman.

Now, under this umbrella of characteristics, she can have all kinds of personalities and still be beautiful. She can be vivacious or shy, colorful or cool, an administrator or a follower. She can be a corporation president or she can bake delicious molasses cookies—or both.

When a woman has God's beauty—a meek and quiet spirit—she isn't threatening to those around her. She doesn't compete; she doesn't "demand her rights," because she's secure. Her trust is in God to exalt her in his own way and time, and he does! He can afford to expand her gifts and increase her place in the world, because she's not grasping for it. That's God's kind of beautiful woman.

Realize how this was true in Jesus' day. The culture of his day was a Roman, pagan, woman-degrading culture. That didn't keep God from honoring the aged Anna, a beautiful woman, with the sight of the new-born Messiah. It didn't keep Jesus from healing Peter's mother-in-law or the woman who was hemorrhaging, or the Canaanite woman's daughter, or the woman who was bent double; or raising to life the synagogue official's daughter, or the son of the widow of Nain. It didn't keep him from freeing the woman caught in the act of adultery, or commending the woman who poured perfume over his feet, or calling attention to the widow who gave an offering of two copper coins, or engaging in a long, life-saving discussion with the Samaritan woman at the well.

It didn't keep Jesus from having some of God's beautiful women as some of his very best friends: Mary and Martha, Mary Magdalene, Joanne, Susanna, and others. Beautiful women were the closest to the cross when he died, and the first to see him when he came back to life.

In the days following, beautiful women were with the men in the upper room those ten days awaiting Pentecost. Dorcas, one of God's beautiful women, was so loved by everybody that when she died God let Peter raise her to life. John Mark's mother was hostess to gatherings of Christians, and Lydia kept Paul and company as houseguests. Aquila and Priscilla, as a married couple together, taught Apollos proper doctrine. (Priscilla must have had a meek and quiet spirit, or her advice would have been odious. But the fact is, she was one of Paul's favorites—truly loved and strategic in spreading the gospel.)

Never think that meekness is weakness. Meekness is strength under control.

God's beautiful women have been used even in mass turnings that have affected whole nations and generations. If you're a woman reading this, one of my sisters in this Western culture, you're an important key to revival in our day. When Paul heard the call to come to Europe for the first time and preach the gospel there, he traveled to Philippi, a key center, and found his way to a group of key women holding a prayer meeting (Acts 16:13). From this small group Christianity spread out until the whole known world was affected by it.

Through the centuries, God's beautiful women with meek and quiet spirits have suffered hardships, rocked cradles, and—you know the rest.

God's longest description of his ideal woman, in Proverbs 31, ends with these words: "These good deeds of hers shall bring her honor and recognition from even the leaders of the nations" (Prov. 31:31, TLB). The woman described here works hard keeping her home and serving the needs of her family, running the household with her head, her hands, and her heart. But she's hardly a pure domestic; she is also in marketing and in real estate and in anything else she wants to put her hand to.

In recent years we have been obsessed with figuring out what a woman should be allowed to do. God says in his Word a woman can do anything; the point is not what she *does* but what she *is*. When a woman is wise, and full of kind words, and hard-working and conscientious, and helpful to her man if she has one, and deeply reverent in her love for God—in other words, if she is a beautiful woman with a meek and quiet spirit—she can do anything in this whole wide world, and the world will praise her for it.

But with all this God-given, legitimate power, how do we as women influence the world for God? By influencing our *personal* worlds to him. And how do we do that? By returning to him first ourselves, with all our hearts. Will it be easy? Of course not. The worthwhile, the best, never is. It will include disciplines—daily disciplines—to change us and change those around us.

If you're a housewife with little ones underfoot, don't chafe! This is not only their training ground, it's yours. David, when he was young, cared for little ones too, sheep and lambs. How could he go straight from sheep tending into the king's palace, playing and singing his original compositions and influencing the highest power of the land? Because he was a self-starter, and while he'd been tending his sheep he'd obviously been using his spare moments composing and practicing and developing his gift.

And take a deep look at those little ones of yours. They're far more challenging than sheep! Only God knows what they'll become when you're giving them Spirit-filled training and love.

But whether mother or not, wife or not, you're a woman—wonderful, unique. And even if you're paralyzed from the neck down, you can be God's beautiful woman. His Holy Spirit within you can give you all the self-discipline you need to focus your attention on him, not yourself, to adore him for large chunks of time, to think on his attributes, to confess your sins to him and experience all the ways which involve life's "top priority," and which concern your central core, the real you. You have every resource to become one of his beautiful women, and to be a great influence on those around you and around the world.

The timing of your life is also unique. It was time for you to read this book. Opportunity, they say, is like a horse. It gallops up to you from nowhere, and pauses. Now it's time to get on. If you don't, he'll soon be gone, and the clatter of his hoofs will be heard dying away in the distance.

Yes, you're a woman—handmade by God to fulfill wonderful plans of his. Do you feel a time-release capsule exploding inside you, urging you to new interests, new opportunities, new horizons?

Is it total revolution for you?

Write me and tell me about it.

> Love,
> Anne Ortlund
> c/o Renewal Ministries
> 4500 Campus Dr., Suite 662
> Newport Beach, CA 92660

For information on "Beautiful Woman" seminars write Anne Ortlund at the address provided above.

HOW TO USE THIS BOOK

THE QUESTIONS AND EXERCISES in this study guide are designed for individual study which will in turn lead to group interaction. Thus, they may be used either as a guide for individual meditation or group discussion. During your first group meeting we suggest that you set aside a few minutes at the outset in which individual group members introduce themselves and share a little about their personal pilgrimage of faith.

If possible, it is a good idea to rotate leadership responsibility among the group members. However, if one individual is particularly gifted as a discussion leader, elect or appoint that person to guide the discussions each week. Remember, the leader's responsibility is simply to guide the discussion and stimulate interaction. He or she should never dominate the proceedings. Rather, the leader should encourage all members of the group to participate, expressing their individual views. He or she should seek to keep the discussion on track, but encourage lively discussion.

If one of the purposes of your group meeting is to create a caring community, it is a good idea to set aside some time for sharing individual concerns and prayer for one another. This can take the form of both silent and spoken petitions and praise.

STUDY GUIDE

NOTE: Before your group begins studying this book, the leader may want to order "Disciplines" notebooks and calendar pages, and at least have the group begin to use them for taking notes, making shopping lists, etc. In chapter 12, "Your Notebook," Anne tells how using a notebook has tremendously helped her and countless other women to organize their lives. But she has found that the "right" sized notebooks and calendar pages are frequently difficult to find. So Anne now makes them available. Order by writing the Ortlunds at Renewal Ministries, 4500 Campus Dr., Suite 662, Newport Beach, CA 92660; or ask for a brochure.

Chapter 1: Your First Decision, and What Follows

1. Which kind of woman are you, the kind who usually "takes life as it comes" or one who, as a rule, thinks ahead and plans for the future? Answer the questions posed by Anne Ortlund on the first page of this chapter and share your answers with the group.

2. What does it mean to "lose your own soul"? In what sense are we "saved" by reaching out to Jesus Christ? From what were you (or do you need to be) saved? *For* what are you saved?

3. Anne speaks of her *thirst* for God and of a time when she wanted "more of God" in her life. What do you think she means by "more of God"?

4. If you had more of God in your life, how do you think your life would be different?

5. Does the word *discipline* bring positive or negative thoughts to your mind? Why?

6. Do you agree with Anne's statement that "the disciplines of life are what get you to where you want to go"? Why or why not?

Chapter 2: Reshaping Your Life to Three Priorities

1. What are your top three priorities in life? List your (honest) priorities, based on how you spend your time and what you think about most of the time.

2. Do you think it is realistically possible to put God first in your life? Describe what a typical day in your life might be like if God were your Number 1 priority.

3. Anne suggests four ways to come to know God. Which of these do you already practice? What changes would you have to make in order to practice all four?

4. Do you agree that we should go to church whether we "get anything out of it" or not? Why or why not?

5. What are the personal implications of Anne's statement that one's "true source of godly love, warmth, nourishment, and togetherness should come from the larger family, the eternal family"? Is this how you view your church? If not, what could you do to make this kind of relationship possible?

6. Anne lists her third priority as the needy people of the world. Who are the needy people in your world? If they were your third priority, which of your gifts would you use to minister to them?

7. See how Jesus' heart reflects these same three priorities in his prayer in the Garden of Gethsemane to his Father: John 17:1–5, 6–19, 20–26.

See how Jesus commands us to live by these three priorities: John 15:1–11, 12–17, 18–27. In what priority are you weak? In what are you strong? How can you adjust your life to better reflect his priorities for you?

Chapter 3: Your Attitude toward Work

1. What color do you think of when you think of your work? Draw a circle and divide your work into three categories, giving each the appropriate size of the pie based on the amount of time you spend in that activity. Now assign a color to each category by how you feel about it. Yellow = exuberant, excited, look forward to it, it's important to you; Red = it's tolerable, important, but not to you, a yawn; Brown = tense, you dread it, it exhausts you and gives nothing in return, you resent having to do it. Share your discoveries with the group.

2. Do you agree that work is God's plan for you or do you wish you didn't have to work? Why does Anne think that work is God's plan?

3. How does following the three priorities on page 31 affect your attitude toward your work?

4. What special gifts are you using in your work? What gifts do you wish you could use? What kind of job could you find or create that would use your gifts more of the time? What would you have to do or give up in order to make this change?

5. What do you feel God is leading you to do in regard to your work? Share this with the group or a friend and ask them to support you in prayer and encouragement as you start taking steps to make this change.

PREPARATION FOR NEXT SESSION:
Before reading or discussing the next chapter, take an inventory of your closet. Notice Anne's list on page 37, but see that her next sentence says, "This may be an entirely different kind of wardrobe than you need." List the categories which *you* need, and count the number of items of clothing you have for each category.

Chapter 4: Your Looks

1. Do you agree with Anne when she says looks are important? How does her formula of spending 1/22 of her time on looks compare with yours?

2. What is your own philosophy regarding physical appearance?

3. CLOSET INVENTORY

Categories of clothing for your particular lifestyle (for instance, dressy dresses, day pants with tops, etc.)	Number of items of clothing
_____	_____
_____	_____
_____	_____
_____	_____
_____	_____
_____	_____

Share your discoveries with the group.

4. If you were to follow Anne Ortlund's philosophy of "eliminate and concentrate," how would your wardrobe change?

Chapter 5: Your Goals

1. How do you view people who set definite goals for themselves? Compare them with those who "fly by the seats of their pants."

2. Has there been a time in your life when you wrote down your life purposes and life goals? Describe how you felt during this period. What did you accomplish?

3. If you currently have your own goals written down, would you be willing to share them with the group? (As Anne says, goals are personal and it would be understandable if you prefer to keep them to yourself.)

4. Review the three categories of goals Anne Ortlund sets for herself, pointing out the distinctions she makes between "life purposes," "life goals," and "one-year goals."

TO THE LEADER: Dreaming and goal setting cannot be done hastily. Therefore, try to allow at least 30 minutes to an hour for the next four exercises.

5. Take a clean sheet of paper and write down your own "life purpose(s)." Be sure to use verbs in your sentences. Otherwise, your thoughts will be vague.

6. Write down your "life goals" (what you hope to do before you die). Anne says to make them *specific* and *large*.

7. Write down your "one-year goals." Now, check to make sure that each one-year goal fits into your statement of life purpose and life goals. If one does not, you need to either eliminate it or rewrite your life purpose and goals so that this goal fits.

8. If there is time, share your goals with your group.

Chapter 6: Your Daily Scheduling

1. How do you handle your daily scheduling? Do you use a calendar? "To Do" lists? A notebook? Or do you try to keep your schedule in your head? Are you happy with your system? Do you make maximum use of your minutes, as well as hours and days?

2. Why is it a bad habit to try to remember to do things instead of writing them down?

3. How much time do you think you "waste" each day due to inefficient scheduling? List the things you do that are time wasters.

4. Add to Anne's list on pages 43–44 the things you want to do when you're tempted to waste time.

5. Now, take three to five minutes to plan tomorrow. Check to see if each activity helps meet one of your "life goals." Share your schedule with the group and explain how it leads to the fulfillment of a goal.

Chapter 7: Your Growing Life

1. What "place" came into your mind when you were reading about Anne's private time with God? Do you have (or have you ever had) a special "place" where you regularly met God? Describe it.

2. How do you identify with Anne's comment that her husband, Ray, is not easily ruffled?
_____ Sounds like me most of the time.
_____ Sounds like me occasionally.
_____ I could be like that if only . . .
_____ Sounds impossible for me.
Explain your answer.

3. What books or articles have you read this year that represent your special interests? What have you read (or are you reading) to "feed your spirit"?

4. How do you study your Bible? Describe the plan that works best for you.

5. If you have not already done so, set a prayer and Bible study goal for this year. Share your goal with the group and plan to report to them on your progress, asking them for encouragement and support.

Chapter 8: Your Life Behind the Scenes

1. Do you agree that one's physical surroundings should be a reflection of God and one's inner self? Why or why not? How close is the organization and appearance of your home to how you view your inner self? _____They are the same. _____They are alike in places. _____They are not alike at all.

2. If your home is not representative of the real you, what keeps you from making it so?

3. Anne refers to God as "organization" and "spirit." What does she mean by these terms? Do you think it is possible to let your mind *dwell* on what is true, honorable, right, pure, lovely, etc., if one has several children at home? How?

4. What is the atmosphere in your house? Choose a number between 1 and 10 to describe the *typical* atmosphere in your home.

1	2	3	4	5	6	7	8	9	10
cheerful									gloomy
1	2	3	4	5	6	7	8	9	10
quiet									noisy
1	2	3	4	5	6	7	8	9	10
uplifting music								agitating music	
1	2	3	4	5	6	7	8	9	10
a refuge									a zoo

Tell the group which numbers you circled and share with them why you did. What do you want to change?

5. What have you decided to do about your wardrobe as a result of reading this chapter and chapter 4, "Your Looks"? Share your decisions with the group.

6. What have you decided to do about your beside table? Your bathroom counter? Your time with God? Share these decisions with the group.

Chapter 9: Your Closest Relationships

1. Take a moment to think of the people on whose lives you feel you have made a lasting mark. Write their names down, or if there are too many, try to think of approximately how many lives you have touched in a significant way.

2. What person has helped you the most as a growing Christian? Was your time with this person structured or unstructured? If you have had the experience of being discipled tell your group how your meetings were structured, comparing them with Anne's design.

3. Anne says that God "constructed us so that we're lonely unless we have firm, deep fellowship with him and with other believers." Does your experience validate this belief? Explain your answer.

4. How do you think a person would know whether or not he or she is ready to disciple another person? What qualifications should a discipler have?

5. If you were to accept God's call to be a discipler, who would possibly be on your first list to disciple? Think of various ways you might propose the idea to them.

6. When would you be able to meet with this (these) person(s)? What steps would you need to take between now and then to prepare yourself?

Chapter 10: Your Public Life

1. Anne says there are two kinds of personalities in the world, those whose attitude says, "Here I am," and those who say, "There you are." Which kind are you? Give reasons for your answer.

2. Think of someone you know who has a "There you are" spirit. Describe this person.

3. Anne advises us to "look quality, think quality, talk quality," and to expose ourselves to quality. On a scale from one to ten, rate yourself by circling a number in each category.

Looks	1	2	3	4	5	6	7	8	9	10
Thoughts	1	2	3	4	5	6	7	8	9	10
Talk	1	2	3	4	5	6	7	8	9	10
Input	1	2	3	4	5	6	7	8	9	10

Now, tell why you selected each number.

4. What can you do to improve in each area?

5. Is your larger circle of friends as large as you would like it to be? Is it too large? How do you differentiate between intimate friends and your "public" friends?

6. Tell the group what you would like your "public" to see in you. What has to be worked on in order for this to be possible?

Chapter 11: Your Desk

1. What do you need to do to improve the efficiency of your desk and filing system? Write down quickly each step you need to take. If you do not even have a desk or filing system your steps may include:
(1) Go by office supply store to check styles and prices of desks and file cabinets.
(2) Talk to _____ about making a desk with a door and slabs.
(3) Clean up _____ room to make room for a desk and file. (Your "file" may be a box which holds manila folders upright.)

2. Next, number your list in the order of which should come first, second, etc.

3. Share your list with the group and add or revise your plan as you hear new ideas from others.

NOTE: If your group is in agreement, you may want to make the next meeting a working session with each person organizing her own notebook.

Chapter 12: Your Notebook

1. Take a few minutes to review how Anne divides her notebook and what categories she uses.

2. List the sections you want in your notebook.

3. If you have decided to make this a working session, go ahead and let each person organize her own notebook. Make sure that more time is spent *doing* than talking.

Chapter 13: Your Reaction to What You've Read

1. Do you agree with Anne when she says that one's quality of lifestyle is determined by her expectation level of God's ability to provide? Why or why not?

2. If you were to raise your expectation level of God, how would you show it?

Chapter 14: What Is a Beautiful Woman?

1. Anne says that a beautiful woman is

disciplined
chaste
discreet

deferring
gracious
controlled
"together"

Write your name on the left side of each word that now describes you.
(Don't be overly modest.) Write your name on the right side of each
word that you believe will describe you in the next few months. Tell the
group why you expect to experience these changes.

2. Think about Anne's statement that "You have every resource to become one of [God's] beautiful women, and to be a great influence on
those around you and around the world." What specific resources do
you have to become a beautiful woman?

3. Do you feel "a time-release capsule exploding inside you, urging you
to new interests, new opportunities, new horizons"? Tell the group
about one new experience you will have this month.

4. Spend a few moments in prayer, lifting up to God the goals, plans,
schedules, and new ideas you have had while reading this book. If you
are studying the book in private, write your prayer—and put it in your
notebook!

Disciplines
of the
Heart

Tuning
Your Inner Life
to God

To my granddaughters, tomorrow's beautiful women:

Mindy Harrah   Lisa McClure
Beth Anne Harrah   Laurie McClure
Krista Ortlund

CONTENTS

FOREWORD

Bookwriting isn't easy.

You write and write and write, and the thing eventually begins to take shape and form and to harden more and more into its own personality. Before you know it, it has a will of its own and has risen up and is looking you straight in the eye and telling you what to do.

"Chapters 3 and 4 need a little lightening," I said, "a bit of humor, a personal anecdote or two. . . ."

"No, they don't." The book had firmly removed the pen from my hand. "Quit fiddling. Don't you change me. Don't you touch me."

Timidly I withdrew. "I was just trying to help," I offered uncertainly. "My other books had more light touches. . . ."

"I'm not your other books," was his reply. "I am the way I am, and that's the way I'm supposed to be."

"But people might have trouble wading through chapters 3 and 4; they might quit reading and miss the important part," I said, struggling to match his authority.

"That's the problem," he answered, and he seemed to have grown until now he was towering over me.

I searched his face—the face I knew so well, line for line. And I dared to like him. In fact, I truly admired him. I have to say it—he's better than me. He has more wisdom than I have; he is *more than me*— far more.

I relaxed.

"You win," I whispered.

1

YOU'RE AT A
CROSSROADS

THERE YOU ARE—a woman.

How is life for you?

Have you too much to do?

Are you loved?

Are you overspending?

Are you gripped by a habit—and worried?

Are you young but unattractive? Beautiful but aging? Losing your health? Wealthy? Shy?

Are you surrounded by clamoring kids? Oppressed by your boss at work? Popular on your campus?

Are you satisfied?

Are you married to a loser? Unusually gifted? Single and fulfilled?

Are you embarrassed over whatever you're like?

There are so many kinds and conditions of women in this world, millions and millions of them—some hurting, some happy . . . some pushers and shovers, others the pushed and the shoved. . . .

But out of them all, only you are you. And here you are, in this special moment, starting to read my book.

This one is a sequel to an earlier book, *Disciplines of the Beautiful Woman*,[1] and I'm praying that through it God will give you individual, personal renewal from your toes up—a renewal as thorough as the one He gave me a few years ago, the one that for me began all this bookwriting!

Disciplines of the Beautiful Woman was the easiest to write of all my books. It speaks of living your external life for God: using a notebook, keeping a desk, organizing yourself and your home. . . . It gives you a hands-on examination of Western culture, middle-class, female Christian living. It's even read by a lot of men, too, because it has to do with

[1] Anne Ortlund, *Disciplines of the Beautiful Woman* (Waco, TX: Word, 1977).

being well managed and goal oriented and productive, and we all want that. I'm glad God let me write it.

But I long that the name *Anne Ortlund* be associated with more than notebooks and closets. For tools to help us live in Christ are only tools.

I can have the latest electric toothbrush and the best toothpaste— and still not brush my teeth.

I can have the most expensive stationery and the finest pen and a supply of stamps—and still not write that letter I need to write.

I can have a wonderfully equipped kitchen and plenty of food—and still not put a meal together. (Don't pursue me on that one.)

Tools are only tools.

I'm painfully aware that I can have my Bible and notebook as close as my elbow—and still snap at my husband, Ray, when my heart's out of tune with God.

You probably know what I mean. The exterior is easier than the interior, isn't it?

The rich young ruler of Mark 10 knew that, too. He said he'd done what he could—but he still had a deep itch inside of him that wasn't satisfied yet. So he came to Jesus—and "Jesus looked at him *and loved him*."

And, oh, the Lord looks at you right now and loves you! He loves your external efforts in His direction; He isn't despising you. Parents love their children's beginning efforts, and God feels tenderly about every external "upward motion" you make.

But how's your interior? Are you discouraged over your progress? Are you feeling you should have gotten farther along than you have?

Or maybe you're just plain becoming disillusioned. You're suspecting the Christian life is overadvertised; you haven't achieved all this peace and power and joy that you hear talked about so glibly. You haven't experienced much victory over the "old nature" still within you. Your circumstances still tend to worry you or depress you, and when you feel you need God the most, He often seems the farthest away.

Well, you don't want to go back to the old life—but surely you missed a turn in the road somewhere! It should have been better than this. . . . Is that how you feel?

So, God is prodding me.

Writing a book on the external life was a start, but the need is deeper. At women's conferences I sense the Christian woman's hunger for God, her hunger to grow, her hunger for solutions to her problems—her longing to *make it* in life, to be looked on as a contemporary "beautiful woman" filled with true godliness and grace.

Interesting as I remember the timing of the writing of *Disciplines of the Beautiful Woman.* . . . One publisher said women weren't interested in getting organized and turned the manuscript down. And when the good people at Word Books accepted it, still some of them wondered if that word *disciplines* in the title wouldn't turn women off and limit sales. But the time for the book was right, and God's women were helped and are still being helped.

I'm convinced that *now the time is right for a book on the "inside job."*

It's later in the world.

Sin is greater now.

The dangers are greater.

The pain is greater.

And your desire for internal answers is stronger.

I believe you will read today more boldly, more deeply, more seriously, perhaps more desperately. You're hungry for more than being organized and productive; you're hungry for a deep heart life of holiness and happiness and serenity.

I believe it's God's time for this book—and I believe *it's your time.*

This one may not duplicate the truths you currently know. It may even ruffle your feathers a bit. So be it.

A famous evangelist's preaching once prompted a critic to say, "Don't you know you're rubbing the cat's fur the wrong way?"

"Then," said the evangelist, "let the cat turn around."

2 and 3

TURN YOUR MIND
AROUND

YOUR WHOLE LIFE—like mine, my friend—is determined by what happens between your ears. That's why the message of this book on a woman's heart life, thought life, between-the-ears life, is so crucially important.

In fact, between your very two ears right now you may be thinking, "This book is starting out a little serious and heavy; I think I'll quit and get a decorating magazine. After all, I only have so much time to relax. . . ." But I'm praying the Holy Spirit will keep tugging at you; you could be at the crossroads of your life and not know it. *(Lord, keep this reader reading, and open up her heart to You.)*

You know about Gallup Polls. Dr. George Gallup, Sr., was a Christian, and one of his last polls before his recent death was designed to probe more deeply into the spiritual condition of his fellow Americans. The poll led him to two conclusions:

1. That religious fervor in America is at an all-time high, and

2. That religious *knowledge* in America is at an all-time low. (That is, fewer know where to find the accounts of the life of Jesus or the Ten Commandments in the Bible, and so forth.)

Dr. Gallup's projection as a result of this poll was that in the years immediately ahead America will go one of two ways. Either:

1. We will experience the greatest spiritual revival we have ever known, or

2. We will see our greatest degeneration into cults and false religions.

I believe the choice will depend on whether American Christians *discipline their hearts*, whether they go deeper internally, whether they deliberately seek for and get settled in God and His Word—or whether they don't.

We're still hanging in the balance.

Religious fervor doesn't seem to have slackened. Ray and I, holding conferences on spiritual renewal all over the world, stay solidly booked several years in advance. And everywhere we go, we're touched at how earnest and tender-hearted God's people are.

It may not be too late. But certainly the direction our country takes depends in part on whether preachers and writers will take the hunger seriously enough and feed people not chaff, but God's truth!

On the other hand, many who aren't grounded in this biblical knowledge are already flocking to new TV shows, new places, new experiences where they're "freed," "made aware," "released," "fulfilled"—sensations on which their "self" dotes, and which appeal to this feelings-oriented age.

"Ray," I asked a while back, "if you were to write a book for a Christian woman about her heart, what would you say?"

"I'd tell her about her great personal need to learn to think biblically," said Ray. "I'd write a book that was a big dose of *truth*, and I'd seek to convince her that the source of truth is the Word of God."

He'd just put into my hands a book called *The Christian Mind*, which has in it this punchy British comment on truth:

> *If schoolboy "X" has got the right answer to a sum, and his eleven companions have got various wrong answers, then "X" would be a fool to compromise by accepting a figure averaged out from the twelve exercise books.*
>
> *Christian truth is objective, four-square, unshakable. . . .*
>
> *[Truth is like] a lighthouse lashed by the elemental fury of undisciplined error. Those who have come to reside in the truth must stay there. . . . Truth is most certainly a shelter.*[1]

Women by the millions today (men, too) are unsheltered, untaught, unfed, and tossing around on stormy, dangerous waves. They're exposed to every opinion and fad, right and wrong. And they're prime candidates to end up on the rocks of satanic religions.

I want this book, then, to be two things:

[1] Harry Blamires, *The Christian Mind* (Ann Arbor, MI: Servant Books, 1978), 113–114.

1. To be rooted in the Bible—to fight against biblical ignorance before it's too late; and

2. To be practical—because your great need is also concrete, measurable obedience to what you learn.

I want to affect you deeply—not just to influence you to start living out of a notebook or cleaning out your closets, but to affect you in your heart, between your ears, in the way you think—where your true living either wins or loses.

I hope you'll have both Bible and notebook in hand as you read this book, and that you'll not only *read* but *do*. Read these first five chapters to get a running start, but after that there will be guidelines for you to follow for on-the-spot obedience. I want the reading of this book to be not only a true event for you, but the beginning of new processes in your life, new "holy habits." Maybe you'll gather a little group of friends and experience it and study it together, holding each other accountable for taking new steps of obedience. Buy yourselves each a notebook to be ready to "do the truth."[2]

And, oh, I want this book to guide you through the Scriptures, so that you see God's reason for reaching for you in the first place and see His grand purposes—with you yourself in mind—behind His Cross: to make you holy as He is holy, and happier than you ever dreamed. I want you to be able to say with no qualifications, as He wants you to say, "Surely goodness and mercy shall follow me all the days of my life!"

---

[2] If you want to buy "Disciplines Notebooks" from me, write for order forms to Anne Ortlund, Renewal Ministries, 4500 Campus Drive, Suite 662, Newport Beach, CA 92625, U.S.A.

3

WHAT KIND OF realistic, nitty-gritty, earthly life does God have in mind for a woman He creates—a woman, for instance, like you?

God wants you to be truly good and truly happy.

Does your heart agree? Does something inside you say that it must be true, that it makes sense, that He didn't go to all that trouble to create you and save you to have you turn out otherwise?

And yet if your Christian life so far doesn't seem particularly good or happy, what do you do? Scale down your expectations?

Maybe you've decided that heaven will come later and your earthly life is still supposed to be full of hassle—but at least it's more bearable than if you weren't a Christian. You've concluded that nobody's perfect yet and that you'll still sin quite a bit, but at least not as much as a non-Christian—and anyway, you're forgiven.

If on a scale of one to ten your expectations are between five and seven, you've got plenty of company. Typical Christians don't really dare to expect too much. Their lives are full of heat and dust and friction, and they've rejected as unrealistic the possibility of being too terrific.

What about you?

Maybe you're a business woman and you certainly love the Lord, but after all, God only made one Mother Theresa. . . . Or you're a homemaker who serves in your church, but you've decided you were never meant to be some sort of Jesus freak. Maybe you've even deluded yourself into thinking your Christian life is "normal" when in fact it's simply stale, commonplace, timid, and ineffective.

For many Christian women life is grey—neither awful nor wonderful.

Their rationale is: if the truly wonderful isn't realistically possible in this life, why expect it and be disappointed? Or if it doesn't seem to be popular, why stick out like a sore thumb?

So in the whole Christian world there's lots of compromise, lots of lethargy, lots of conformity to the mediocre, lots of tolerance of sin and therefore lots of sin. And because of sin, there's lots of pain—you can be sure God sees to that.

With an eased-up view of sin, the heavy emphasis is on grace and forgiveness so that the idea becomes "God forgives us; let's forgive each other. Then we can do anything and still accept each other." Romans 6:1 is shocked at this kind of attitude: "Shall we sin to our heart's content and see how far we can exploit the grace of God?" (PHILLIPS).

The Bible smashes that kind of thinking. God overturns it all like overturning money tables in the temple. May this book strongly say to you, "THUS SAYS THE LORD"—not "Thus says the majority"! Reader, like a little child, hear His Word freshly and turn your mind around.

God didn't plan for your Christian life to be grey. No, no, no!

Take the book of Proverbs, for instance. Proverbs doesn't say that your life should be somewhere between awful and wonderful. Proverbs says the fool's life is awful and the believer's life is *wonderful!*

Period!

People weak in the Bible are uncomfortable with such black-and-white pronouncements. They "think grey"—so they live grey, have grey friends, sin a little or a lot, and hurt a little or a lot. And probably they're bored, bored, bored.

Proverbs, however, says black is BLACK:

> *The way of the wicked is like deep darkness; they do not know what makes them stumble (4:19).*

> *[They] lie in wait for their own blood (1:18).*

> *[The house of the adulteress] leads down to death. . . . None who go to her return (2:16–19).*

Satan tries to make the wicked look . . . well, shades of grey somewhere between soft dove and sophisticated charcoal. The "scoundrel and villain" of Proverbs 6:12–15 we're supposed to half admire; he seems bad, steely cool, and kinda cute—like the hero of some TV or movie detective plot. He's the one who

> goes about with a corrupt mouth,
> who winks with his eye,
> signals with his feet

and motions with his fingers,
who plots evil with deceit in his heart—
he always stirs up dissension.

But God's future for him is death:

Therefore disaster will overtake him in an instant;
he will suddenly be destroyed—without remedy.

The life of the fool, says Proverbs, isn't even a pretty lacquer black—
it's ugly and dirty: "The name of the wicked will rot" (10:7)!
On the other hand, dear lady, if you love God, take a look at *what He
says your life is to be like*, reasonably and realistically:

[You] will live in safety
and be at ease, without fear of harm (1:33).

When you lie down, you will not be afraid; . . .
your sleep will be sweet.
[You will] have no fear of sudden disaster
or of the ruin that overtakes the wicked,
for the Lord will be your confidence
and will keep your foot from being snared (3:24–26).

No shades of grey here! Blessings will crown your head (10:6). You'll
point the way of life to others (10:17). You'll be granted what you desire
(10:24). You'll stand firm forever (10:25)—you'll never be uprooted
(10:30). You'll win favor and a good name in the sight of God and man
(3:4) . . . and on and on.
Does God lie, or does He even exaggerate? Then do you dare think
this is all too good to be true?
The grey Christian woman tends not to take God really seriously.
Even her "believing" is grey, so she gets a life about the same shade.
What about you?
Will you read another chapter and lift your eyes to the possibility that
your life could really be *wonderful?*

4

DARE TO BELIEVE
YOUR LIFE COULD
BE WONDERFUL

IF YOU HAVEN'T before, deep inside your heart begin to believe a daring truth: God doesn't want you to live a mediocre life. In fact, here's His flat-out goal for you:

That you may become blameless and pure, children of God without fault in a crooked and depraved generation, in which you shine like stars in the universe (Phil. 2:15).

That you may be able to discern what is best and may be pure and blameless until the day of Christ, filled with the fruit of righteousness (Phil. 1:10–11).

You don't have to "live grey," feeling dirty, unworthy, mediocre, unfulfilled, and guilty.

And, my friend, whatever God asks you to be, He enables you to be! Second Peter 1:3 says that His divine power has given you *everything you need* for life and godliness! He says that you may even "participate in the divine nature and escape the corruption in the world caused by evil desires" (2 Pet. 1:4).

"How can such a thing be?" we ask in wonder, the way the Virgin Mary asked of the Christmas angel. And back from Colossians 2:9 comes the lofty magnificence of this bold statement of truth:

In Christ all the fullness of the deity lives in bodily form, and you have been given fullness in Christ!

Then how could you or I insult Him by living a cheap, grey, inconsequential life? He has promised that "He will be the sure foundation for your times, a rich store of salvation and wisdom and knowledge" (Isa. 33:6)!

And how does the power for this come to you?

Ray was walking one day on the beach near our Southern California home, thinking about the power of God in our lives.

Just then he happened to come upon a dead sea gull washed up on the shore. He thought, "If I threw the carcass of this gull up into the air, gravity would make it fall to the ground with a thud. On the other hand, over my head sea gulls are flying everywhere."

What was the difference? It was life. The power of gravity was just as great on the living gulls as on the dead ones, but the greater power of life within lifted the living ones and overcame gravity's downward drag.

So Romans 8:9–11 says,

> You . . . are controlled not by the sinful nature but by the Spirit, if the Spirit of God lives in you. . . . And if the Spirit of him who raised Jesus from the dead is living in you, he who raised Christ from the dead will also give life [that lifting, overcoming life-force] to your mortal bodies.

God's resurrection power is the greatest upward force of all forces; that's the power for godliness that He's put within your very own body.

And the Apostle Paul prays that you will *understand this power*, dear person feeling downward pulls in your life! So few do understand—and understanding makes all the difference, as you'll see in the next chapter.

He prays "that the eyes of your heart may be enlightened" (would you ask God to open the eyes of your heart?)—

> that you may know . . . his incomparably great power for us who believe. That power is like the working of his mighty strength, which he exerted in Christ when he raised him from the dead (Eph. 1:18–20).

Talk about getting a drink from a fire hydrant. . . .

When you take this seriously, you want to ask, "Lord, is that an economical use of power? Was there some reason You really needed to take the most gigantic upward force in the entire universe and put it inside lil' ol' me?"

Picture J. Paul Getty drawing from his vast financial resources a coin to make a phone call. Then maybe you can begin to understand that you have absolutely unlimited power for godly living, and that when you draw on it every minute from here to eternity, the amount you'll use will be laughably, ridiculously small compared with the amount that's left still available for you.

5, 6, and 7

LEARN TO LET GOD
WORK IN YOU

THEN WHY DO so many Christians live grey, struggling, carnal lives? Because they haven't comprehended the vastness of the power within them and what to do with it.

"Well, what *are* we to do with it?" you're asking.

And I answer, "Nothing."

"What?" you squawk. "That's crazy. Of course we're to do something. We have to do something to take advantage of all that power."

A woodpecker was once pecking away on a great tree. Suddenly a huge bolt of lightning struck the tree and with enormous noise and force split it right down the middle, straight to its very roots.

The poor little woodpecker found himself on the ground nearby, half-dead, his feathers torn and singed. And when he gathered himself together he croaked, "I didn't know I could do it!"

So God desires to show His great power in our lives, and we croak, "Now, what shall I do? I certainly have to do something to make this happen."

The answer is really "Stand back!" It's "Take God seriously! Accept His enormous power in your life; believe it, and be ready for miracles!"

"What must I do," asked the Philippian jailer, "to be saved?"

And Paul answered, "Believe. Just believe, and you'll be saved— that's all it takes. Don't 'do'; you'll just get in the way. Let God do the 'doing'!"

And that night, as the jailer simply "[came] to believe in God" (Acts 16:34), the Lord God Almighty mysteriously reached down out of eternity and chose him, applied the eternal work of the Cross to that man's account, wrote his name in the Lamb's book of life, washed him of his sins, caused him to be born into His heavenly family, breathed into him eternal life, removed all condemnation from him, deposited in him His Holy Spirit as a "down payment" of more to come, bestowed on him all the riches of His grace, eternally predestined him to be conformed to the image of His Son, made him a co-heir with Christ of all things, called him, justified him, sanctified him, glorified him—and so much more that it will take all eternity for that jailer to discover what God "did" the instant he believed!

When we're itchy to "do," it's usually because we really *don't believe*, so we're trying to help God out. In Jesus' hometown, "he did not do many miracles because of their lack of faith" (Matt. 13:58). They didn't take seriously His supernatural power so available for them, so He didn't use it! And when we don't understand His resurrection power within us, we develop an activist religion that crowds out the possibility of that giant, explosive power's working in our lives.

Now, the confusion comes because we don't see clearly that there are two sides in Christianity: His side and our side, His dazzling white and our black. (Face it: in ourselves, in our own strength, we're black.) Most Christians mix the two—some of God in their lives, some of themselves, some white, some black—and come out grey.

But God wants to take over completely and use His power to make you, my friend, as dazzling white as Himself!

Just as he who called you is holy, so be holy in all you do; for it is written: "Be holy, because I am holy" (1 Pet. 1:15–16, Lev. 11:44–45).

"It is God's will that you should be holy" (1 Thess. 4:3).

Now, if you're objecting, "But I can't; that's impossible," you're absolutely right. Whew, you see it! That's so important. If you thought you could, you'd be another woodpecker.

You can't be holy. You can't be truly good. You can't, in yourself, be "pure and blameless" and all those things God seems to be insisting you must be.

Take a look at the two sides of this thing.

Ray and I have a big porcelain conch shell in our kitchen, and sometimes I fill it with fruit. I had a gorgeous peach in it recently, a soft gold with a perfect rosy blush on it. At just the right moment I carried it to the sink, leaned over, and took a big bite. Yuk! I hadn't noticed the other side; it was black with rot and mold. That peach had two sides.

When I saw only one side of my peach I described it as perfect. Someone seeing the other side would say, "No, that peach is rotten."

Now, there are two distinct sides in Christian righteousness, and they are totally different and must not be confused.

God's part is to work—with all that divine, all-encompassing power.

Our part is to trust Him to do it.

A century ago Christians knew this truth well. But we forgot it, and our egos took over, and we became such busy little woodpeckers that our heads hurt! Then we got stressed out, so we've given up and settled for less.

Certainly there's plenty of work to be done. We are trapped in bad habits and self-centeredness and temper and all that opposes God. Those things are the *fruit* of sin—that we worry about and try to keep somewhat under control, or at least under cover.

But the real problem is even more serious. It's the *root* of sin—that consistent, basic tendency to sin which made Paul cry out, "What a wretched man I am! Who will rescue me from this body of death?" (Rom. 7:24).

You can't rescue yourself.

> Were the seas water
> And all the land soap,
> If Thy blood not wash me,
> There is no hope.[1]

So God does the work! He steps in and rolls up His sleeve and bares His mighty arm, and does it all.

Oh, my friend! If you could understand what He's done for you— and what He's doing—and what He will yet do—!

As Isaiah 63:1–10 explains it, Jesus Christ our Lord,

Dismayed over the death-sins in which we're totally—and willingly—enmeshed,

Feeling intensely the loneliness and rejection of being the only One who cares enough to do something about it,

Dons His soldier's garb and takes sword in hand and comes down to do what He knows, for love's sake, He must do.

He battles us sinners to the death—His death—becoming totally bloody and ruined and eternally stained and scarred—

For what?

To rescue the very ones He's battling—to rescue us, His enemies, whom He loves so passionately—to rescue the ones who fight Him, bloody Him, hurt Him, defeat Him, wound and kill Him,

To rescue us so that He can rise, scarred and bloodied, to enfold us tenderly to His breast and gently clear our vision so we can see how deeply He loves us, and then to spend eternity pouring out His kindness

[1] John Donne (1573–1631).

upon the precious ones He's rescued, comforting us and sustaining us and doing uncounted good things for us all the days of our eternal lives.

Alleluia!

So, there are two sides. His part is to do it all. And our part is to let Him do it—and hopefully to thank Him and praise Him and marvel over it all!

But when we speak of resting and trusting, it's not as though nothing were happening. Everything is happening! He is thrilled over you, the one He's restored to Himself, and He is constantly, powerfully working on your behalf.

There was a time when God rested: on the seventh day of creation, when He had finished all His creating work (Gen. 2:2). But then Adam and Eve and all the rest of us sinned, and God hasn't rested since. Jesus said, "My Father is always at his work to this very day, and I, too, am working" (John 5:17). And God won't rest again until you are totally redeemed, and until all sin and death and everything that hurts you is completely destroyed (1 Cor. 15:24–28). He loves you so much!

But does it gall you to think of just letting Him do everything?

Between your two ears, my friend, your successful living depends on your seeing the difference between these two sides. Unless you understand the mighty, eternal, efficient, sufficient work of God for you, you'll try to lend a hand and you'll mess up your life.

A few decades ago, when we forgot the ancient, biblical truth of God's work and our rest (our theological roots), then certain hymns fell out of favor. Hymns that emphasized our part of trusting Him sounded as if Christianity had had the juice turned off, as if it was no go, as if it was dead in the water.

With all there is to *do* in the Christian life, why would we sing songs like this—

> Jesus, I am resting, resting
> In the joy of what Thou art;
> I am finding out the greatness
> Of Thy loving heart?

Forget this resting stuff; let's get busy! Let's GOFORIT!

Jean Sophie Pigott wrote that wonderful hymn I just quoted in 1876, just one year after Bradford Torrey wrote this next one. It's even quieter, so it died even sooner.

Right now, do something interesting: read this hymn as an activist, roll-up-your-sleeves-and-hit-that-target modern Christian, and see how it will turn you off. Then read it a second time in the light of the full-orbed, unceasing, supportive, caring energies of God on your behalf, and see how it will turn you on.

Here's the hymn:

> Not so in haste, my heart!
> Have faith in God and wait.
> Although He linger long,
> He never comes too late.
>> He never comes too late;
>> He knoweth what is best.
>> Vex not thyself in vain;
>> Until He cometh, rest.
> Until He cometh, rest,
> Nor grudge the hours that roll;
> The feet that wait for God
> Are soonest at the goal,
>> Are soonest at the goal
>> That is not gained by speed;
>> Then hold thee still, my heart,
>> For I shall wait His lead!

Are you feeling tense these days? Are you overworked, stressed out? Keep reading! Do yourself a favor and keep reading.

I spoke recently to the Fellowship of Christian Airline Personnel in Dallas. (What a wonderful bunch they are!) I asked Pam, a pretty flight attendant, for illustrations on what it means to trust in God and let Him work.

Pam was great! First she told me how hard it is to diaper her one-year-old.

"You never saw such a squirmer," she said. "If she would just relax and let me be in control, I could put on her diaper in half the time, and then she could go have fun again." (Christian, think about it.)

Then she told me about her sister's little boy's getting his first haircut. That barber had to be quick! Just as he'd be ready to snip, Jason would wiggle, turn his head, or get bored and want out of the chair. Many rubber-duck-squeaks later, the job was finally done, but that was getting a haircut the hard way. Jason had trouble being quiet to let the barber do his work.

I told Pam about how my fair skin doesn't like California sun, so now and then I have to have the dermatologist remove sun damage. This last time it was everything on my face at once. You better believe I lay absolutely quiet on that operating table while the doctor froze, cut, and burned.

Listen, when it comes to getting the power to live a holy, happy life—let's you and me admit it's not our strong suit. Let's stay quiet and let Almighty God do for us everything we need done. "Be still before the Lord," says Psalm 37:

> Commit your way to [Him];
> > trust in him and he will do this:
> He will make your righteousness shine like the dawn.

Now Work Into Your
Life What You've
Been Reading

If the message of this book from God's Word is going to be life-changing for you, you must insist on a dead boulevard stop at this point.

Don't race on to the next chapter.

Tell God you have this tendency to St. Vitus' Dance—to nervous rushing which keeps you living on the surface instead of going underneath!

"Current Christianity," said someone, "is seventy-three miles wide and half an inch deep." Will you personally help to reverse that trend?

Within the next twenty-four hours, before you go on to chapter 6, take a full thirty minutes to reread this fifth chapter. Then, just *sit before the Lord.*

"Be still," as Psalm 37:7 commands, and during that time write in your notebook a prayer to Him.

Surrender your heart to Him, telling Him you want to turn a new corner in your Christian life.

Surrender your mind to Him. Tell Him you want to learn to think well, to think biblically, to walk in truth, to be established and settled in His doctrine.

If you are several in a group, end your meeting now with a time of silence. Afterward, if the Spirit leads, humbly pray together about your new determination. Then make the thirty-minute experience your "homework" before meeting again.

6

I HAVEN'T TOLD many stories and entertained you much so far, have I? That's because, as I said, I believe you're ready to read more boldly, more deeply, more seriously. Here's a truth for you that could truly establish and strengthen and settle you in God:

God is at work in everything.

Do you believe that? You won't truly rest and trust if you believe He's only at work in some areas of your life, and the rest is up to you. Then you'll come out grey! And hassled. And tired.

Grey Christians think God is at work in some activities but not in others. Sometimes I've heard Christians pray when they come to a church meeting or a retreat, "Lord, it's so good to come back to You out of the bustle and stress. . . ." I want to interrupt, "He's been with you all the time! How tragic if you've been living until now as if you were on your own!"

Grey Christians think God is at work on Sundays but not from Monday to Saturday. They come to church with their empty buckets, in a sense saying, "Fill 'er up, preacher! It's got to last me another whole week!" They don't know that Jesus said, "Whoever believes in me . . . streams of living water will flow from within him" (John 7:38). Or that He told the Samaritan woman at the well, "The water I give [the believer] will become in him a spring of water welling up to eternal life" (John 4:14).

We need to understand that we live in fullness, that God has made us artesian wells! We come to church with God's fullness within, to contribute and share as well as to receive. And all week long the same fullness is within—nourishing, purifying, sustaining us. We're given a never-ending supply of Him!

Grey Christians think God is at work in healings but not in sicknesses.

Yet wonderful King Hezekiah said after his sickness, "Surely it was for my benefit that I suffered such anguish" (Isa. 38:17).

The Apostle Paul, who admired Timothy's "sincere faith" (2 Tim. 1:5), told him, "Use a little wine because of your stomach and your frequent illnesses" (1 Tim. 5:23).

And Paul himself, after praying three times to be freed from his "thorn in the flesh" (probably eye trouble) had this testimony:

> [God] said to me "My grace is sufficient for you, for my power is made perfect in weakness." Therefore I will boast all the more gladly about my weaknesses, so that Christ's power may rest on me. . . . For when I am weak, then I am strong (2 Cor. 12:9–10).

Grey Christians think God is at work in good times but not in bad.

Have you noticed Jonah's ups and downs (or should I say ins and outs)?

"The Lord provided a great fish" (Jon. 1:17) to rescue him from drowning.

"The Lord God provided a vine" (4:6) to shade him.

Then "God provided a worm" (4:7) to destroy the shade.

And then "God provided a scorching east wind, and the sun blazed on Jonah's head" (4:8).

The Lord provided them all: two goods, two bads.

Or think about Joseph; "the Lord was with him" in great times and in terrible times:

> *His master saw that* the Lord was with him *and that the Lord gave him success in everything he did (Gen. 39:3).*
>
> *While Joseph was there in the prison,* the Lord was with him *(vv. 20–21).*

Joseph lived serenely through it all because he understood that God was at work in everything in his life. So he could say to his brothers who had abused him, "Don't be afraid. . . . You intended to harm me, but God intended it for good" (Gen. 50:20).

Indeed, you have that sweeping statement in Romans 8:28 that says flatly that God is at work in everything for you: "We know that in all things God works for the good of those who love him, who have been called according to his purpose."

Grey Christians don't see this. They go to church and maybe worship or serve the Lord with all their might, and then they go home and worry over things. Their Christianity is fractured and compartmentalized—and so are their hearts as well.

Grey Christians carve up their lives into "sacred" and "secular." They have the impression that prayer, Bible reading, church attendance, and "fellowship" are sacred acts that make God happy. Then there's eating, sleeping, lovemaking, working, recreation, and all the rest that are secular acts. For these they sort of apologize to God and look on them as necessary waste. And the upshot is that they feel uneasy most of the time and consider themselves "basically secular" Christians.

But the dogged, can't-get-away-from-it fact is that they're Christians—so they have to keep crossing back and forth all their lives between sacred and secular. And their inner hearts tend to break up into dividedness, purposelessness, frustration.

Says A. W. Tozer,

> *They try to walk the tight rope between two kingdoms, and they find no peace in either. Their strength is reduced, their outlook is confused and their joy is taken from them.*[1]

There is terrible danger in considering yourself a "basically secular" Christian! It gives you a low self-image, a feeling of weakness and failure, and a sense of standing on the threshold where it's only an easy step to a little drugs, a little sexual permissiveness, a little this or that.

Jeremiah lived among grey believers, and he cried,

> My heart is broken . . .
> because of the Lord
>   and his holy words.
> The land is full of adulterers. . . .
>   "Even in my temple I find their wickedness,"
>   declares the Lord
>
> (Jer. 23:9–11).

In that day, too, "consenting adults" behind closed doors were polluting society, and God cried,

> Can anyone hide in secret places
>   so that I cannot see him? (v. 24).

[1] *The Pursuit of God* (Harrisburg, PA: Christian Publications, 1948), 119.

Oh, my friend! It is radical and revolutionary and cleansing and purifying for you to see that *God is at work in everything*—and then adjust your life accordingly!

William Law (1686–1761) wrote in his book, *A Serious Call to a Devout and Holy Life,*

> *He . . . is the devout man [or we'll say woman] . . . who considers God in everything, who serves God in everything, who makes all the parts of [her] common life parts of piety, by doing everything in the name of God, and under such rules as are conformable to His glory.*[2]

Jesus' life was like that. He'd given His whole human life to the Father (Heb. 10:5, 7), and the Father made no distinction between act and act. Jesus ate, He preached, He went to parties, He did miracles, He rested—and He said, "I always do what pleases him" (John 8:29).

If you read *Disciplines of the Beautiful Woman,* you may remember that I suggested a list of things to do when you're tempted to dawdle. Every one of those acts can be bright with the glory of God:

1. Exercise.

2. Memorize Scripture.

3. Look over your coming calendar and prepare what to wear.

4. Give yourself a pedicure.

5. Write a list of your blessings.

6. Walk around your house critically: adjust, rearrange, throw out, give away.

7. Cook ahead for the freezer.

8. Cream yourself all over.

9. Read part of an important book.

10. Clean out your cosmetics drawer.

11. Write a letter to an old friend.

12. Do your nails.

13. Weed your garden.

[2] (Philadelphia: Westminster, 1948), 1.

14. Bring your recipe file up to date.

15. Encourage a Christian friend by telephone, someone you don't usually call.

16. Put all those old photos into albums.

17. Take a walk in the park.

18. Nap on a slant board, or with your feet up.

19. Have a prolonged time talking with God: partly on your knees, partly standing with hands raised, partly on your face before him on the floor.

20. Polish the silver.

21. Write a poem (don't be silly; everybody does).

22. Write your pastor an encouraging note.[3]

We may have done those activities as God's "beautiful women" to fill our time more profitably and live more efficiently. But now see a deeper dimension. In your thought life, in your heart life, judge each of those twenty-two acts. We are in God, and He is in us. *He in us* writes a letter to an old friend, weeds the garden, has a prolonged time of prayer! "It is the Father, living in me, who is doing his work" (John 14:10).

All is filled with God. All is in Him and before Him. All is done in humble submission to His will. "In all thy ways acknowledge him [in memorizing Scripture, in giving yourself a pedicure], and he shall direct thy paths" (Prov. 3:6, KJV). He will order your schedule; He will enjoy everything you do (and you will enjoy everything He does!) as you live in Him, and He in you. Your life is synchronized, in harmony with His. His works are superimposed on yours—and yours on His!

And that's how He tells you to live (Col. 3:17)!

Open your eyes, my friend, and fill all your life with the brightness of the splendor of God! Live all your life seeing your powerful, loving Lord at work everywhere, in everything, in all your circumstances, in all your moments. Psalm 119:91 says, "All things serve [him]." Romans 11:36 says that "From him and through him and to him are all things."

[3] Ortlund, *Disciplines of the Beautiful Woman*, 65–66.

Then nothing—nothing—is without God's wonderful meaning in it. "The earth is the Lord's, and everything in it" (Ps. 24:1). "The whole earth is full of his glory" (Isa. 6:3)! He knows when every sparrow falls, and He knows even the number of the hairs on your head (Matt. 10:29–30). He has established all governments (Rom. 13:1), and the hearts of all governmental rulers are in His hand, doing what He pleases (Prov. 21:1).

If God is truly at work in everything, you have brand new ground rules for living your Christian life.

Literally:

You're to cast all your anxiety on Him because He cares for you (1 Pet. 5:7).

You're not to repay anyone evil for evil; " 'I will repay,' says the Lord" (Rom. 12:17–19).

You're not to fear anything, because He's with you (Ps. 23:4).

You'll never lack anything, because He's your Shepherd (Ps. 23:1).

When you pass through hard times, He'll see that they don't get the better of you (Isa. 43:2).

Says Hannah Whitall Smith,

> *[No action] can touch us except with [the Father's] knowledge and by His permission. It may be the sin of man that originates the action, and therefore the thing itself cannot be said to be the will of God; but by the time it reaches us it has become God's will for us, and must be accepted as directly from His hands.*
>
> *No man or company of men, no power on earth or heaven, can touch that soul which is abiding in Christ, without first passing through His encircling presence and receiving the seal of His permission. If God be for us, it matters not who may be against us; nothing can disturb or harm us, except He shall see that it is best for us.*[4]

Only if this is true does 1 Thessalonians 5:18 make sense: "Give thanks in all circumstances, for this is God's will for you in Christ Jesus."

God is at work in everything. Are you believing practically at this minute how great He is—how great He is *for you?* It should begin to relax your muscles even as you read.

"Be still," says the psalm.

"Let your hands hang down," says Hebrews.

---

[4] *The Christian's Secret of a Happy Life* (Westwood, NJ: Barbour, 1985, originally published 1870), 151–152.

Hear it again: you won't really rest and trust if you believe that He's only at work in some areas of your life, but that the rest is up to you. Do you have a grey mind, like most Christians, that mixes a little white and a little black and is confused, directionless, fractured?

Or will you *let God be God?*

Now Work Into Your Life What You've Been Reading

Write down in a list in your notebook each area of your life—how you spend your time. Following each of these areas write this prayer: "Lord, I give this area of my life to You. Do what You want with it. Subtract it or strengthen it or cleanse and purify it."

List your bad circumstances. Thank Him on paper for each one (1 Thess. 5:18)! Turn each one over to Him, asking Him as you write to heal your thought life concerning:

1. Your resentment

2. Your worry

3. Your tendency to take the matter into your own hands, or whatever.

Don't hurry.

Ask Him to give you an attitude of worship, praise, and rest each time one of these circumstances confronts you.

Remember, your living is between your ears!

Memorize Isaiah 26:3. Hold yourself accountable to someone who will hear you say it.

If you are reading this book in a small group, allow plenty of silence for this writing, and then share all that you're able of what you've written down. Pray for each other and memorize together.

7

SAYS RICHARD FOSTER, "In our day heaven and earth are on tiptoe waiting for the emerging of a Spirit-led, Spirit-intoxicated, Spirit-empowered people.[1]

I hope in the last few chapters you've been thrilling to the truth of God's possibilities for your life and His greatness on your behalf.

To believe it, to accept it, is the first step—but then you must walk on it and live in the light of it and be obedient to it, one day at a time. Then you will not only be "Spirit-empowered," but really and actually, as Foster said, "Spirit-led" and "Spirit-intoxicated," too. Oh, I do believe the time has come when God's people will grow their roots down deep in knowledge and grow their trunks and branches up tall in holiness and happiness! I think you and I have "come to the kingdom for such a time as this"!

You heard me say "you must" in that last paragraph. Did you catch it? And you're saying, "Hold it, Anne Ortlund! You've been saying that God's part is to do the work and our part is to rest and trust. Then what's this 'you must' business?"

I'm glad you asked that question. You're sharp to pick up on it and not let it pass!

The foundational truth is that there is God's side and there is our side. The work, the accomplishment, is only His. You in yourself can't be holy and happy, but Christ *can* be—in you and through you—and He will be if you ask Him to and let Him.

"The Lord will accomplish what concerns me" (Ps. 138:8, NASB).

He establishes "the work of our hands" (Ps. 90:17)—our hands, His establishing.

Said Isaiah to the Lord, "All that we have accomplished you have done for us" (Isa. 26:12).

[1] *Celebration of Discipline* (San Francisco: Harper & Row, 1978), 150.

Here's a glove, empty and limp. I hold it up by its wrist and it can't wave, it can't pick up anything, it's helpless. Then I slide my hand into the glove, and my fingers fill all its fingers. Then it can seem full of dexterity and power!

"My, what a wonderful glove!" someone says. "It's so clever and gifted! It's brilliant!"

No, the glove is helpless in itself; it's the hand inside that's brilliant. And you know what? Any old out-of-fashion, funny-looking glove will do!

Your part is to relax and let Him work in you; His part is to achieve fabulous goals in you and for you. "He who trusts in himself is a fool, but he who walks in wisdom [in Christ] is kept safe" (Prov. 28:26).

Now, in the rest of the book I'm going to be mostly exhorting you and urging you—but you must understand it in the light of God's side and your side, or nothing much will happen. When your heart leaps up and you respond to something—"Oh, yes, that's what I want to be or do!"—then in the next breath say to God, "This, too, I surrender to You, Lord, to let You do the work in me. I rest in Your fabulous ability; I'm on tiptoe to see You do this wonderfully in my life. And I will give You the credit!"

Day by day, morning by morning, begin your walk with Him in the calm trust that *God is at work in everything*. George Mueller used to say, "It is my first business every morning to make sure that my heart is happy in God." He was right! It is your personal business, as a discipline of your heart, to learn to be peaceful and safe in God in every situation.

Some of my mornings I read this written in my notebook:

> The light of God surrounds me;
> The love of God enfolds me;
> The power of God protects me;
> The presence of God watches over me;
> Wherever I am, God is.

Remember, friend, where your real living is going on. In your thinking, in your reacting, in your heart of hearts—here is where your walk with God begins and continues. So when you start to move into trusting Him, *stay there*. Don't wander out again into worry and doubt!

Here's an old-fashioned illustration that's so good I can't think of a more modern one to replace it.[2] A piece of iron, in itself and by itself, is

---

[2] Illustration taken from *The Message of Keswick* (London: Marshall, Morgan, and Scott, new edition 1957), 44.

cold, black, hard, and ugly. But hold it in a furnace, and what a change takes place!

I saw this once with my own eyes at Lukens Steel Mill in Coatesville, Pennsylvania. The coldness was gone, the blackness was gone, the hardness was gone, the ugliness was gone—the iron had been transformed. The fire and the iron were still distinguishable from each other; the iron was certainly still iron. But as long as that iron was held in the fire, it had entered into a new experience, and it was hot and glowing and purified.

You ask me what I, Anne Ortlund, am in myself, and I can tell you that I'm "cold, black, hard, and ugly"! But as long as I remain in the fire of Christ, I'm hot and glowing and purified. From moment to moment it's my privilege to remain there, to "abide in Him"—and He Himself is my life and purity and power. Only He sets me free from the law of sin and death (Rom. 8:2)—but, oh, He does set me free!

Can I boast that this is true? Hey, I know very well what I am in myself.

Do I "know the Lord"? I've barely begun. Just the same, as Meister Eckhart said, "No one knows better what heat is than the man who is hot."[3]

Or do I mean I've come into some kind of sinless perfection? *I wish!* It would be my greatest delight, and it would make my life even happier and easier than it is now. But that rascal "self" keeps exploding out from the fire and has to be shoved back in again. Says 1 John 1:8, "If we claim to be without sin, we deceive ourselves and the truth is not in us."

But what a release, what a freedom indeed, to be delivered from trying to manage my own Christian life and to let Him take over! "The [person who] has discovered this secret of simple faith has found the key that will unlock the whole treasure-house of God!"[4]

I love J. B. Phillips's picture of this life in his translation of Romans 5:17: "Men by their acceptance of his . . . grace and righteousness should live all their lives like kings"!

Comments Oswald Sanders,

What a fascinating picture of Christian living this vivid picture portrays: nobility, charm, authority, wealth, freedom. Our God invites us to believe that these spiritual qualities and prerogatives may and should be enjoyed by every child of the King of Kings. If

[3] *Meister Eckhart,* ed. James M. Clark (London: Thomas Nelson and Sons, 1957), 176.

[4] Hannah Whitall Smith, *The Christian's Secret of a Happy Life* (Westwood, NJ: Barbour, 1985, originally published 1870), 42.

we do not manifest and enjoy them, it is not because they are beyond our reach, but only because we are living below our privileges.[5]

I stop writing and sit a little taller. My heart shouts halleluia! As you read, are you joining me? Let's tell Him we never again want to live below our privileges — not when He has gone to such lengths to provide them, and not when He so delights in our receiving them!

[5] *Spiritual Maturity* (Chicago: Moody, 1962), 125.

Now Work Into Your
Life What You've
Been Reading

Consider as yours, right now, the qualities Oswald Sanders says every child of the King should enjoy. In your notebook list each one, and then write beside them how they relate to Christ's own characteristics. Thank Him for each of these qualities and ask Him to live them out to the fullest in your life:

1. Nobility

2. Charm

3. Authority

4. Wealth

5. Freedom

If you're studying this book together in a small group, allow silence for this writing, and then share together as much of what you've written as you're able.

Follow with a time of joyous praise, perhaps with singing as well as prayer.

8 and 9

WHY GOD MUST DO THE WORK: YOU AND I ARE BOTH WEAK AND WICKED

NOW WE NEED just two chapters to see how cold, black, hard, and ugly iron is—to get motivated to stay in that fire!

Are you willing to look hard at you and at me? Sin is such a big part of what God's Word has to say to you that to ignore it would be to ignore God. To shut your eyes to sin would be to stay outside the sheltering lighthouse of truth and to be exposed to all those satanic rocks.

You're aware of it: there are plenty of false religions today that never mention the word *sin*, and they're all out to make you one more convert on their list. But if you haven't examined the blackness, the awfulness of your sin so far in your Christian life, it's time.

That remarkable Christian Blaise Pascal (1623–1662) said, "We can only know God well when we know our own sin. And those who have known God without knowing their wretchedness have not glorified him, but have glorified themselves."[1]

What a description of today's Christianity!

(Am I rubbing the cat's fur the wrong way? Then turn around, cat! Popular ideas of the day don't nullify the Word of God. "Not at all! Let God be true, and every man a liar," Rom. 3:4.)

Christian, you must understand thoroughly what you are (remember the woodpecker!) if you're to *remain willing* to trust in God only for all His power in your life.

Jesus told about a fellow who went to the temple and prayed, "God, have mercy on me, a sinner." And because that man was willing to flat-

[1] Sherwood E. Wirt, ed., *Spiritual Disciplines* (Westchester, IL: Crossway, 1983), 19. You may be interested to know that Pascal, who was sickly and only lived to be thirty-nine, was a physicist who discovered "Pascal's Law," which laid the foundation of modern hydraulics. He also invented the barometer and the calculator, the latter being the forerunner of today's computer. He was a Christian who, some have said, wrote the finest prose ever written by a Frenchman.

out admit his sin, Jesus said, "I tell you that this man . . . went home justified [—totally justified—] before God" (Luke 18:13–14). Wow!

Grey Christians think they're a mixture of good and bad. Revelation 3:16 says that makes Jesus gag. Only because He pronounces us totally bad is He able to make us totally good—without any propping up or polishing up on our part at all.

In ourselves we are blacker than iron—black, black. Unless we see that, we will never hate sin and fear sin and be repelled by sin enough to stay in the fire. (Says Tozer, "The Holy Spirit is first of all a moral flame.")

I began this book telling about Dr. George Gallup's last poll, which reveals the fact that Christians today are at a dangerous crossroads— high in religious fervor, low in knowledge—exposed and vulnerable.

I see another trend—moral deterioration. How can I say that, when earlier I said we're ready for broad-scale renewal? Because both trends are true; that's why we're indeed teetering in the balance.

But there's no doubt of it at all: we *are* deteriorating morally. With so many out of the fire, we're cooling off and getting blacker. I see evangelical Christianity passing from the wonderful height of its acceptance *IN* this world to the depth of its acceptance *OF* this world.

I see how when liberalism waned and we evangelicals rose to popularity and were listened to—we could have given our authentic message and cried to the world, "Repent! Be radically cleansed of your sin! Receive Jesus Christ's purity and holiness for your lives!"

But instead, in that time of golden opportunity, we lost our courage. We became embarrassed by our "separation" from the world, and we cozied up to it and joined it. We Madison-Avenue-trivialized our glorious gospel. And we stained ourselves with the world's adulteries and fornications.

I heard a respected old pastor comment recently at our lunch table that just as in the last twenty years Christians have accepted and gotten comfortable with adultery (through divorce), so in the next twenty years they will equally accept and get comfortable with abortion and homosexuality. I see it happening already: church families are secretly murdering little fetuses within their single daughters and ignoring the fact that their church musician is gay because he "helps the people to worship. . . ."

We're getting colder, blacker, harder, uglier! We must weep; we must mourn! We must hate with a holy hatred our blackness, our sin, our ugliness, our coldness, our hardness—that wrenches and tears our Father's heart and makes the pain of Jesus' cross go on and on!

None of the ransomed ever knew
How deep were the waters crossed;
Nor how dark was the night that the Lord passed through
Ere He found His sheep that was lost.[2]

* * *

For all that He suffered,
   in Gethsemane,
   in Gabbatha,
   in Calvary,
For the pain,
   the shame,
   the curse, of the cross,
That He deigned to be betrayed
   and that by His own disciple,
That He deigned to be sold,
   and that for thirty pieces of silver;
   to be troubled in His mind,
   to be weary,
   to fear,
   to be exceeding sorrowful, even unto death,
   to be in an agony,
   with strong crying,
   and tears,
   to sweat great drops of blood, . . .
   to be left alone,
   and denied by Peter,
   and that with an oath,
   and a curse;
   to be subjected to the powers of darkness,
   to be laid hands on,
   taken as a thief,
   bound,
   carried away,
   hurried to Annas,
   Caiaphas,
   Pilate,
   Herod,
   Pilate the second time,
   the Praetorium,

[2] Elizabeth C. Clephane (1830–1869), "The Ninety and Nine."

Gabbatha,
the cross.
Thou that wast silent before the judge,
restrain my tongue.
Thou that didst deign to be bound,
restrain my hands. . . .
In that Thou was struck with the palm of the hand
before Annas,
accused before Caiaphas,
attacked by false witnesses,
condemned for blasphemy . . .
stricken,
spit upon,
reviled,
blasphemed:
Thy head was crowned with thorns,
and struck with the reed,
Thine eyes dim with tears,
Thine ears filled with reviling,
Thy mouth given to drink of gall and vinegar,
Thy face marred with spitting,
Thy back ploughed with the scourge,
Thy neck bent down with the cross, . . .
Thy feet pierced with nails,
Thy heart oppressed with grief,
Thy side pierced with the lance,
Thy Blood flowing . . .
Thy Soul in bitterness,
and Thy cry of agony,
"Eli, Eli!" . . .
Thou, Who didst deign
that Thy glorious head should be wounded,
forgive thereby whatever, by the senses of my
head, I have sinned.
That Thy holy hands should be pierced,
forgive thereby, whatever I have done amiss
by unlawful touch,
or illicit operation.
That Thy precious side should be opened,
forgive thereby whatever I have offended
by lawless thoughts,
in the ardor of passion.

That Thy blessed feet should be riven,
forgive thereby whatever I have done
   by the means of feet swift to evil. . . .
And I, too, Lord, am wounded in soul;
   behold the multitude,
   the length, the breadth, the depth of my wounds;
   and by Thine, heal mine.[3]

Let us pray separately—you, reader, and me—in our shame for our having done this to our Lord. Let us ask Him to forgive our unwashed praises before Him, our sillinesses, our ignorances.

Let us see how our coldness, hardness, blackness, ugliness becomes colder, harder, blacker, uglier—unless in terror we wrench ourselves free and rush to His precious fire! Let us see again in Romans 1 the progression of moral ruin:

1. Knowing God

2. But not praising and glorifying Him as God,

3. Not giving Him thanks,

4. Becoming futile in our thinking,

5. Becoming darkened in heart,

6. Becoming idolaters,

7. Becoming lesbians and gays,

8. Practicing every known sin,

9. Having pleasure in others who do the same. . . .

> *God our Father,*
> *Lord Jesus Christ our Savior,*
> *Holy Spirit, purifying, white-hot Fire,*
>   *We rush to You.*

---

[3] *The Private Devotions of Lancelot Andrewes* (New York: World, 1956), 185–190.

Now Work Into Your Life What You've Been Reading

1. Let us weep and mourn for our sins: write to God, on paper, confessing to Him. (You may want to put your confession on a separate sheet of paper, read 1 John 1:9, and then completely tear up your list. Those sins are gone forever!)

2. Read Isaiah 63:1–10 again and meditate on how much He loved us, His enemies (Rom. 5:10). Thank Him, thank Him—writing in your notebook as eloquently as He will give you words.

If you are studying this book in a small group, allow a time of silence for the writing of number 1. Then read and discuss Isaiah 63:1–10 and spend much time in prayer together for thanksgiving.

YOU MUST COMMIT YOURSELF to moral purity. No matter where you're starting—from this moment on, you must. First Thessalonians 3:13 says this begins when you "strengthen your heart," so do it right now. Say "yes" to 1 Thessalonians 4:3–8, which begins, "It is God's will that you should be holy."

You don't need to pray to see if it's His will for you to have sex with that wonderful Christian you love and are soon to marry; for your church to hire that homosexual who's such a glorious musician; for you to wed that respected, long-time Christian whose divorced wife is still alive . . . for you to embrace fornication, homosexuality, or adultery in any form—all defined in 1 Thessalonians 4:3 by the Greek word *porneia*, from which comes our word *pornography*.

"Abstain," says God. He doesn't say "Be careful" or "Pray about it"—He says, "Abstain! Run from it! Don't touch it! Have nothing to do with it!"

Stay pure and blameless. If you don't, God will suffer most of all. (When we sin, *God* loses!) But He will also let you share in His suffering by punishing you (1 Thess. 4:4–8)—through anxieties, conflicts, guilt, disease, or worse.

(A telltale sign of moral weakness and susceptibility to temptation is excessive interest in the physical—food, clothes, fitness—and a weak interest in the spiritual—prayer, the Word, fellowship, ministry. Judge yourself before the Lord.)

Now, let me picture for you as strongly, as vividly as I can that God wants you to stay away from sin. Read carefully a lesson from history.

Practically from the first, Amalek was an enemy of God. He was the grandson of Esau by a concubine (Gen. 36:12), and his tribesmen were the first to try to hinder Israel from escaping the Egyptians (Exod. 17:8–16). For that reason, on the spot God promised Moses that He'd eventually destroy the Amalekites (Exod. 17:14–16; Deut. 25:17–19).

During the following centuries, the Amalekites fought God's people at every opportunity—plundering them, killing them, hassling them, oppressing them—until finally God told King Saul, in effect, "Enough! The sins of the Amalekites have reached full measure, and it's time to wipe them and all their possessions off the face of the earth" (1 Sam. 15:1–3).

Unfortunately, Saul didn't happen to share God's views. So he wiped off the face of the earth the part of the Amalekites that didn't look good to him—and spared the rest for his personal use, hoping God wouldn't notice.

But here came God's prophet Samuel! Sounding as hearty and business-as-usual as he could, Saul chirped, "The Lord bless you! I have carried out the Lord's instructions" (1 Sam. 15:13).

"What then," interrogated the prophet sarcastically, "is this bleating of sheep in my ears? What is this lowing of cattle that I hear?" (v. 14). Saul hadn't fooled him a bit!

And because King Saul didn't hate what God hated and didn't destroy what God wanted destroyed, God took away his crown and his reign.

God hasn't changed today. You must hate what He hates and destroy what He wants destroyed. He knows the damage these enemies do to His children, the hurt and anguish they cause to His precious ones, and when He says "kill them"—*do it!*

Colossians 3:5–8 is this kind of command. God says,

> *Put to death, therefore, whatever belongs to your earthly nature: sexual immorality, impurity, lust, evil desires and greed, which is idolatry. . . . Rid yourselves of all such things as these: anger, rage, malice, slander, and filthy language from your lips.*

Friend, if you don't think they're as awful as God thinks they are— and if you let some of them hang around instead of ruthlessly killing them—understand right now that, as He did to Saul, God will remove your stature, He'll cut down your influence, He'll give you disgrace.

Look carefully at these things listed in Colossians 3, and ask yourself if you hate each one as God hates them. Do you let any of them hang around? Do you let them coexist in your life as if they were acceptable? Are you tolerating God's enemies?

Nehemiah didn't. When he came back from a trip and found Tobiah put up as a guest in God's house—Tobiah, who'd been God's enemy from the start—do you know what Nehemiah did? He literally threw out all Tobiah's stuff with his own two hands and had the room cleaned up and restored (Neh. 13:6–9).

Listen, the world is full of Christians who pass around little "spiritual" books and go to Bible classes and say "praise the Lord" a lot—at the same time showing no desire to put to death the characteristics of their earthly natures.

To people like these, the love of Jesus crucified is pure sentimentality. And whether they know it or not, they are utterly without power in their lives.

True Christianity costs. It costs plenty. You kick out all the enemies. You put to death everything God tells you to put to death.

Lust must go—wham!

Greed, likewise—pow!

Filthy language isn't funny—kill it!

And if any of these enemies comes to and raises his head, bash him again.

To love God and to please Him is worth everything, everything. Your sexual immorality must go, your evil desires and greed must go, your anger must go, your malice must go, your slander must go. All of them must go—forever! Be ruthless. Whatever the sins are that right now make you feel guilty and uneasy—hate them! Murder them! Get them once and for all out of your life.

And don't you dare read these words just to have read one more Christian book—just for a little evangelical tickling and entertainment. Let these words jar you to instant obedience.

What lurking thing are you hosting, coddling, hanging on to, putting up with? You know how your Lord Christ feels about it.

You say you're "only a woman," and it doesn't even seem ladylike to think so tough?

General Sisera was an enemy of God, the commander of a Canaanite army which cruelly abused God's people, Israel. So Jael— "only a woman," "just a housewife"—lured him into her tent, offered him rest and a snack, got him covered up and cozy and off to sleep, quietly picked up a tent peg and a hammer, and—THUNG! She drove that thing right through his temple (Judg. 4:4–21).

You know what sin you have to put to death.

Do it with all your strength.

Personally.

Quickly.

Now Work Into Your
Life What You've
Been Reading

Confessions, like trash collections, have to be regular and thorough. The alternative to continual repentance and confession is:

1. Guilty feelings, man's greatest underminer, which lead to . . .

2. The crippling, addicting habit of lying to oneself ("I'm not all that bad"), which leads to . . .

3. A self-deception of being partially good, partially able, which leads to . . .

4. False starts, "new year's resolutions," with no power of implementation, so that each produces more disillusionment and hopelessness than the one before, which lead to . . .

5. Manufactured excuses ("Oh, well, we're all human"), blaming others or circumstances, and lowered expectations of future performance, which lead to . . .

6. A general, habitual malaise due to low self-esteem and self-pity, and a temptation to further sins.

In contrast,

1. Repentance and confession look squarely at reality. ("I am a vile, helpless, hopeless sinner, worse than I know, and my personal attitudes and actions are repugnant to a pure and holy God.")

2. Repentance and confession submit to God's own assessment of the situation: that He isn't mad at you, that He cares about

you totally and considers you too precious to lose, that He was willing—even eager—to go to the Cross to redeem you.

3. Repentance and confession qualify you for His immediate and complete forgiveness and cleansing from all your sins, both known to you and unknown (1 John 1:9), and the throwing over you of Christ's robe of absolute righteousness in His eyes (Isa. 61:10).

4. Repentance and confession, then, as a way of life, cause you to know very well what you are in yourself but to walk in the light, balanced and with head up (1 John 1:7). You live not in your flesh but in the Spirit (Rom. 8:5–9). Your human tendency is death—but you are alive with life (Rom. 8:10–11)!

Get on your face before Him (why not literally?). Confess to Him your sins, your repentance, and your total acceptance of His cleansing. Don't hurry the process.

If you're in a group, this can be one of the most meaningful and life-changing sessions you'll ever have. Get at least on your knees and be as honest with Him before each other as His Spirit controls and allows in His delicate taste and wisdom. (There is far more you will confess to Him only in private.)

He will make it a holy and cleansing time.

10 and 11

BREAK THE BACK OF
YOUR OWN EGO

JESUS SAID, "Blessed are the meek, for they will inherit the earth" (Matt. 5:5). Blessed—happy, to be congratulated—are those who understand exactly what they are and don't try by pretense or posing to deny it or cover it.

Grey Christians aren't much into meekness. To them it sounds weird—and not very desirable. Of course they love the "inheriting the earth" part; coming into a huge piece of real estate sounds terrific. ("The whole earth? Wow!") And they say they take God's Word as truth. But getting an inheritance by becoming *meek?* In reality they shrug off the parts of the Bible that don't have a good, twentieth-century-American ring to them.

Then our Christ, in love, explains to us more what He means by meekness:

> *Come unto me, all ye that labour and are heavy laden, and I will give you rest. Take my yoke upon you, and learn of me; for I am meek and lowly in heart: and ye shall find rest unto your souls. For my yoke is easy, and my burden is light* (Matt. 11:28–30, KJV).

Do you know what your burden is—the one that Jesus wants to remove? It's a burden you manufacture all by yourself between your ears. And most people carry it, are "heavy laden" by it, are dragged down and depressed and discouraged and exhausted by it all their lives.

It's the burden of ego.

How much emotional energy do you spend protecting yourself from every possible slight, challenging every word spoken by either friend or enemy which demeans you, cringing under every cool look, tossing at night because someone else seemed preferred over you? How much emotional energy do you spend trying to doctor up your image and "look good," trying to say only what's "cool," trying to do only what's accepted, trying to appear only in a way that will make you admired, trying to sustain a subtle publicity campaign that says you are more, do more, have more . . . ?

Exhausting, isn't it?

It's a cruel, crushing burden, and it never lets up. It never lets you relax a minute to recoup. It wears away your strength, your morale, your life. We may call it "stress," but its real name is "ego."

Ego may be open or subtle, worldly or Christianized. It may mean smashing enough faces and brains to wow the world of boxing. It may mean taking over enough companies to wow the corporate world of business. It may mean getting enough church members or adherents to wow the religious world. Or individually, memorizing the most verses, visiting the most shut-ins, teaching the biggest Bible class—whatever makes the rest say "wow!"

Or ego may mean writhing and seething because you *haven't* made it to the top: you lost the match, your company was outclassed, your ministry is struggling. . . .

Ego keeps you forever tense and dissatisfied, forever in agony lest someone else appear better, smarter, richer, more liked, more successful, more admired, more spiritual, more "blessed." . . .

Ego is a terrible, terrible burden.

Jesus says, "Let me give you rest. Learn of Me. I am meek!"

Meekness is the opposite of ego with its pretense, pride, competition.

"I will give you rest," He says. "Accept the blessed relief of being only what you are. Then I can do it all!

"Quit pretending. Quit striving. My dear child, quit trying to be some cocky little god competing with Me—maybe, worst of all, some cocky little *religious* god. Come down off your silly, rickety throne.

"Only my Father is worthy of a throne! Bow to Him only, and give Him all the glory, and let Him be all and do all, in you and for you!"

When you think of it, that's how Jesus Himself was meek. He was willing to do only the Father's will—to do only what the Father told Him to do and say only what the Father told Him to say.

Meekness sounds awful, though, to grey Christians—like they'd come out losers, nerds, nothings.

That's the devil's lie.

What made Satan fall in the first place? It was his determination to exalt his own ego. He swore,

I will ascend to heaven;
I will raise my throne

Above the stars of God . . .
I will make myself like the Most High
(Isa. 14:13–15).

Satan wanted to be "self-made"! God wouldn't have it (Luke 10:18).

Satan, in his fallen state, tried to tempt the Lord Jesus to do the same thing—exalt His ego:

The devil led him up to a high place and showed him in an instant all the kingdoms of the world. And he said to him, "I will give you all their authority and splendor. . . . If you worship me, it will all be yours" (Luke 4:5–7).

Jesus refused and instead took the meek way—to the cross. He really did put His head in the noose, didn't He? He walked into it with His eyes wide open!

And did His meekness make Him a loser? Did the Cross make Jesus Christ a nerd, a nothing?

No, no, no, no! Because He resolutely turned His back on ego and chose meekness, in the end all will bow down to Him—not just those kingdoms of the earth that Satan displayed to Him, but every knee "in heaven and on earth and under the earth" (Phil. 2:10)—more, infinitely more.

Long before the devil tempted Jesus, he also tempted Eve to exalt her ego: "When you eat of [the fruit] your eyes will be opened, and you will be like God" (Gen. 3:5).

Unlike Jesus, however, Eve obeyed Satan and *fell.* She didn't go up, she went down. And she fell so far that the magnitude of her fall dragged the whole human race down with her. Talk about a crash!

Now, "he who has an ear, let him hear what the Spirit says" (Rev. 2:7). Listen to the quiet voice of love, with its sweet reasonableness, wanting the best for you (a "best" so good we can't imagine it):

Come to me, all you who are weary and burdened, and I will give you rest.

"I have no desire," He says, "for you to go on being crushed under this great burden of trying to be what you're not and trying not to be what you are. Let it roll off. Let it go. What an enormous yoke it is! My dear, you're all exhausted from posing, from exaggerating, from hiding, from trying to *appear* instead of just *being.* Let Me help you take this ugly thing off. Poor child! Here, put on Mine instead":

Take my yoke upon you and learn of me, for I am [meek] and humble in heart, and you will find rest for your souls. For my yoke is easy, and my burden is light.

Says Christ, "My name is 'I AM WHO I AM,' as Exodus 3:14 puts it. I don't try to defend Myself or to appear to be different than I am. Satan, on the other hand, 'masquerades as an angel of light' (2 Cor. 11:14), and all his followers try to do the same. It's part of their death struggle; they're on their way out.

"I never had to do that," He continues, "and neither do My children. You are who you are: accepted in the Beloved, precious in My sight, and in the process of becoming perfect as I am perfect—a process so sure that I already see you that way!

"Isn't that enough? Aren't you satisfied with My plan?"

Humble yourselves, therefore, under God's mighty hand, that he may lift you up in due time (1 Pet. 5:6).

"Lift you up in due time"?
Lord—like maybe, "inherit the earth"?

Now Work Into Your Life What You've Been Reading

1. In your notebook, writing your new determination to God, take off the burden of ego you've been wearing. List and describe the characteristics of your personal ego, and after each description write, "Right now, Lord, I let this roll off." At the end of this process deliberately sit taller and take a long, deep, fresh breath of air.

2. Then describe on paper to your wonderful Christ your action of putting on His easy, comfortable yoke of meekness and honesty of heart. Do it with eager enjoyment and prayer, in the power of the Spirit. Understand how much He's enjoying this, too! He loves you very much.

If you are studying this book in a small group allow silence for the individual writing of number 1. Then in conversational prayer describe to Christ what you see of His own yoke and express in prayer, with thanksgiving, your act of putting it on.

If this isn't easy before each other, understand that learning to walk together "in the light" (exposed, knowable, open) as He is in the light is your only way to true fellowship together and to cleansing (1 John 1:7). Christ in you (remember the hand in the glove?) will be the help you need to begin a new habit—of being yourself!

11

GOD, YOUR DEAR FATHER, is the One before whom you humble yourself. As you get to know Him, you rush to Him not only to get "hot, glowing, and purified," but because He's so wonderful to come to!

He's the north star from which we all get our bearings. He's the tuning fork by which we derive our pitch. He's the fact of facts. He's the beginning and the end of all. He's the magnetic field of attraction to which everything is drawn.

We come to Him because frankly it's such an easier way to live, and so much more fun—exhilarating, challenging, important, noble. Jesus Christ is Square One, and anything not related to Him is ultimately meaningless and futile.

And yet we know what it is to withdraw from His fire and start getting occupied again with ourselves and bugged with each other, fidgeting with our "self-images" and trying unsuccessfully to play "I'm okay, you're okay."

We know what it's like to "worship" Him when we're too far from the fire. We get very aware of shutting our eyes and raising our hands and noticing with sidewise glances who *isn't* shutting and raising—or very smugly aware that *our* kind of church is certainly not the sort to get into shutting and raising. . . . God help us all.

When we get back into the fire, we're aware of God again—and suddenly we're humble! We see who we really are, and we're just as embarrassed as that fellow Jesus talked about (Luke 14:7–9) who glided gracefully to the best seat at the wedding and had to be asked to move.

We'll suddenly understand and identify with the Pharisee at the temple (Luke 18:11) who "prayed about himself, 'God, I thank you that I am not like all other men—robbers, evildoers. . . .' "—posturing there, making a fool of himself, and absolutely unaware that his hearers couldn't decide whether to laugh or throw up.

When we get back in the fire, when we're abiding in our blessed Lord, then when He tells us to humble ourselves—hey, we won't think it's some big-deal spiritual project; we'll know it's just common sense.

Lectured Evelyn Underhill at one of her retreats,

> *If we and our interesting little souls and their needs and experiences are still in the foreground of the spiritual landscape; if we are still making man the measure of things; if our thanksgiving is complacent and all about our being such splendid creatures . . . we are not yet clear of that unreal, anthropocentric, man-centered religious world which is from beginning to end the creation of human pride.*[1]

As she says later, "He and His will matter—not us and our satisfaction and enlightenment!"

Meister Eckhart in the thirteenth century said it more simply:

> *Whoever wishes to receive from above must be below in true humility. . . . Nothing is given to him who is not truly below, nor does he receive anything at all, not even the smallest thing. If you consider yourself in the least, or anything or anyone, you are not below, and you will not receive anything. But if you are altogether below, you will receive fully and completely.*[2]

Do you wonder what books of today ring with such bedrock truth that they'll be cherished seven hundred years from now? Read with conviction these further words of Eckhart, written so long ago:

> *Some persons want to see God with their own eyes, just as they see a cow; and want to love God, just as they love a cow. You love it for the sake of its milk and cheese and for your own profit.*
>
> *So do all those who love God for the sake of outward wealth or inward consolation; they merely love their own advantage. It is the plain truth that everything you put foremost in your thoughts and purposes that is not God Himself, however good it may be, cannot fail to be a hindrance to you on your way to the highest truth.*[3]

---

[1] *The Mount of Purification* (London: Longman, Green, 1960), p. 22.
[2] *Meister Eckhart*, 174.
[3] Ibid., 147–48.

Of course he's absolutely right on both scores—that we must come humbly and that we mustn't come just for what we'll get out of it.

But do you think that's the end of the matter as far as God's concerned? Not on your life!

Look at the prodigal son in Luke 15.

He *did* come to his father humbly; his planned speech said, "I am no longer worthy to be called your son; make me like one of your hired men" (v. 19).

But he also came for what he would get out of it; he said to himself, "How many of my father's hired men have food to spare, and here I am starving to death! I will set out and go back to my father. . . ." (vv. 17–18).

Both issues his father impatiently brushed off. Hired man? His father saw him coming a long way off, ran to him, threw his arms around him, and kissed him—the Greek verb is continuous, meaning he kept on kissing him and kissing him!

"Eat the servants' food? Are you kidding? I'm ordering a feast with everything and the very best clothes for you and—let's see, you need a really handsome ring to complete the look. . . ."

My friend, *our* part is to humble ourselves in sincerest penitence before Almighty God. But He is such a lover—and He loves to love! He will insist on raising you to look right into His eyes—insist that you have fellowship with Him heart to heart as best friends, His mind having fellowship with your mind on ever deepening levels; insist that you have everything you need and more, as befitting one favored by the great God of all gods and King above all.

Do you know that your groveling before Him even makes Him impatient? Making ourselves nothing in order to make Him everything really turns Him off. (Ray and I understand that; I can't abide for him to put himself down, and neither can he stand it when I belittle myself. That's the way lovers are.)

It *is* our place to remember what we are, in ourselves, in order to appreciate all that we are in Christ! But self-occupation (whether we're saying "I'm wonderful" or "I'm a louse") is sin, and God won't have it.

Think about Moses. God planned a fabulous walk through life with Moses. But when He began to broach the subject to Moses—

> Go down, Moses,
>   'Way down in Egypt land;
> Tell ol' Pharaoh,
>   "Let my people go!"

—Moses began making objecting noises: "Who am I . . . ?" (Exod. 3:11); "Suppose I . . ." (3:13); "What if . . ." (4:1); and then just outright, "O Lord, I have never been eloquent. . . . I am slow of speech and tongue" (4:10).

God's answer was quick: "Who gave man his mouth? . . . Is it not I, the Lord? Now go; I will help you speak" (4:11–12).

And when Moses was still self-demeaning, God's anger "burned against" him (4:14). He can't stand to have His cherished children reviled by others or even by themselves.

His side, your side: understand the difference.

You stumble to the door of a castle—ragged, filthy, embarrassed, insecure. . . .

And when you go in, the King Himself eagerly takes over. He welcomes you with all His heart, bathes and clothes you gorgeously, and makes you the guest of honor at a royal feast.

But *you must receive it all*. Don't you dare sit in a corner miserable because you're remembering who you are and where you came from. That wouldn't honor your Host! He loves you, and He did it all to give you the time of your life.

And *you must stay there*. Well, who would be so rude—or so foolish—as to leave?

"The king has brought [you] into his chambers" (Song of Sol. 1:4). The friends are standing around rejoicing and delighting in you.

Relax! Enjoy! Forever!

Now Work Into Your
Life What You've
Been Reading

In your notebook, make a list of all that you've come into as an adopted child of the King. If you need help, look at Ephesians 1:3–14. Thank Him, in your own words, for each thing He's given you.

If you are studying this book in a small group, read and discuss Ephesians 1:3–14 together, writing in your notebook all the aspects you see there of your new position in Christ. Then have a time of thanksgiving in prayer together.

12

MOVE OUT OF THE WORLD OF "THINGS"; MOVE INTO THE REAL WORLD—

IT'S FABULOUSLY TRUE, my friend, that the King of heaven has brought you into His chambers and endowed you with every treasure He can assemble, and that He asks you only to believe and enjoy and let your new life become more and more real to you!

But there's one more important clue to making sure that the awful burden of ego is lifted from your back, so that you're truly freed to receive all your royal Sovereign wants you to have.

Do you remember the scene in the musical, *My Fair Lady*, when Professor Higgins took the flower girl Eliza Doolittle off the streets and had his maids scrub her and burn her clothes so he could give her new ones? Remember the way she howled? She was comfortable with her dirt, and she liked her old clothes! Many a Christian woman (man, too!) says by her attitude, "I prefer the old rags and trinkets that I've acquired all by myself. They're mine!"

Albert Edward Day has an important insight here:

> Left to itself, the ego is persistent in acquiring and keeping. Sharing is not one of its passions. . . .
> Giving is not a trait of the ego. Owning is! "Mine" is its dearest adjective. "Keep" is its most beloved verb.
> The ego is possessive. Its possessiveness in property manifests itself as stinginess, miserliness, greed. Its possessiveness of people makes jealous friends, husbands, wives, parents.
> Most persons who are possessive never recognize the fact. So complete is the domination of the ego that it is unconscious.[1]

Woe to him, exclaims Jeremiah, who props up his ego with, for instance, real estate:

[1] *Discipline and Discovery* (Nashville: Upper Room, 1977), 80.

He says, "I will build myself a great palace
    with spacious upper rooms."
So he makes large windows in it,
    panels it with cedar
    and decorates it in red.
Does it make you a king
    to have more and more cedar?

(Jer. 22:14–15).

That's a probing question: "Does it make you a king . . . ?" Or we would say, "Does it make you a queen . . . ?" The world says yes. God says no:

Do not worry about your life, what you will eat or drink; or about your body, what you will wear. . . . Look at the birds . . . they do not sow or reap or store away in barns, and yet your heavenly Father feeds them. . . . See how the lilies of the field grow. They do not labor or spin. Yet I tell you that not even Solomon in all his splendor was dressed like one of these. If that is how God clothes the grass of the field, . . . will he not much more clothe you? (Matt. 6:25–30).

If God clothes the grass so gorgeously, He may see fit to give you a big house, too—paneled with cedar and decorated in red! Then again, He may not. But the point is not what you have or don't have! That's not what makes you a queen; *God* makes you a queen (Rev. 5:10, KJV)! *You are a queen* in any case, not by your work, but by His work.

The point is not, I say, what you have materially or don't have. *Your living is between your ears*—whether you trust this area of your life, like the rest, to Him, or whether you're fascinated by "things," doting on them, worried over them, trying to get more of them, equating them with status.

"Do not worry," says Matthew 6:25.

"Why do you worry?" says Matthew 6:28.

"Do not worry," says Matthew 6:31.

"Do not worry," says Matthew 6:34.

My brother Bobby and I used to play marbles on our living room rug. He always won, but I was a sucker and we'd keep playing until Mother called us to dinner.

We never thought to ask each other, "Do you think we'll get any dinner tonight? Do you think Daddy brought home any food? Do you think Mother cooked it? What if they've forgotten us? What if they've decided not to feed us any more? Should we have done something to earn it, so they'd keep giving it to us?"

Hey, we were their *kids*. Our job was to play marbles, and their job was to supply the grub!

If you get momentarily anxious over finances, picture yourself a little kid playing on the floor. Your job is basically just to wait for the dinner call. This is not to say you shouldn't work and have a sense of responsibility (2 Thess. 3:6–13), but *your source of supply is not your paycheck from your work*. Your source of supply is your heavenly Father, who knows better than you do what you need (Matt. 6:32) and has promised to supply just the right amount.

Ego is very uncomfortable with this plan. Satan whispers through your ego, "Ridiculous! You'll probably be a pauper. Say you trust Him if it makes you feel better, but you'd probably also better do a little scrambling on your own!"

Then he triumphantly throws in his counterfeit Bible verse, which he made up all by himself: "Don't forget—God helps those who help themselves." And he grins, thinking of the millions of grey Christians who believe his "verse."

Is Satan right? Will you be poor?

Think about how God made you so thoughtfully and how He cherishes you, and think about how lovers delight in giving to the ones they love. Think about how the father clothed the prodigal son he loved so much. Think about how Matthew 6:30 says, "If that is how God clothes the grass of the field, . . . will he not *much more* clothe you?"

"Well," you say, "what about all the poor Christians and even starving ones around the world?"

The former president of World Vision told me, when I asked him outright, that he had never heard of a Christian anywhere starving to death. He said he knew stories that sometimes they get very hungry—and then when they pray they're thrilled to see God come through for them. Dr. Wilbur Smith used to say that in the last two thousand years of world history, those nations which have regularly repeated "give us this day our daily bread" have never experienced starvation.

Standards of living differ, expectations differ, needs differ—but no child of our Father has ever known Him to go back on His often-repeated promise to take care of His own.

> I was young and now I am old, [wrote David,]
>   yet I have never seen the righteous forsaken
>   or their children begging bread
> (Ps. 37:25).

So how wrong is Satan? Does God want you rich? Well, could your ego handle it? God is most concerned about what happens in the disciplines of your heart.

"Trust Me," He says. "Trust Me. Trust Me."

And then He gives you one dynamite, measurable, black-and-white way to trust Him—by regular, planned, sacrificial giving to Him! Writes Albert Day,

> Because of the possessiveness of the ego, the practice of generosity is very significant. It is a denial, a repudiation of the ego. Faithfully practiced, generosity weakens the ego's authority.[2]

Giving is the way to riches, because you can handle the riches when your ego has been gotten out of the way:

> Give, and it will be given to you. A good measure, pressed down, shaken together and running over, will be poured into your lap. For with the measure you use [in giving], it will be measured to you (Luke 6:38).

But will God give you all this just so you can more and more feather your own nest? Says 2 Corinthians 9:11, "You will be made rich in every way so that you can be generous on every occasion."

My friend, if this is the life you want—this life of trust and rest and richness in Christ—deliberately turn your back on the touchable, material world and concentrate on the *real* world.

The real world is everywhere around you. It's not a future world; it's right now on all sides of you—more stable, more lasting, and of far greater value than the world you've been temporarily looking at:

> There is something in man which longs for the Perfect and Unchanging, and is sure, in spite of the confusions, the evils, the rough and tumble of life, that the Perfect and the Unchanging is the real.[3]

> So we fix our eyes not on what is seen, but on what is unseen. For what is seen is temporary, but what is unseen is eternal (2 Cor. 4:18).

[2] Ibid., 80.
[3] Underhill, *Mount of Purification*, 239.

If you open your eyes to the real world of God, to rest in it and enjoy it, trusting Christ and having fellowship with Him moment by moment, more and more, you'll find you've become more truly human and sensitive and alive.

If you live in the grey world of trying to combine God and materialism, you'll become more and more earthly, self-centered, dull, flabby, bloated, insensitive, and out of touch. The choice is up to you.

If you choose aliveness in God, you won't withdraw *out of* the world; you'll love it, with a cleansed and pure love, and want to serve it more than ever before. Still, in your heart there'll be a sense of separation, of detachment, knowing that world is fading away (Isa. 51:6).

"Oh, pastor," exclaimed a woman once to Charles Spurgeon, "I'm afraid the world is coming to an end!"

"Never mind, my dear," that great preacher answered. "We can get along without it."

Friend, turn from being consumed by fabrics and furniture and food. Move out of obsession with that external world into the real world— where your heart is a bona fide naturalized citizen, and where your thinking processes and habits are becoming more and more at home.

But then, when you consciously begin to "live and move and have [your] being" (Acts 17:28) in the real world, you come to an amazing discovery. You begin to understand that "things" are not only external to you; they're actually subservient to you. You thought you were moving away from them—but that was only between your ears. Material things are still available. They are created by God just so He can meet your external needs while you give your focus and attention to what is real.

When, in your mind, you're freed from possessing, then you possess all things!

All things are yours . . . and ye are Christ's; and Christ is God's (1 Cor. 3:21, 23, *KJV*).

Seek first his kingdom and his righteousness, and all these things will be given to you as well (Matt. 6:33).

He who did not spare his own Son, but gave him up for us all—how will he not also, along with him, graciously give us all things? (Rom. 8:32).

Now Work Into Your Life What You've Been Reading

1. Right now read out loud to Him this prayer: "O Lord, open my eyes to the world of reality! Open my eyes to see what You see, to love what You love, to hate what You hate, and to use with ease what You give me to use."

2. Read Hebrews 1:14 and then read aloud this prayer: "O Lord, give me the habit of continual awareness of the angels assigned to serve me. Make me grateful for them."

3. Read 2 Kings 6:15–17 and then read aloud this prayer: "O Lord, give me the habit of continual awareness of Your armies surrounding and protecting me, and may I enjoy that protection."

4. Write to Him your own decision, whether first time or reaffirmed, to give to Him regularly, generously (tell Him, if possible, a minimum of how many dollars every week you will give Him — 1 Cor. 16:1–2), to turn your back on the possessiveness of your own ego and of this world.

5. Release to Him, on paper, everything else you have tended to "own": people, your reputation, your gifts — everything to which you've attached the pronoun *my*. Give them, one by one, to Him.

6. Write your own concluding prayer, worshiping Him in this surrender of all and in your enjoyment of moving into the valuable, the real.

If you're studying this book in a small group, read in unison together the prayer in the first paragraph above.

Read Hebrews 1:14 and pray the prayer in unison.

Read 2 Kings 6:15–17 and pray the prayer in unison.

In silence, individually write to God about your decision to give and release to Him the things you tend to "own."

Share with the group as much as God directs you about the prayers that you wrote, and close with prayers together of surrender and worship and joy.

13

—OF FEARLESSNESS
AND CALM

YOU'LL HAVE TROUBLE believing this next story, but it's true. For many years my father was a general in the U.S. Army. He wasn't the typical image of an army general. He was a "velvet-covered brick"—strong and decisive, but so warm and gracious and encouraging in the process that he came across as if his greatest pleasure was to help his subordinates do their jobs well. Every command he had, officers asked to serve under him.

At the age of eighty-one, Daddy lay in a hospital, dying of stomach cancer. He was weak and thin and in terrible pain, near the end of his long struggle. Then a nurse across the room dropped something. Daddy sprang out of bed and retrieved it for her!

He didn't really mean to do it; he was embarrassed by it and probably exhausted by it. What he did was simply reflex action, the habit of so many years.

Well, "abiding in Christ" can be pictured a lot of ways, but think about the image of my dear Daddy in his hospital bed trying to help a nurse far more capable than he. The point is, abide in Christ and *stay there*. For your own good, rest in Him and let Him do His work. He doesn't expect you to do it for Him, and you can't, anyway. You're too weak to do the kind of business that only God can do.

Ego can get us in the habit of feeling accountable for all the ills of the world! We can try to carry a load that only God can bear—to feel guilty over all the pain and injustices on our planet, to groan under the weight and to think it all wouldn't happen if only we would "do" something.

The late Pope John was once begged by a very concerned cardinal to relieve the ills of the world. The story has it that Pope John put his arm around the cardinal and said he'd been helped recently by a dream he'd had. He said in his dream an angel came into the papal bedroom and said, "Hey, there, Johnny boy, don't take yourself so seriously."

Understand God's side, understand our side! His side is to let sin play itself out to the end of its rope and then to come in mighty judgment and set the world right. Our side is to pray, to give, to serve and help to the uttermost as He guides us—but still to hug to our hearts the secret knowledge of the sovereignty of God. He is at work. He knows. In the big picture, all is well. We trust Him. We rest in Him.

J. I. Packer speaks of "the gaiety, the goodness, the unfetteredness of spirit which are the marks of those who know God."[1] That's not a self-centered withdrawal from the world's pain; that's *knowing God!* Understanding the end and purpose of history frees you to reach out and help—in His name.

And in the meantime—the first page of my notebook always carries this paraphrase of Psalm 90:14: "He fills us each morning with his constant love, that we may sing and be glad all our life"!

Remember I told you that George Mueller used to say, "It is my first business every morning to make sure that my heart is happy in God."

This is characteristic of the iron only as it stays in the fire, not otherwise. There you develop a relief, a lightheartedness, an exhilarating joy and fun that knows God is truly God!

Ray and I were the speakers on a Caribbean cruise a while back, and on the cruise one day we ran into a lanky black crew member ankling down one of the ship's corridors, snapping his head back and waggling his elbows. "You gotta loose up!" he was chortling, "loose up!"

Hey, he was *right!* Resting in Christ *doctrinally* should "loose us up" *emotionally*. We won't be so tense! We won't get hurt so often. We'll laugh more.

Resting in Christ should "loose us up" *intellectually*. We can stretch to be less dogmatic on the fine points. Much as I hate to admit it, I'm probably not right nearly as often as I think I am! If we're rigid in our pet opinions, we're probably rigid in our muscles, too.

And speaking of that, resting in Christ should "loose us up" *physically*. We get so bloomin' serious over our foods and fear of foods, our exercises and fear of exercises, our medicines and fear of medicines, our sicknesses and fear of sicknesses.

[1] *Knowing God* (Downers Grove, IL: Inter-Varsity, 1973), 21.

Resting in Christ should "loose us up" *relationally*. We can be free to be ourselves and allow others the same privilege, receiving them as Christ receives us (Rom. 15:7).

And resting in Christ should "loose us up" *spiritually*. We may discover that what we thought was zeal for God was actually just a self-destructive intense personality.

—Yes, of course we should "burn out for God"; I want to, too—to live all my life for Him. But we don't need to burn out for Him like gasoline—explosively, burning everybody around us in the process. We can burn out like charcoal—slowly, steadily, over a long period of time, and good to the last golden marshmallow!

Rest, my friend. "Make every effort to enter that rest" (Heb. 4:11). *Loose up*.

Right now, relax. *Loose up.*

Be humble, don't argue, be teachable. *Loose up.*

Smile. Look up. *Loose up.*

It's God's way. There are troubles and pressures all around. But discipline your heart to *loose up*.

Are you exhausted? Your first need isn't a vacation; you'd come back from that and just get tired again. Your first need is to move into that position of trusting and resting in Christ—to *loose up*.

Are you in a deadlock with a teenage child, at an impasse with a friend or an employee? Your first need is not to kick them out, turn them off, fire them. First run to God. He'll *"loose you up."*

"[The Lord] will keep in perfect peace him whose mind is steadfast, because he trusts in [him]" (Isa. 26:3). He will not only give you solutions; He will give you settledness in the process.

Friend, *it's not your circumstances that shape you.* They are outside you and beyond; they can't really touch you. It's how you *react to your circumstances*. That's between your ears, and that affects the "real you."

And what controls your reactions? Abiding in Christ (John 15:4–10, KJV). Staying there. "Loosing up."

Then what if you find, for instance, a lump in your breast? Of course you'll make a doctor's appointment immediately—but that's external. What happens within? *Lord, nothing important has changed. You love me. Your eternal, perfect plans for me are continuing on schedule. I will praise You; I will worship You. I will rest in all You're continuing to do in my life.*

Or what if you lose your job? You'll be your vigorous, efficient self in looking for another—if, indeed, He wants you to have another. But all that's external. What happens within? *The Lord is my Shepherd; I shall*

*not want. I will fear no evil, for You are with me. My cup overflows. I
praise You for this opportunity to praise You!*

Or what if you're confronted with any trauma at all? Psalm 112 is a
wonderful psalm describing the godly person, and it says "He will have
no fear of bad news; his heart is steadfast, trusting in the Lord. His heart
is secure, he will have no fear" (vv. 7–8). God's Word is God's Word!
He's practical; He's realistic; He gives you every expectation of living on
an even keel.

I've been growing in this—lagging behind Ray, but growing. Several
years ago we acted with our hearts instead of praying first, and we
cosigned for a loan for a dear friend. (We knew perfectly well Proverbs
6:1–5 says never to do that, but we acted impulsively.) When the fellow
went bankrupt, the bank came after us and really cleaned us out. For a
few months we expected to lose our home, our only real material asset.
But God held our minds in the palm of His hand, and we were able to
say, "We deserve whatever He does; we got into this scrape all by
ourselves. But what if we live the rest of our life in a rented apartment?
We still have the Lord. If we're really cleaned out, still all is well. Praise
Him."

Grey Christians live from Monday to Saturday as though there were
no God at all. They live as practical atheists, so they never "loose up."
They fear sickness. They fear death. They fear what will happen to their
children. They fear losing their money. They fear moral breakdowns.
They fear failure. They fear being inadequate. They fear others' thinking they're inadequate! They fear unhealthfulness in their food. They
fear burglars and murderers and "ghoulies and ghosties and long-leg-
gety beasties and things that go bump in the night"!

God doesn't want you that way. *He wants you unflappable.* Don't
"become easily unsettled or alarmed," He says (2 Thess. 2:2).

In his devotional classic, *My Utmost for His Highest,* Oswald Chambers writes about what it means to abide in Jesus:

> *God means us to live a full-orbed [inner] life in Christ Jesus, but
> there are times when that life is attacked from the outside, and we
> tumble into a way of introspection which we thought had gone.
> . . . Self-consciousness is not sin; it may be produced by a ner-
> vous temperament or by a sudden dumping down into new cir-
> cumstances. It is never God's will that we should be anything less
> than absolutely complete in Him. Anything that disturbs rest in
> Him should be cured at once, and it is not cured by being ig-
> nored, but by coming to Jesus Christ. . . .*

Never allow the dividing up of your life in Christ to remain without facing it. Beware of leakage, of the dividing up of your life by the influence of friends or of circumstances; beware of anything that is going to split up your oneness with Him and make you see yourself separately. Nothing is so important as to keep right spiritually. The great solution is the simple one— "Come to Me." . . .

Whenever anything begins to disintegrate your life with Jesus Christ, turn to Him at once and ask Him to establish rest. . . .

Take every element of disintegration as something to wrestle against, and not to [allow]. Say—Lord, prove Thy consciousness in me, and self-consciousness will go and He will be all in all.[2]

In another place Chambers writes,

Think of the things that take you out of abiding in Christ.—Yes, Lord, just a minute, I have got this to do; yes, I will abide when once this is finished; when this week is over. . . .

Begin to abide now. In the initial stages it is a continual effort until it becomes so much the law of life that you abide in Him unconsciously. Determine to abide in Jesus wherever you are placed.[3]

Remember, *your real living is between your ears!*

Then make a constant prayer-wall around you that distances you from all outer circumstances, while within it you rest in the love of God. You're at peace with His work; you rejoice in Him. Let there be encircling you that shield of continual trust in His continual work.

"Surely I will be with you always," He says (Matt. 28:20):

> The Lord delights in those who fear him,
> who put their hope in his unfailing love
> (Ps. 147:11).

"But," you say, "shouldn't I at least have one fear—shouldn't I fear Satan? Shouldn't I fear what he could do in my life?"

What should be your attitude, as God's child, toward that terrible enemy, Satan? The classic passage given us in Scripture on how to handle him is Ephesians 6:10–18, and it says that your defense is simply to put on the armor God gives you and then to stand:

[2] (New York: Dodd, Mead, 1953), Aug. 19.
[3] Ibid., June 14.

Therefore put on the full armor of God, so that when the day of evil comes, you may be able to stand your ground, and after you have done everything, to stand (v. 13).

And what is the armor? Truth, righteousness, readiness with the Gospel, faith, salvation, the Word of God, and prayer (vv. 14–18)—all aggressively positive and happy!

Little sheep certainly do need a healthy fear of wolves. But if their egos lead them to think their safety depends on their own powers of confrontation, they could get *too* fearful and too "wolf-occupied." The most important thing their fear of wolves should do for them is make them stay close to their strong shepherd!

As we take up truth, righteousness, God's Word, prayer, and so on, we *are* close; we're within God's prescribed circle of protection. And we've become identified with all power and authority, so that in Christ our victory over the devil is already assumed.

> The Prince of Darkness grim,
> We tremble not for him;
> His rage we can endure,
> For lo! his doom is sure;
> One little word shall fell him.[4]

Then "cast all your anxiety on [the Lord] because he cares for you" (1 Pet. 5:7). He takes the responsibility. You can "loose up"!

Note that word *all* in the verse I just quoted. Sometimes we can get hung up on just one problem.

I know a pastor's wife who functioned beautifully through the years until her daughter became a rebel and married poorly. Then this woman took this care upon herself. And she went into such grieving that for the rest of her life she was disconsolate. She was a poor wife, a burden to her friends, a discredit to God. Her entire mental focus was on the disgrace of her daughter.

Cast on Him *all* your anxieties—every one. And if they come back into your mind? Cast them on Him again, and keep casting them on Him as often as you need to. Tell Him, "Lord, I can't carry this burden. You carry it for me. And let's make a deal: I'll take Your peace instead!" (see John 14:27).

But then, what if the thing you fear the very most of all happens to you? What if the most terrible possible thing happens? What if God

---

[4] Martin Luther (1483–1546), "A Mighty Fortress Is Our God," tr. Frederick H. Hedge.

does to you what He did to Shadrach, Meshach, and Abednego—throws you into a fiery furnace?

The basic truth is that God is good, and he loves you to the end, and your reasonable expectation is that He'll give you what you hope for in your life. But *"even if He does not"* (Dan. 3:18)—He is still good, and He is still in charge. He will still take care of you. You can even experience a holy, happy carelessness! You can "loose up"!

Is it a fiery furnace you're in—or is it indeed the fire of the Holy Spirit of Christ keeping you hot and glowing and purified?

Now Work Into Your Life What You've Been Reading

1. Take inventory of the state of things between your ears. Are you aware of the "gaiety, the goodness, the unfetteredness of spirit which are the marks of those who know God"? Enjoy the measure that you do know God already and tell Him on paper how you anticipate reflecting that knowledge more and more.

2. List the bad situations in your life and, after recalling each one, write, "I flee to Your arms and rest there, my loving and caring Abba [Daddy]." Don't go on to the next situation until your heart is truly "loosed up," resting and praising Him in each one.

3. Memorize Psalm 119:14.

4. Put on the floor beside your bed a piece of paper that your feet will hit the first thing as you get up. On that paper write these words: "He fills us each morning with his constant love, that we may sing and be glad all our life" (Ps. 90:14).

If you are studying this book in a group, allow silence so group members can do numbers 1 and 2.

Then have a period of group prayer, sharing aloud with God and each other as much as He directs you to reveal of the business you've been transacting with Him.

Memorize together Psalm 119:14.

Number 4 will be "homework."

14

—OF RESTEDNESS
AND STRENGTH

FOR YOU TO REST—that is, to live in total acceptance of God's way—demands quiet.

I don't mean a "quiet *time*," a period for Bible study and prayer, preceded by and followed by the old frantic rat race. Doing that gives your brain mixed signals; it breeds confusion; it gives you a grey life.

Resting demands quiet *all the time*. However active your external life may be, He wants you to develop between your two ears, in the discipline of your heart, a lifelong attitude of rest in Him.

To rest in God permanently means to hand over each activity, each situation of your life, to Him and to learn the habit of trusting Him to *work for you*.

We don't naturally rest. Naturally we are stewers, tinkerers, and fussers.

I asked you on the first page of this book, *"Have you too much to do?"* Could it be because you're stewing, tinkering, fussing? Or are you taking on yourself what God didn't intend for you?

I know I'm rubbing the cat's fur the wrong way! Christians have copied the world's hunger to go faster and do more, to achieve and to be applauded. The only difference may be that when a worldling says "I'm beat," he'll head for a massage or a psychiatrist, but the Christian may try to keep going, keep smiling, and keep saying "Praise the Lord!"

Have you too much to do? Are you pushed, rushed, harried?

Said George Fox long ago, "Come out of the bustlings, you that are bustling."

To guard your inner life, you must guard your outer life. How's your pace? Are you too busy? Is your lifestyle allowing you only enough time to race through this book, or does it also give you time to react to it?

Does your pace allow you to *keep in touch with yourself*—with your inner needs and feelings and longings? Does it allow you time to think, plan, make changes? Does it allow you time to observe carefully the dear ones around you and care for their needs—physical and emotional? Do you have time to really *live?*

If not, do you have the courage to change? When you see the terrible pace and stress around you, could you dare to say no to it? Could you gear down to a different tempo? In the midst of all the craziness around you, could you live poised and serene?

Asian theologian Kosuke Koyama says that in human affairs God moves at something like three miles an hour, the pace at which a person walks, not runs! Are you synchronized to your world, maybe even to your Christian world, but out of sync with God?

You probably won't change just because you become aware of the terrible damage an overbusy life is doing to yourself, to your family, and to your relationship with God. Habit alone will keep the nervous St. Vitus' Dance going, driving you forward pell-mell—like a smoker who knows that every cigarette cuts fourteen minutes off his life but keeps reaching for another.

You will change when your inner life changes. But I just said your inner life is affected by your outer life! Then is the whole thing a vicious circle that can't be stopped?

No, the change begins with a decision. Your heart is your headquarters. Even as you read this chapter, make the decision, by a conscious act of your will, that you will learn to rest in God both in your inner life and your outer life. Once the decision is made—and you implement it as God opens your eyes to ways to implement it—gradually, gradually, over the weeks or years, the changes will come. Your heart will start listening to a different pulse deep within you, and with joy you'll begin to match your steps to that lovely, restful beat.

"Make it your ambition to lead a quiet life," says 1 Thessalonians 4:11. What a radical reversal of today's typical goals!

But you're hesitating about the decision. Why?

What's keeping you from "loosing up"? What's destructive in your life—what's driving you? Put your finger on it; it's not from God.

He says to you, "Do not let your hearts be troubled" (John 14:1). Don't allow it! Don't stand for it! "May the Lord of peace himself," writes Paul, "give you peace at all times and in every way" (2 Thess. 3:16).

What is it that's driving you?

Is it perfectionism? That's pure ego. You'll self-destruct! Confess your perfectionism to God and ask Him for deliverance.

Is it desire for excellence "for the sake of your witness"? Whose excellence, yours or God's?

Is it pure social pressure? Maybe you need to say no to some activities that "everybody"—even Christians—are involved in. They're sapping more energy from you—or more finances—than you can afford to lose.

Is it love of money? This is so serious it's frightening. Jesus says you cannot serve both God and money (Matt. 6:24); you must choose one or the other. Wrestle that one to the ground and have done with it forever!

Maybe you really do need to quit your job and rest in God to supply. Would you have to scale down your standard of living? Maybe so, maybe not. God knows the economic level best for you, and He's committed to supply that as you're obedient to Him.

Slowing down may mean a new style of living for your children. You lift from them the burden of "too much"—all the ballet lessons, swimming lessons, Cub Scout meetings, piano lessons, charm lessons, 4-H (all good, but too much). And you shelter them to make their own play, take naps, or just sit and dream.

You may need to lock up the television except for a few pre-chosen programs. Rediscover the "family devotions" of an earlier generation: regular Bible reading and memorization and prayer as a gathered family. Play table games together, or jacks or hopscotch. Get your aerobics jumping rope with your kids.

Or just sit! Be near. Be available when the questions and decisions come. Be rested; don't let any seemingly good thing keep you from being rested.

It will take the discipline of your heart to shift down. For a while you'll feel restless, guilty that you're not "doing" something every minute. You'll want to "get busy," maintain the former pace, rectify every situation by your own nervous efforts. Who said it would be easy? "*Make every effort* to enter into that rest . . ." (Heb. 4:11).

But if you do learn to slow down, before long you'll know yourself better. You'll know the ones you live with better. And you'll have become a little island of poise in a mixed-up world. Your family, according to whatever measure of control and influence you still have, may become one less candidate for divorce, drugs, tragedy.

And you will say by your very lifestyle that you have time for life and for God—that He is the active One, working in you that which is well pleasing in His sight.

Now Work Into Your Life What You've Been Reading

How easy it is to say, "Yes, yes, our society certainly needs this chapter. . . . My sister-in-law needs this. . . . My neighbor needs it. . . ."

Let me, Anne Ortlund, tell you, "*I* need it." In fact, God has just brought along a situation for me not to fuss over but to pray extra about. (Any tinkering on my part would needlessly bristle some personalities.) *I rest in You, Lord. Help me to learn the lessons I'm writing about!*

1. As you think about this chapter, if you know it, hum a little of "It's me, O Lord, standin' in the need of prayer"!

2. Make a list—written, or if you're in a group, verbal—of possible eliminations to make your home life more serene and oriented toward God.

3. If you're a parent, study Deuteronomy 6:4–7 and write in your notebook, or discuss with your group, how you're doing in that role. Set specific goals to help you shape a godly family life.

4. Write your prayer or pray as a group, asking God for the courage to "live godly in this present world," resisting the pressures of the age.

5. Praise and thank Him for His power to answer your prayers more than you could ask or imagine (Eph. 3:20–21)!

15

—OF YOUR OWN
UNIQUENESS

IN THIS BOOK so far, if you've not only read it but "done" it, you've taken three bold new steps:

1. You've accepted the fact that God plans for you a wonderful life.

2. You've admitted your own helplessness and sin, and you've determined to "abide" in Christ and His power for righteousness in your life.

3. You've faced the problem of today's frantic pace, and you've shifted down to allow that habit of "abiding" to take hold.

You've made three new steps to do two things: to get clean and to get rested.

Do you realize what you've done? You've left the defense and you've gained the offense in your life. Now let's go back to number 1 and see just what this wonderful life is that God has planned for you. Oh, my friend! You are just about to stumble on wonder after wonder, and every wonder will be true.

See, for instance, that God has made you a divine original, a one-of-a-kind miracle.

There are more than five billion people on this planet, and there's no one like you—nor has there ever been, nor will there ever be. Then dare to be His miracle! And enjoy it to the fullest!

God has made you uniquely wonderful, and living your life is a totally personal, between-your-ears miracle, shared by only you and Him. When you're sick, others can be with you, but they can't be sick with you. When you're depressed or when you're happy, no other person, no matter how close, can feel your feelings.

Except God. He has fused you to Himself (John 14:20), and He eagerly planned that fusion even before the creation of the world (Eph. 1:4).

You are His precious, one-of-a-kind treasure. Do you really believe that? Said William Ellery Channing (1780–1842), "Every human is intended to have a character of his own; to be what no others are, and to do what no other can do."[1] From the very beginning, when you were only a much-loved concept in God's mind, you've been a combination of materials like nobody else.

Don't shrink from being what you are. Ethel Waters used to say, "God don't sponsor no flops!"

Accept your limitations light-heartedly. He made you exactly right. Are you below par in some way? Read Exodus 4:11 and John 9:1–3 and believe with joy.

Accept your strengths, too, with humility and gratitude. He knew what He was doing when He put you together. Assess yourself "with sober judgment, in accordance with the measure of faith God has given you" (Rom. 12:3).

Assess yourself honestly, and then—

Live in the sunshine! Abide in Him. Stay in your Lover's love (John 15:9) and don't wander out of it.

As you live there, my friend, you can learn gradually to be yourself, to become what God had in mind when He made you. This is so important that it takes skill, thought, and growth—to develop into being only who you are, your true self.

Baby Christians have to copy others, and that's all right. When Samuel was a little boy and heard God's voice for the first time, he had no idea how to answer. So he just copied what old Eli told him to say: "Speak, Lord, for your servant is listening" (1 Sam. 3:9). For his stage, that was fine.

But when Samuel grew up, he and God were deep, good friends and shared many joys and agonies and adventures together. Eli was no longer on the scene, but never mind, Samuel didn't need him to copy any more.

Grey Christians all their lives copy others. They're originals, too, of course, but they never realize it, and they don't mature into their uniqueness. They never grow up inside; they have no deep individual roots, so they spend their life parroting Christian externals—the Christian words, phrases, and ideas that are currently "in." And they all sound bland and alike—their conversations, their teaching, their Chris-

[1] Laurence J. Peter, ed., *Peter's Quotations* (New York: Bantam, 1977), 374.

tian songs—like pleasant tapes played over and over. They must be terribly boring to God! He hears the same few words and ideas repeated over and over around the world, as in a giant nursery school.

But you? Expect to graduate out of the baby stage. Look forward to moving beyond copying others to a wonderfully mature knowledge of God and His Word—and friendship with Him—that will bring you into your own focus and style.

Look forward to becoming *only what you are*. (Then you can really contribute to this world, because nobody else is what you are.) Begin to learn to "eliminate and concentrate"! Have you heard those two words before? You have if you read *Disciplines of the Beautiful Woman*.

Eliminating must be a very long, careful process, lest you eliminate both "bathwater" and "baby." Be careful what you're reacting against. Ask God for perspective; otherwise you could throw out important things—and throw out your graciousness and your tolerance as well. Use discretion and restraint in all your process of eliminating.

Nevertheless, as your eyes are fixed on Jesus Christ, you'll find yourself shedding what no longer represents you, what is inconsistent or superfluous. It will happen. Said Richard of St. Victor long ago, "The essence of purification is self-simplification."[2]

You'll find that you're deliberately unifying your life, your person, your style, your interests, your flavor, your thrust. God is one, and in Him you will discover more and more your own inner integration and coherence and order.

M. Dunnam wrote,

> *Isn't this our desire: to move through our days not as programmed and driven machines but as deciding, creating persons? Don't we want to be centers of spiritual power and harmony, having at least hints of life infused with and empowered by a sense of the Divine Presence?*[3]

Writes Meister Eckhart,

> *All creatures struggle and strive by a natural impulse that they may be like God. . . . Whether you like it or not, whether you know it or not, nature in her inner-most recesses secretly seeks and aims at God.*[4]

---

[2] Quoted in Underhill, *Mount of Purification*, 3.
[3] Maxie Dunnam, *The Workbook on Spiritual Disciplines* (Nashville: Upper Room, 1984), 125.
[4] *Meister Eckhart*, 179.

We have to admit it's true! God must have planted that within us. So when Dunnam asks, "Don't you want to be centers of spiritual power and harmony?" your answer and my answer is yes, yes!

And Eckhart pushes bravely even further into unexplored territory:

> *When God makes man . . . He loves His work. . . .*
> *Now I will say what I have never said before: God savours Himself. In the sweet savour in which God savours Himself, He enjoys all creations, not as creatures, but as creatures in God.*[5]

We tremble, we're awed. When we've fallen so far, can this still be true? Yes, the whole shout of the New Testament is that God in Christ has restored you to a far more exalted state than even Adam and Eve ever knew! It's true! It's true! God treasures you, He cherishes you, in Christ.

My friend, you're so forgiven, you're so perfectly cleansed because of the cross of Jesus Christ that you can really stand tall for all the universe to inspect. In Him—as you abide there—you are personally free to grow, to express your own will, to develop yourself.

Someone has said, "Love God and do as you please." And that's right, because when you truly love God *you please what He pleases*—and you and He are both thrilled.

Then live your inmost life in God. You are a twosome, and you and He can chart your course and make your agenda together.

Let every part of your life—your person, your style, your direction, your flavor—be in Him. When you're in Him, then you're based on truth. You'll be honest and genuine through and through; you'll be coordinated, all of a piece; you'll be in harmony with yourself. And then you can grow within yourself to unlimited dimensions—and all because you're in God.

Faddish lives age quickly. They're not based on God, who is greater than all culture and all generations, so twenty years from now they'll seem faded and "out of it." Anchor yourself to the great "I AM," and you will develop more and more into a woman who is ageless, whole, true, and at rest.

Goethe said, "The spirit tends to take to itself a body." And your inner life in God will shape the outer you in concrete ways. Only He knows what ways, but the result will be uniquely you from the toes up, whether you're presiding or helping or selling or studying or creating. It

[5] Ibid., 182–183.

will be uniquely your style, built on your convictions. It will be your part of God and you!

And my friend, when you abide in Him, when you truly focus on Him until you specialize, then that kind of centeredness and concentration will cause something remarkable to emerge. In the "specializing" God will accent the "special"! You won't just be living in the sunshine, but you yourself will have taken on characteristics of the sun.

God will be developing in you the power to radiate and affect things and structures and people.

Truth is so powerful! Righteousness is so dynamic! Get on your face before Him and surrender yourself to Him, that this might be so.

If you're truly abiding in Him, *you'll affect things*. If you're artistically creative, putting together music or stitchery or buildings or lithography or poetry or cities or whatever, you'll depend less and less on copying what's already around you, and you'll draw more and more from the resources of the life of Christ deep within your own self. He is ultimate Truth, and you'll begin to reflect His integrity and wholeness in your own creations.

Ray and I must not write by copying other popular Christian books around us, saying what they say and hoping to sell as they sell! We'd be liars and phonies. We must write what comes deeply out of what God puts into us—what we've experienced and what we've learned. Whether our books sell or not, before God we must be true to our inner selves.

If you're abiding in Him, you'll also affect structures. If your job is to put together and manage people (you're a female office manager, factory foreman, politician, minister, company president), you won't outline your people in boxes and squares to look good in reports; you'll study their true situations, their work loads, their gifts, and their needs, and you'll work at building your people from the inside out. (As a mother, you'll do the same.) That's integrity. That's managing in truth.

If you're abiding in Him, you'll affect people. Jesus' last command was to disciple others (Matt. 28:18–20). And whether you're a butcher or a baker or a candlestick maker, you're to choose people to gather close to you, to teach and love and affect them for Him. (See my book *Discipling One Another.*[6])

To do this you must live in truth—sincere and genuine and transparent. An authentic Christian can say without embarrassment, as Paul did, "Join with others in following my example" (Phil. 3:17) and "I urge you to imitate me" (1 Cor. 4:16). But such a Christian is also

[6] (Waco, TX: Word Books, 1979).

willing, as Paul was, to expose his own failures as well as strengths. A Christian who walks in truth never hides his struggles on the way to holiness; discipling demands honesty. So Paul could say, "We speak before God with sincerity, like men sent from God" (2 Cor. 2:17)—like facets of truth sent from *the* Truth.

Now, becoming authentically you, a unique original, doesn't mean you'll say what no one ever said before or do what no one has ever done. It simply means you'll say exactly what God tells you to say and you'll do what God tells you to do. Jesus explained it like this—and He's our beloved model: "The words I say to you are not just my own. Rather, it is the Father, living in me, who is doing his work" (John 14:10). Said Thomas Carlyle (1795–1881), "The merit of originality is not novelty; it is sincerity. The believing man is the original man."[7]

Then will you dare to be God's unique miracle? Will you assess honestly what God has made in making you—and then have the courage to love that and be that with all your might and no other? Will you fear only your sin, but fear nothing else?

My friend, dare to live fully in Him, with godly enthusiasm! (Franz Josef Haydn, the composer, was once asked why his church music was so cheerful, and he answered, "When I think of God, my heart is so full of joy, the notes dance and leap from my pen!")

Dare to enter into personal friendship with God as He waits for you to do. Dare to walk with Him and be absolutely free—in Him and with Him!

In yourself you're cold, black, hard, ugly iron—a worthless sinner. But in the fire you're hot and glowing and purified; in Christ you become "blameless and pure" (Phil. 2:15). One day soon the iron itself will be forever changed (1 John 3:2)—oh, praise the Lord!—but in the meantime . . .

Stay in Him! Live His plan for you with all your might! Be happy in Him; be happy in your life in Him; be happy in all He gives you and in all He takes away; be happy in what you do; be happy in what you can't do; be happy in all He makes you to be; be happy in what He never allows you to be. Be happy in you! Be happy in Him!

No more drifting, wandering, doubting, complaining, living in confusion.

Don't let anyone judge you (Col. 2:16).

Don't let anyone disqualify you (Col. 2:18).

Don't let anyone discourage you (2 Chron. 20:15).

Don't let anyone deter you (Mark 9:39a).

[7] *Peter's Quotations*, 373.

Don't let anyone detract you from your goal (James 1:4).

God has made you alive with Christ (Col. 2:13), and you have been given fullness in Him (Col. 2:10). He is a shield around you, your Glorious One, Who lifts up your head (Ps. 3:3).

Then, from your stance in Christ, produce! Achieve! GOFORIT!

Perhaps you'll become so focused, so concentrated, that your sunbeam will narrow to a laser beam. People like this become the geniuses, the prophets, the ones with maximum intensity of power to affect.

Open yourself wide to whatever He desires.

Now Work Into Your Life What You've Been Reading

This chapter takes time to digest, doesn't it? Read it over again, stopping at the points mentioned below to take it in for yourself.

1. On page 195, after rereading the paragraphs that say, "accept your limitations" and "accept your strengths," write a list of your strengths and another of your weaknesses (not your sins). Below the lists, write Him a prayer of thanksgiving for them all.

2. On page 196, after rereading the paragraph that says eliminating things from yourself or your life must be a long, careful process, make a list of what some of those might be. Hebrews 12:1 calls them "weights" or "hindrances"; they're not bad, they just don't reflect *you* any more.

3. As you finish reading the chapter, pray as Mary did, "Behold the handmaid of the Lord; be it unto me according to thy word" (Luke 1:38, KJV; Ps. 123:2).

If you're studying this chapter in a group, bring as homework what you wrote for these three sections, report on them or read them, and then pray for each other together. Perhaps you need to agree to check on each other periodically, to hold each other accountable for really eliminating "weights" and "hindrances," clutter and extras, from your lives.

16

—OF COMMUNION
WITH GOD

"DEEP WITHIN YOUR vast interior space," writes John White, "is a tabernacle God built to commune with you. From it He calls you with tender urgency."[1]

Have your inner chambers been unused and silent when they should be busy with God? Hannah wept over being barren: like a womb that's empty month after month, is your interior tabernacle empty—when God meant it to be a house of prayer?

Maybe that word *prayer* threw up a roadblock in your mind and you're back in your former rut of saying, "I'm so busy, I really don't have much time for prayer."

Listen, the issue of prayer really isn't prayer—it's God.

When Ray and I are in a crowded room, we may be doing different things and talking to different people, but we're more or less aware of each other. If one of us has an obvious need, it won't be long until the other has noticed and done something about it. And when other conversations end and other duties get finished, somehow, somehow, we find our way back to each other.

It isn't that we're trying so hard to stay in touch; eventually we'd be exhausted from the intensity of the effort. It's just that we're in love.

The command to "pray without ceasing" may seem like an impossible chore if you're "too busy" for even ten minutes a day. Hear it again: the issue of prayer isn't prayer—it's God. Prayer is simply the measuring device for the state of your relationship with Him.

If you're still a grey Christian, away from Him and living by your own energies, you're praying very little. And you're "out of sync" with God's whole universe, and everything goes wrong. God isn't pleased with you; He rebukes you and hassles you and punishes you. He doesn't

[1] *The Fight* (Downers Grove, IL: Inter-Varsity, 1976), 22.

prosper your living; He doesn't honor you. He's a faithful Father who disciplines His children.

But if you have an honest desire to surrender everything to Him and abide in Him and let Him have His way with you—oh, my dear! You'll discover how wonderful He really is—how nice, how friendly, how eager to commune with you, how comforting and strengthening and delicious, how easy to live with!

When you look in the Bible at the people who set their hearts to follow hard after the Lord—see how the Lord actually winked at their faults and overlooked their failings! Besides, if you really desire God in your life, He desires it, too; He warms up to a person like you; you're what He's looking for! He will treat you well. He will bless you.

Well, then, that gives you confidence to start talking to Him, doesn't it?

And when you do, the blessed God of all grace meets you where you are, and moves you from there at the pace of your capacity, even at the pace of your choice.

> He tends his flock like a shepherd:
>   He gathers the lambs in his arms
> and carries them close to his heart;
>   he gently leads those that have young
> (Isa. 40:11).

Start talking to Him. Talk to Him right now. Tell Him you'd like to learn the art of communing and communicating with Him.

Wrote Madam Jeanne Guyon (1648–1717), who was often in prisons for her faith,

> *Nothing is so easily obtained as the possession and enjoyment of God. He is more present to us than we are to ourselves. He is more desirous of giving Himself to us than we are to possess him.*
>   *Listen! You who think yourselves to be so dull and fit for nothing! By prayer you may live on God Himself with less difficulty or interruption than you live in the vital air.*[2]

Obeying something is always better than just reading about it. As you read this chapter, stay in constant touch with Him. Before another word, just breathe "Father. . . ." He loves it, and so do you. "The

[2] Sherwood E. Wirt, ed., *Spiritual Disciplines* (Westchester, IL: Crossway, 1983), 72.

farthest reaches of your inner space," to quote White, are echoing back His call.

Something inside you is saying that this is more important to your well-being than aerobics or natural foods. Let this truth get a firm grasp of your heart.

Writes F. P. Harton,

> The Christian life is essentially God dwelling in us, and the fruit of that indwelling is the soul's participation in the divine life.[3]

How can it happen—that He lives in you and you respond by living in Him? At first, given the hard facts of living in this world, it seems about as practical and real as a trip to Mars. But—

> There is a way of ordering our mental life on more than one level at once. On one level we may be thinking, discussing, seeing, calculating, meeting all the demands of external affairs.
>
> But deep within, behind the scenes, at a profounder level, we may also be in prayer and adoration, song and worship, and a gentle receptiveness to divine breathings.[4]

If the world briefly calls for total concentration, so be it. But as surely as a freed homing pigeon turns home again, so before long your interior consciousness will begin to turn back to God. When you love Him, it happens without effort. It's what you most want. It's the least taxing and most pleasurable thing you can do. Says Frank Laubach, "To see anybody will be to pray! To hear anybody . . . will be to pray!"[5]

Listen, this isn't something you add to your already busy life. This is what you do while you do what you are doing! It won't take *more* of your time—it will take *all* of your time.

I'm aware of Him as I write this. I can't speak to Him in whole sentences, but I'm calling to Him to help with the words, and just now as I tore a sheet from my yellow pad I said, "I love You."

Be doing the same as you read. (What a mysterious link that gives you and me!) In between paragraphs, breathe "alleluia," or whatever comes to mind. Just as you breathe air with your lungs—automatically and almost unconsciously—breathe Him with your spirit. "Glory to You, Lord." You hardly knew you said it.

[3] *The Elements of the Spiritual Life* (Bungay, Suffolk, Great Britain: Richard Clay, 1933), 9–10.
[4] Thomas Kelly, *A Testament of Devotion* (New York: Harper, 1941), 124.
[5] *Learning the Vocabulary of God* (Nashville: Upper Room, 1956), 33.

It may be a quick request shot up—a quick telegram, almost wordless, but you and God both understand it. Notice Nehemiah 2:4: "The king said to me, 'What is it you want?' Then I prayed to the God of heaven, and I answered the king. . . ."

Pray always (Luke 18:1). Pray continually (1 Thess. 5:17). Pray on all occasions (Eph. 6:18).

Where do you pray? In church (Ps. 111:1), in private (Matt. 6:6), in the open (on the beach, Acts 21:5; in a garden, Luke 22:41), on your bed (Ps. 149:5)—everywhere (1 Tim. 2:8)! "Pray in the Spirit on all occasions with all kinds of prayers and requests" (Eph. 6:18).

Prayer is for all the time. You pray when you iron, you pray when you jog, you pray when you take the train to work. But prayer is more than that, too.

A *life of prayer is also a regular discipline.* It includes a scheduled time when you lay aside everything else and give Him your undivided attention. Why do I say this? Because God gives us plenty of glimpses in His Book of the private lives of godly people, and this is what they did.

David was a busy king, but 2 Samuel 7:18 says that he "went in and sat before the Lord." In Psalm 55:17 he said he prayed "evening, morning and noon."

The writer of Psalm 119 prayed seven times a day (v. 164), including midnight (v. 62).

Daniel prayed on his knees in his upstairs room three times every day (Dan. 6:10).

Isaac was praying in the evening when he first saw Rebekah and fell in love (Gen. 24:62–65).

Peter prayed at noon (Acts 10:9), and Peter and John went together to the temple to pray in the midafternoon (Acts 3:1).

Jesus prayed early in the morning (Mark 1:35), and even sometimes through the night (Luke 6:12). Luke 5:16 says that withdrawing to pray was His constant habit—and you notice He didn't just do it when there was a lull between events; He withdrew to pray in the thick of things and even when He could have been sleeping.

Scheduled withdrawing to God is what will establish, strengthen, settle you in the disciplines of your heart. Said Christ in John 15:7, "If you remain in me and my words remain in you"—that's Bible reading—"ask whatever you wish, and it will be given you"—that's a bold, free prayer life for total success. How can you turn down a deal like that?

And the Scripture must accompany your prayers. Oh, your need and mine is to know the Book!

Ray and I read through the Bible every year. This is our seventeenth year, and every year we see more of the Lord in His Word—more truths, more connections, more amazing structures. There is nothing like getting a sweeping, overall view of the whole, over and over and over.[6]

Stay in the Word even to catch the flavor of how to pray! There seems to be much prayer in our day with great authority but little humility. And yet godly ones in the Bible seemed to pray no "commanding" prayers; they never seemed to stridently confront situations, spirits, or powers. Indeed, Jude warns of "godless men" who have no awe of celestial beings. And he points out that even the great archangel Michael never dared to rebuke the devil; he only prayed that the Lord would rebuke him (Jude 9). Sometimes I cringe when dear believers loudly, almost arrogantly, "claim" this or "pray against" that.

Stay immersed in the Scriptures to learn how to speak to the Holy One, your dear Abba Father:

1. Read out loud the prayers in God's Book, so that your own voice can climb inside the words (for instance, Dan. 9:4–19; 2 Sam. 7:18–29; 1 Sam. 2:1–10; 2 Chron. 6:14–42).

2. Put a Bible prayer in front of you, and use its form and general idea to shape your own prayer.

3. Study the postures of those who prayed in the Scriptures— and their emotions.

How should we pray? Seventeenth-century school children used to pray, "Grant that I may worship and pray unto Thee with as much reverence and godly fear, as if I saw the heavens open and all the angels that stand around Thy throne. Amen."[7]

Everybody's private living will work out prayer differently.

At this point in my life, I give Him the late morning. I don't eat until I have my time with Him, and I like that because the pangs of hunger prompt and accompany my desire to meet the Lord. I couldn't do that when I was feeding a family breakfast, but now I can wait, and for an hour or so I sit having brunch as I read and underline and take notes and write my prayers.

---

[6] Why don't you do what we do and subscribe to *Daily Walk*, P.O. Box 80587, Atlanta, GA 30366? It will guide you through in about twenty minutes a day.

[7] William Law, *A Serious Call to a Devout and Holy Life* (Philadelphia: Westminster, 1948), XXV.

Then several years ago I thought about "the Lord's prayer" that Jesus taught us, and I realized I never used it unless I repeated it in a church service. And I thought, "If He suggested we use that prayer as a model, then I want to do that regularly."

So I do. As soon as I think of it in the morning, I start silently saying it—well, actually whispering, to concentrate. I may be out running or walking. I may be putting on my "face" before the mirror. (You may have trouble doing this if the house is full of kids!) I don't listen to any radio or television or make phone calls or get any outside input into my mind until I've spoken "the Lord's prayer" to Him.

It sounds different every day.

I may begin, "O my heavenly Father, more wonderful than any earthly daddy, may Your reputation be hallowed, respected, honored, revered—by me, and even by others through me." I chew over those ideas a while.

"May Your kingdom come soon. Lord, it will be wonderful! The lion will lie down with the lamb. Pollution will be conquered; nature will be balanced. People's creativity will be poured not into weapons but into peaceful pursuits—how fabulous. 'Even so, come, Lord Jesus.' "

Eventually I begin the next paragraph: "May Your perfect will be carried out everywhere in the universe, Lord—not spottily, in some places but not in others, as it is now. I pray that soon every created thing and being will be united in doing Your will; You deserve it. May every knee bow, and every tongue confess You."

Maybe by now I'm halfway around the park in my sweats; wherever I am, the conversation continues:

"Give Ray and me this day our daily bread—and how I thank You for Your faithful supply! Lord, give us wisdom for earning, for spending, for saving, and for giving." And so on, through the prayer.

Then I release my mind to the day's news or to other input, but I look forward in a few hours to a dead-boulevard-stop time to get alone with Him.

However you plan your daily walk with God, plan it! I give my next week's schedule to my small group each time we meet, so that it's there in black and white in advance for me to follow and for one of them to pray over. Then I'm held accountable for my life—for my walk with Him—the way I want to be.

Work to keep your quiet time enlivened and fresh! It will probably fall through the cracks if somebody isn't specifically praying for you about it and holding you accountable, and it will also fall through the cracks if you're not active when you have it! Write or sing or talk out loud or at least whisper.

Ray is as busy as I am, but his withdrawing time is just as urgent. Ray sings to the Lord every day; he keeps a few hymns of praise pasted in his notebook. And some of his notebook pages contain his prayer subjects: one page for each family member, one for our finances, another for Renewal Ministries. There's a page for his broadcasting on Haven of Rest, one for churches and fellow pastors he loves, one for the President and those in authority, and so on.

We pray together as well. In the car, going any distance, we pray conversationally back and forth. Every night in bed, last of all before sleep, we pray wrapped in each other's arms. (In Australia a fellow was shocked over that and asked if it was reverent. But we know our Father really enjoys it. We even thank Him and praise Him for our loving.)

Sometimes on Sundays I pray for all Christians around the world. I pray for those in the Orient who rise to worship Him first. Then I picture the wave of risers-and-worshipers as it moves westward with the morning sun. I particularly pray for our friends in Afghanistan, where we lived, who believe and therefore suffer. I pray for Israel, and for Christians in Communist countries and in Europe and Africa. I pray for the brothers and sisters in the Americas, who get up and praise Him last—except for the Pacific islanders, who rise and add the final amen!

> God Himself is with us.
>   Hear the harps resounding!
>   See the crowds the throne surrounding!
> "Holy, holy, holy"—
>   Hear the hymn ascending,
>   Angels, saints their voices blending!
> Bow Thine ear To us here;
>   Hear, O Christ, the praises
>   That Thy Church now raises.[8]

What a lofty, all-encompassing business prayer is! We lift our hearts to God, and we discover we have joined a numberless company around the world and in heaven itself! We have left time and moved into eternity! We have, in a sense, shed our mortal bodies and moved, ahead of schedule, into our future glory with Him!

And, indeed, "prayer changes things." Wonder of wonders, it even changes the mind of Almighty God (Exod. 32:14; Jon. 3:10; Amos

[8] Gerhard Tersteegin (1697–1769).

7:2–6)! In prayer we have become "God's fellow workers" (1 Cor. 3:9)! We are no longer our little selves.

> *Deep within your vast interior space . . . is a tabernacle God built to commune with you. From it He calls you with tender urgency. And from the farthest reaches of your inner space an ache of yearning echoes back His call.*[9]

> *O come, let us worship and bow down.*

---

[9] John White, *The Fight* (Downers Grove, IL: Inter-Varsity, 1976), 22.

Now Work Into Your
Life What You've
Been Reading

1. In your notebook write to Him your thoughts and hopes and longings of this very moment.

2. Then, according to your need, pray through one of the following psalms, changing the words where you like to make them your personal prayer to the Lord:
   a. To worship Him—Psalm 145.
   b. To admit your sin and be cleansed—Psalm 51.
   c. To lay out before Him a problem—Psalm 20. (Add words to make it specific.)
   d. Just to talk to Him—Psalm 25.
   e. To rejoice in His safekeeping—Psalm 91.
   f. To thank Him—Psalm 116.

If you're meeting in a small group, allow a time of silence for number 1. Then any of the psalms listed above can be prayed out loud, one verse for each person, still changing the words to pray according to your needs.

Perhaps you'll want to agree to pair off to hold each other accountable for daily quiet times, for as long as each person desires and until the habit is firmly established.

17

—OF BEING EQUALLY
AT EASE WITH LIFE
AND DEATH

I WAS SITTING in the back of the car listening to my two Ray Ortlunds talking together up front. The senior Ray, veteran of thirty-six years of ministry, was commenting on preaching to the junior Ray, fresh with his Ph.D. from the University of Aberdeen, Scotland, and just starting to pastor a church. Ray, Jr., is so smart (where did this kid come from?), and he feeds his people sermons from the Word of God that are thoughtful and finely honed.

"But remember," said father Ray to son Ray, "not many of your flock will ever be great biblical scholars. Teach them from the Bible mainly two things: how to live and how to die."

I sat there thinking, "My book is on how to live, but it needs a chapter on how to die. Both are so important for us all."

One of your heart's disciplines must be a complete, relaxed acceptance of your coming death. To dread death is both ignorant and un-Christian. In fact, one of the reasons Christ died was to "free those who all their lives were held in slavery by their fear of death" (Heb. 2:15).

(I had to take a break just now for an errand, and I was wandering through a department store. So many kinds of eye shadows, knee-highs, notepaper, strapless bras, candlesticks, clip-on earrings, fondue cookers, stereos, candies, fabric belts, machine-made Persians, overnighters, li-quors, plastic cannisters, colored toothpicks—on and on and on and on. . . . "O God," I thought, "I'm on my way through all these trinkets to go write on death! How exciting! How eternally important and ennobling!")

Search your own heart. Do you fear the thought of dying? Let me give you three ways to break that chain and be freed.

1. Call death by its right name.

Death is death. You don't have to glamorize it the way some Eastern mystics do or dread it like the humanists. And don't get trapped into speaking of death in lovely but empty sentiments—"pleasant fancies of a half-held creed." Poor morticians—they have to think up every pink fuzzy phrase they can to substitute for the word *dead*; their clients might not be able to handle the plain reality.

2. *See death for what it is: both an enemy and a friend.*

Without Christ, it's the ultimate enemy. God told Adam that if he sinned he would die (Gen. 2:17), and he did—so he did! And ever since, sinners have had to concentrate on their sinful present because they're "deathly" afraid of their future: " 'Let us eat and drink,' [they] say, 'for tomorrow we die!' " (Isa. 22:13).

A woman without Christ had better get whatever happiness she can scrounge from eye shadows, knee-highs, notepaper, and strapless bras—because death will be the end of all that and the end of everything in any way pleasant to her.

But for grey Christians to copy that—how terrible! For them to clutch at the trinkets of this world as if they were all there is—how unnecessary, and how tragic!

Now, we do have to say that death is also the Christian's enemy, in the sense that it tears us away from those people we love best. Ray and I often say it: "What would I do without you? How could I stand it?"—even though we know God's tender grace.

We've told the Lord we'd love to die together—if Jesus doesn't spare us that by coming first! But we know He gives "dying grace" only to the dying; we don't need it ahead of time. So we rest content in that and meanwhile hug to ourselves every day that we have together.

But still—I'm very curious about my own death, and very excited over it, and in a great sense eager for it; aren't you?

Dr. Carl Henry has written, "Death is a transition from life to life—that is, from creation life to resurrection life."[1] And of the two, which is better? Do you go up or down? We have a friend who chuckled, "If Christians had any idea how wonderful heaven is, we'd all commit suicide!"

"What a friend we have"—not only "in Jesus," but in death! Death is your dear friend who will bring you through the door and into His very arms.

Then you can keep light touch on your scheduling ("if it is the Lord's will"—James 4:13–15) and have a holy carelessness about death's interrupting it all.

One time, as a total surprise to Ray, he and I got whisked off by friends for a week in Hawaii. He thought those seven days were solidly filled with appointments and work. But I had secretly rescheduled everything and packed our bags, and before Ray could catch his breath

---

[1] "The Road to Eternity," *Christianity Today*, 17 July 1981, 32.

we were suddenly transported to soft Hawaiian sunshine, strains of uku-
lele music, wonderful food, rest, and fun! Hey, heaven's going to be
even better than that! And death is your transportation into the very
arms of God.

One of my friends told me her little girl one day had a great insight.
"Mamma," she said, "I know how Jesus gets people to heaven."

"How?" said her Mother.

"He kills 'em!"

How do you explain that one? Well, in a sense it's true, because
"flesh and blood cannot inherit the kingdom of God, nor does the
perishable inherit the imperishable" (1 Cor. 15:50).

Now, if Satan—poor loser that he is—gets in one final kick on his
way out, never mind. Any sickness, weakness, pain, or even blood will
be covered by God's kind hand.

And here's the point of it all: "Though worms destroy this body," said
Job (now, there's your Grisly-Thought-for-the-Day), "yet in my flesh
shall I see God." The end will be the beginning—glory, victory, and a
bright and shining forever!

No wonder the woman of Proverbs 31 can "laugh at the days to
come" (v. 25)!

If we live, we live to the Lord; and if we die, we die to the Lord.
So, whether we live or die, we belong to the Lord (Rom. 14:8).

3. *Learn how to live in constant readiness for death.*

This means, first of all, not concentrating mostly on your notebook
or your wardrobe, but on the disciplines of your heart. That's the inner
you—the part that's eternal, and you need to get yourself ready for your
entire future.

> My flesh . . . may fail,
>   but God is the strength of my heart
>   . . . forever
> (Ps. 73:26).

You say you're only twenty-three and you can't relate to this? My
brother Bobby barely had twenty-four years. My mother's sister had only
two.

> Man's days are determined;
>   [God has] decreed the number of his months
>   and [has] set limits he cannot exceed
> (Job 14:5).

Our pioneer American forefathers slogged across valleys and mountains and open prairies until they came to a settling place, where they'd stake a claim. Then on the spot they usually put up some rude lean-to until they could build a snug little home out of sod or timber.

What if the wife had said, "Henry, I don't want to move! I don't care if you have built a better place; I just want to keep crawling into this little lean-to for the rest of my life"? Henry would rightly call her crazy.

So God describes our bodies as disposable tents, and he says that fortunately "we have a building from God, an eternal house in heaven, not built with human hands. Meanwhile we groan, longing to be clothed with our heavenly dwelling" (2 Cor. 5:1–2). My word, yes! Who wants girdles and permanents and aches and pains forever? And when God describes our future body to us, He's limited to earth-words; it's the only language we know. But He means far, far more than what He says.

Therefore, my friend, detach your affections more and more from what you taste-touch-see. Don't detach your affections from the world itself—you're too needed (Phil. 1:21–26)—but detach yourself from a debilitating closeness to it.

Now, let's pursue this a little more: how can you prepare yourself for your own personal death, the only one you'll ever have?

By learning to experience solitude. By learning to enjoy being alone. It will get you ready for the ultimate "alone" experience of dying.

If you've clogged and saturated and stuffed your life with unceasing companionship, abundant advice—always the group, always the crowd—you won't know what it is to be an individual. And then if you're suddenly forced to walk single file when it's not familiar, it could be a panicky experience.

Get used to withdrawing. Get used to the sweet presence of Immanuel, who will never leave you or forsake you.

Solitude is essential if your roots are to grow deep. "Each heart knows its own bitterness, and no one else can share its joy" (Prov. 14:10). "Know thyself"—which means, fortunately, not being an eccentric loner but getting very familiar with being a twosome with God.

Where can you go for solitude? "Jesus often withdrew to lonely places and prayed" (Luke 5:16). In a city, lonely places are hard to find. We live by the ocean, and Ray knows stretches of beach where few people go. There he talks to and listens to God.

Find a closet; find a spot behind your house; find a hiding place. Incessant sound will dull you, desensitize you. You were made for quiet. The silent forces are the great forces: sunbeams, gravity, dew. There is strength in aloneness, in listening, in observing, in prayer.

"Be still, and know that I am God," He says (Ps. 46:10). In your kind of world, full of noise pollution, *listen, in the discipline of your heart, to the still, small voice of God.*

Elijah stood at the mouth of a mountain cave, and along came a wind so violent it shattered rocks—

> *But the Lord was not in the wind. After the wind there was an earthquake, but the Lord was not in the earthquake. After the earthquake came a fire, but the Lord was not in the fire. And after the fire came a gentle whisper [a still, small voice]. When Elijah heard it, he pulled his cloak over his face (1 Kings 19:11–13).*

Oh, the holiness of that moment! I think Elijah pulled his cloak across to humble himself, but also to shut out every other sound.

Some of our foremothers just threw their aprons up over their heads. Tune out . . . and tune in.

Only those who live well, die well.

Now Work Into Your
Life What You've
Been Reading

Ponder on your own, or discuss in your group together, how you will apply this chapter.

If you've prepared realistically for your own death, you have no assignment at all. If not, consider these possibilities:

1. Make a will.

2. Arrange for godparents to raise your children if needed.

3. Update your insurance program.

4. Consider assigning particularly treasured possessions to each of your children, buying a cemetery plot, or whatever appeals to you. Know that what happens to your remains is relatively unimportant and temporary, until Christ transforms it all in glory!

If you're in a group, discuss together an exchange of ideas on personal preparations. Follow with a time of prayer, thanking God for
—Believers gone on before,
—His promise of resurrection,
—Your own peace of heart.

18

MOVE IN BEAUTY
WITHIN YOURSELF

WELL, YOU'RE COMING to the end of this book.

If you read *Disciplines of the Beautiful Woman*, the companion book to this one, you were challenged to make whatever is your own private living space a place of beauty and organization and serenity.

You put a pretty basket for your makeup on your bathroom counter. You've allowed no more than a picture and a bud vase and a small book on the nightstand beside your bed. You're working at keeping clutter and confusion from the area intimately surrounding you.

But this time, reading this book, shrink the space even smaller—to within yourself. Dear feminine friend, if your environment is serene but your heart is not, you lose; isn't that true?

Right now, eliminate from mind even the closest circle surrounding you, and concentrate on your soul. Surrender to God. Relax; sink down into His terms. Let Him create in your spirit beauty and peace and rest.

> Hidden in the hollow
>   Of His blessed hand,
> Never foe can follow,
>   Never traitor stand;
>
> Not a surge of worry,
>   Not a shade of care,
> Not a blast of hurry
>   Touch the spirit there.
>
> Stayed upon Jehovah,
>   Hearts are fully blest;

Finding, as he promised,
Perfect peace and rest.[1]

Now you may be joining Madam Jeanne Guyon and Mother Theresa and many others—women who through the centuries have lived in loveliness and peace and power without depending on any exterior at all. They've moved in beauty even in prisons and slums! Even if their most intimate surroundings have been beyond their control, in their hearts has been elegance and rest and God Himself.

Perhaps this book has found its way behind iron or bamboo or other curtains. You say you live in a totalitarian state and you have little or no freedom? Hear the good news: in the only area where it really matters, you can be totally free.

And a light shined in the cell,
And there was not any wall,
And there was no dark at all,
Only Thou, Immanuel.[2]

Or perhaps you say you're chained to an impossible husband. Think about Abigail: so was she. Nabal was rich but selfish and insensitive—a drunk and a bum, "surly and mean in his dealings" (1 Sam. 25:3).

And what was Abigail like? She was not just an escapist; she was realistic enough to call her husband a fool (v. 25). But she hadn't let him ruin her. When she talked to David, her speech revealed such a long-term inner nurturing of godliness that her words came out almost like poetry:

The life of my master will be bound securely in the bundle of living by the Lord your God. But the lives of our enemies he will hurl away as from the pocket of a sling (1 Sam. 25:29).

Regardless of the crudeness around her, here was a woman of inner delicacy and sensitivity and beauty. Abigail's life was hidden in God. David recognized it immediately, and when God in His own time terminated Nabal's wretched life, David was quick to marry her. He knew a good thing when he saw it.

[1] Frances R. Havergal (1836–1879), "Like a River Glorious."

[2] Amy Carmichael, "Light in the Cell," in *Toward Jerusalem* (Fort Washington, PA: Christian Literature Crusade, 1936, 1977), 144. Copyright material used by permission of Christian Literature Crusade, Fort Washington, PA 19034.

But Abigail didn't become lovely in the course of being David's wife; *she had already become lovely while she was the wife of Nabal.* Her real living was between her ears!

Or perhaps you say you're single and lonely: think about Ruth. She'd been widowed at an early age; she was childless; and she lived in a country far from her own home with a depressed mother-in-law (Ruth 1:20–21)!

But Ruth lived in God. Whatever her external situation, she was happy, helpful, modest, sweet—everything God wanted her to be. Her real living was in secret, and her Father who saw in secret rewarded her openly: He gave her a wonderful second husband and made her an ancestor of Jesus Christ (Matt. 1:5).

Or perhaps you say it's too late; you're getting old, and your whole life has been terrible: think about Miriam.

As a little girl, one of millions of captive Jews cruelly oppressed in Egypt, Miriam could remember when Pharaoh had ordered all male Hebrew babies to be drowned (Exod. 1:22)! So her parents had hidden her tiny brother, Moses, in a basket and made her responsible for protecting him. Unfortunately, Pharaoh's own daughter had discovered him and confiscated him and so permanently split up the family. And Miriam had lived all her life as part of a tormented captive people.

Then, when Miriam was in her upper eighties, something good finally happened to her! Was it too late to take advantage of it? Here were her two younger brothers, who had survived their ordeals but were now aged eighty-three and eighty, finally leading all the Hebrews out of the land.

Do you think Miriam complained about leaving her home or about the length of the walk? Listen, as soon as the opportunity for leadership emerged, she was right there. And when everybody started singing the great song Moses had made up about their escape,

Miriam . . . took a tambourine in her hand, and all the women followed her, with tambourines and dancing. Miriam sang to them:

> "Sing to the Lord,
>   for he is highly exalted.
> The horse and its rider
>   he has hurled into the sea"
> (Exod. 15:20, 21).

Her choice was in the disciplines of her heart: to be just one more little old woman in the world, or to rise to fulfill God's great plans for her life. She chose the latter, and for the next forty years she joined her two brothers in leadership!

Or perhaps you say your problem is different: you're raising your children in a godless community full of pressures toward immorality—so you have a right to stew, not for yourself but for your children.

Think about Mordecai—a man, it's true, but a substitute mother. Mordecai was one of thousands of captured Jews in Persia, where the culture was so pagan and oppressive that if the name *God* had appeared in the book of Esther that tells his story, the book wouldn't have survived for us to read.

Mordecai had assumed the responsibility for raising his little orphaned niece, Esther—and this in a situation where neither he nor she had any personal freedoms whatsoever. So when King Xerxes was looking for a new queen, neither of them could object when Esther was taken and put into the harem of girls being tried out for the king!

How would you feel?

Well, Mordecai had parented his little niece as best he could, and both of them were in the capable hands of Almighty God. So when Esther was away from Mordecai's influence and even in impossible circumstances, God gave her courage, and she saved her entire captive people from on-the-spot extermination.

How big is your God? Do you try to "manage" and "control" yourself and everybody around you? Is your mothering colored by every worry and fear, as you try to drive your children from behind?

Or do you lead them visibly from up front, modeling for them a life of rest and trust? Good leadership says, "Watch me. . . . Follow my lead. . . . Do exactly as I do" (Judg. 7:17)! Are you close enough, exposed enough to your children that your serenity and joy in Him can be caught? Do you "talk about [the Lord] when you sit at home and when you walk along the road, when you lie down and when you get up" (Deut. 6:7)? Are you abiding in Him as you live in the wonder of seeing Him work it all out eventually for good (Rom. 8:28)?

I'm in process in my life, too. The children are grown, and now Ray and I travel and speak full time for a living. And when I wake up in the morning, sometimes I have to think whether I'm in Cedar Rapids or Tokyo. We get jetted to time zones where our bodies rebel. We get put into very hot places and dirty places and cold ones; we can be paid well or not at all, given a luxurious bed or hard cots. . . . For a "nester" like me all this could be destabilizing—if circumstances controlled the inner me.

But I'm Noah in the ark! God has given me only one window, and it's overhead, so wherever I am, the view is the same. When I "blue sky," I'm being realistic—because my view is God!

> Be we in East or West, or North, or South,
> By wells of water, or in land of drouth,
> Lo, Thou hast put a new song in our mouth,
> Alleluia.[3]

Whatever is happening around you, first of all nurture your hidden life. Become a beautiful woman—one whose heart is nourished and lifted by daily Bible reading and disciplined prayer. Luke says, "Be careful, or your hearts will be weighed down" (21:34). Don't let it happen! Insist on trusting Him! Insist on abiding in Him! Insist on enjoying Him!

He will also be in you. Then, like a glove sheathing a hand, you'll move only as He moves in you. He may move you to be busy or slow-paced, but it will be right, and it will carry out His majestic purposes.

There is no other way.

Settle your mind. Be steadfast in God. And there, inside of you, He will create a heart of beauty and peace, rest and hope, love and singing.

Alleluia! Alleluia! Alleluia!

And the direction of your life will not be from outside to inside, so that after all your good resolves, people and circumstances will crush you and defeat you again.

No, "though he slay me, yet will I trust in him" (Job 13:15, KJV)! And the direction of your life will be from that inside of trust to the outside—to your family, your friends, your church, your work, your neighborhood, your city. . . .

Now hear a sentence from *Disciplines of the Beautiful Woman* in a deeper context: "And from that well-tended, precious center of you the circle will enlarge . . . and enlarge . . . and enlarge"![4]

My reader friend, were the proddings I felt about this book right? Was it time for me to write it? Was it the time in your life for you to read it?

---

[3] Amy Carmichael, "We Conquer by His Song," in *Toward Jerusalem* (Fort Washington, PA: Christian Literature Crusade, 1936, 1977), 107. Copyright material used by permission of Christian Literature Crusade, Fort Washington, PA 19034.

[4] Ortlund, *Disciplines of the Beautiful Woman*, 101.

I want you to know that I, too, am subject to its message. I was fussing to Ray that I didn't have enough time to get it finished by the deadline—and then my own book got to me.

I said to him, "Ortie, guess what; good news! You won't hear me fuss any more about that manuscript, because God's very words from my pen have rebuked me, and from now on I have peace in my heart that He'll give me whatever time I need to do it right."

My living, too, is between my ears.

So let's you and me, reader and writer, bow together before Him. He has worked on us both—in the reading, in the writing.

Lord, the two of us kneel at Your feet.

We live in a grey world—neither hot nor cold. We repudiate that. We vigorously turn from it. We spit it out of our mouths, as You do. We hate what You hate.

Lord, we are worse than we had realized.

Lord, You are more wonderful than we'd realized!

Lord, Your love for us, Your pardon of us, Your righteousness available to us are all greater than we knew.

> *Love so amazing, so divine*
> *Demands my soul, my life, my all.*

Now Work Into Your Life What You've Been Reading

1. Write down what steps you're taking, in courage and obedience, to help you establish an inner life of rest and trust in God—steps to establish disciplines for your heart.

2. Share these steps with one meaningful person in your life—or share them in your group—so you can be held accountable and have prayer support.

3. Write and tell me about them. I'd love to hear. I'm praying.

Love,
Anne Ortlund
c/o Renewal Ministries
4500 Campus Dr., Suite 662
Newport Beach, CA 92660

Disciplines
of the
Home

To

My beloved Ray;

Sherry and Walt,
　　　Mindy,
　　　Beth Anne,
　　　Drew;
Margie and John,
　　　Lisa,
　　　Laurie,
　　　John IV,
Ray, Jr., and Jani,
　　　Eric,
　　　Krista,
　　　Dane,
　　　Gavin;
Nels

CONTENTS

> Today's society is an impending
> avalanche sliding toward hell.
> Is your family caught in the slide?
> How can you gather up your
> loved ones and make a drastic
> leap to solid ground?

INTRODUCTION

WE USED TO HAVE Sunday dinner sometimes at Rosemary and Alfred's. The table was always beautifully set; the food was always delicious; and best of all, we were so warmly welcomed! We were always truly wanted.

And so were a ninety-five-year-old man who drooled a lot, and a blind lady, and a very fat lady, and others. People at Alfred and Rosemary's table weren't invited because they were classy but because they were genuinely loved.

God's circle is like that. It's a tender, warm, nourishing place for all kinds of people—some of us not too bright, some smart but without much courage when the chips are down, some good-looking but pretty stupid—everybody a little funny, one way or another.

But whatever, one thing is certain: the Lord really loves and wants us. He enjoys helping us improve and making us happy. He desires us around His table. We don't have to stand off in a corner, we don't have to eat in the kitchen—we belong. We have a place. We're welcome.

Is your home anything like that?

Probably you've got some kind of combination of bodies under your roof: you're a married couple with no kids, a married couple with kids, a single mom or dad with kids; maybe some parents are with you or foster kids or grandchildren—you know your own setup. Ogden Nash says a family unit is composed not only of children but of men, women, an occasional animal, and the common cold.

The big questions aren't, How sharp are all of you? and, How much money are you making?

The big questions—no matter how odd your assortment or what their histories or deformities or problems—the big questions are . . .

How do you get along?

How do you help each other and lift each other?

Is your home a place where your young ones can get prepared for tomorrow's world?

Your old ones get comforted?

Your unwise ones get tender guidance?

Your producers get recharged?

Your hurt ones get healed?

Or if God has included under your roof any of His lambs who are truly inadequate for this world—is home still where they're loved, where they know they belong?

In other words, is your home a restoring, nourishing, comforting, inspiring place?

God's is, and He wants yours to be.

I'm excited, writing this book. The need is so great, and God has such powerful solutions!

Maybe you've already read *Disciplines of the Beautiful Woman,* for help in living your external life for God: using a notebook, keeping a desk, organizing your wardrobe.

Then you may have read *Disciplines of the Heart* for help with your interior—your heart life, thought life, between-the-ears life.

(Some people said to me recently, "Anne, in the first book you threw rubber-tipped darts at us. In the second one you used knives!" Oh, dear.)

But "no man or woman is an island," as they say. And when my friends at Word Publishing asked that I make the "disciplines" book a trilogy, with this third one on the home, I was glad to say yes.

This book, too, has study suggestions. Maybe you'll want to gather a group and study all three books in a series—hopefully for a triple whammy.

May God greatly lift your sights and give you new visions of what your very own home can become for Him—"a restoring, nourishing, comforting, inspiring place."

PORTRAIT: JOE AND
BETTY SWEET

JOE AND BETTY met in 1914 under a tree. Rural, Irish Catholic Joe, strongly built but not handsome, immediately fell in love with gorgeous, dark, willowy, Presbyterian Mary Elizabeth Weible—a city girl, delicately raised. The tree was on the campus of Kansas State Agricultural College, where Joe had struggled to pay for every minute of his so far two years of studies, and Mary was a new freshman fully supported by her family.

Joe was to be my father, and Mary, my mother. But at that point they couldn't have been more different—too different to be suitable to marry each other.

Joe's birthplace had been a nice two-story family home in Denver, which his gambling father lost soon after little Joe was born. Moving to a small farm to begin again, Joe's father and mother both slowly sickened with tuberculosis and eventually left their four young sons and two tiny daughters orphans to fend for themselves.

Was Joe the "Cinderella"? The other boys had their father's dashing good looks; the little girls were beautiful; Joe was homely. In any case, it was eleven-year-old Joe, third of the four boys, who dropped out of school to farm and care for the two little sisters and help put his brothers through college.

Ten schoolless years later, when the boys had their diplomas and the girls were situated in homes as domestic help, Joe himself started back to school, crammed junior high and high school subjects to pass an entrance exam, and put himself through college as well.

The third fall on campus, when Joe saw incoming freshman Mary Weible under that tree—for him, everything was new. He proved to her his worth through outrageous effort: he worked both day- and night-jobs, he got straight A's, and he became colonel of the college

R.O.T.C. And from the beginning, he romanced her and won her and tenderly nicknamed her Betty.

Six years later, when Joe had his new commission in the U.S. Army, he and Betty were married. Almost immediately World War I called him from his nearly completed Ph.D. program and put him on active duty. That changed their life direction, and thereafter Mother was his "lady"—through thirty-plus years in the Army and twenty-plus more years as editor-in-chief of a military publishing company.

Strong, proud, erect, everything-is-under-control Joe, who to many was Brigadier General Joseph Burton Sweet, was just "Daddy" to four of us: my older brother Bobby, me, and our two little sisters Mary Alice and Margie. We children heard him tell plenty of fun stories about his childhood—Daddy was a great storyteller. But the real truth of his bitter struggles and deprivations and childhood sufferings we had to piece together from others, even after his death.

Daddy and Mother were similar in that both were earnest, hard-driving workers; and when in their mid-thirties they accepted the Lord into their lives, that's the kind of Christians they became—true leaders who for nearly half a century taught Bible classes and tirelessly counseled and shepherded others.

But there was an unspoken sadness in their differences. Daddy was an idealist, a romantic, an irrepressible lover. He said "I love you" to Mother and Bobby and his three girls a thousand, thousand times. On the other hand, inherently shy, good, practical Mother would brush all that "silliness" away—and so her children figured "Oh, that's just Daddy," and did the same. He made us all feel very secure in our worth, but it never occurred to us to give security back to him; Daddy was Daddy. It wasn't until after his death, when we were full-blown adults, that we realized Daddy, too, was inherently shy, and he, too, had had needs. . . .

Perhaps that difference between them accounted for a lot of their frustrations and the way they often tended, in the little daily moments, to misunderstand and irritate each other.

How, then, did Joe and Betty Sweet initiate a family tree with thirty-nine descendants so far, who are all (except the littlest ones) happy, settled, productive Christians?

*   *   *

They were faithful to three crucial disciplines of the home:

1. *They built strong habit patterns that affirmed their love for each other.* They always stood up for each other with unquestioned loyalty. Their friends were all mutual friends. Their times of recreation were spent together. And after they met the Lord their life direction together became even more focused—teaching His Word and caring for those around them.

2. *Together they built strong habit patterns that affirmed their love for their children.* Daddy continually hugged, praised, and encouraged us; Mother exhorted and spanked; we needed both. Both parents spent time with each of the four of us. Daddy helped when we needed assistance with homework and gave us extra quarters for good grades. Mother helped with scouting and piano lessons and other extracurricular activities.

3. *And together they built strong habit patterns that affirmed their love for God.* Churchgoing was as regular as breathing. Every day ended with family Bible reading and prayers. Each parent and each child knelt individually at their own bedsides for final nightly prayers. Nothing—not travel or vacations or house guests—ever altered these routines.

And daily, year after year, until their deaths, Daddy prayed out loud with Mother for every child and every grandchild by name.

THE THREAT

"The only way to get this world back on track is to go back to the basics: how we raise our kids. . . ."
— Lee Iacocca

WE'VE LOST THE WORLD of Joe and Betty Sweet, and we can't ever get it back. "Everyone is really scared," writes Elizabeth Schorr.

She's talking about the present world's response to the thousands of kids today who are out of control—kids who've produced a labyrinthine system of cops, courts, camps, schools, foster homes, and treatment programs.

Why? These young people have learned to disdain right conduct—conduct basic to our functioning as a civilized world. Business leaders are beginning to guess that unless something changes, they could soon be faced with a "major shortage of educated, trustworthy workers."[1]

"The upheaval is evident everywhere in our culture. Babies have babies, kids refuse to grow up and leave home, affluent Yuppies prize their BMWs more than children, rich and poor children alike blot their minds with drugs."[2]

My own state of California has now hit all-time highs and (per capita) leads the nation in numbers of youngsters in foster care and juvenile detention.

And throughout the United States, at the beginning of the 1990s, of the nearly 63 million youngsters under eighteen, these facts are true:

- Almost a million are in foster, group, or institutional care.

- Over a million run away from home each year.

[1] "Kids Out of Control," *Los Angeles Times*, 18 May 1989, V5.
[2] Jerrold K. Footlick, "What Happened to the Family?" *Newsweek* special issue, winter/spring 1990, 16.

- 14 million are poor.

- Almost 10 million have no regular source of medical care.

- 20 million have never seen a dentist.

- Over two million are reported each year as suspected victims of abuse or neglect.

- Over a million are not in school.

- Each year over half a million of the girls become mothers.

- An estimated three million have a serious drinking problem.

- And the suicide rate climbs and climbs.[3]

Furthermore, say criminologists Professor and Mrs. Sheldon Glueck, "A delinquent child often grows up to produce delinquent children—not as a matter of heredity, but of his own unresolved conflicts which make him an ineffective parent." These criminologists also say they foresee no letup in this trend.[4]

"The nation's children are in trouble, and we've got to join hands and help them," says Mrs. Roseann Bentley, President of the National Association of State Boards of Education. Her organization has linked up with the American Medical Association and others for one purpose—to search for ways to prevent teen drug and alcohol abuse, smoking, AIDS, and pregnancy.

She says 77 percent of U.S. teen deaths are the result of drinking and drugs. "Education alone will not change behavior. We have to involve the community."[5]

To which I say, "The community is not enough. We have to involve specifically the home—and most specifically, the Christian home."

One social worker explains the way she sees it:

The world's complicated. Pressures on parents are increasing . . . not only for single parents who struggle to put meals on the table, but also for the Yuppie moms and dads hard pressed to make their BMW payments. . . .

[3] *USA Today,* 4 Oct. 1989, 11A.
[4] From an interview in *U.S. News & World Report* (April 1965), and cited in *Dare to Discipline* by James Dobson (Wheaton, IL: Tyndale House—Regal Books, 1970), 92.
[5] *USA Today,* 20 Sept. 1989, 1A.

Parenting takes more energy than most tasks, but when parents come home drained from a day of coping with modern life, there's not much energy left for child rearing.[6]

Already, even among the offspring who seem to "succeed," we're producing a big crop of Type A's—people who are restless, anxious, time-urgent, angry, hyperaggressive, ego-driven, and basically insecure. Why are they like this? Because, say the researchers, in their formative years important people in their lives didn't care—or were perceived as not caring.

Neighborhoods, churches, schools, and families are all generally weaker than earlier in our history; values of right and wrong often aren't being taught. The result? Many children often don't "succeed" at all. And when ever-growing numbers of kids mess up, there's almost never enough system or money or personnel to salvage them.

Peter Forsythe, head of a New York foundation dealing with juvenile delinquency, says kids don't go bad the day they hit junior high:

Parenting is a learned skill. Control starts early. If you lose it early, there's no reasserting it.

Research shows society has more luck helping bad families become functional than it does helping rotten kids become good ones. The knee-jerk reaction when a kid gets out of control is to break up the home. Got a bad kid? Send him somewhere. But that usually makes the kid worse. At a minimum, you destroy the laboratory in which the child and parents can learn to solve the problem.[7]

"The laboratory!"

Precious laboratory it is. Have you any idea how much God loves families, His own invention? How much He loves *your* family? How much He loves your kids, who are His, and how concerned He is for them?

In the very beginning of human history God established the family. In fact, three times when He's wanted to begin something special, He's started with a new family:

1. Adam and Eve and their children;

2. After the flood, Noah and his wife and children;

[6] Ibid., 2A.
[7] Ibid., 3A.

3. After the Tower of Babel, Abraham and Sarah and their offspring.

This third family grew to become the world's most stable social system—a system with father, family, clan, tribe, and nation.

Up the ladder, everyone was *accountable to.*

Down the ladder, everyone was *responsible for.*

Eventually, sin began to split the structure apart, from the top down.
Around 600 B.C. the Hebrew nation was broken up and scattered, and
with it, its tribes.

Clans went on for centuries, both Jewish and Gentile—extended
families living near each other. Eventually, with increased mobility,
these too were broken up and scattered.

Just since World War II, an escalation in the divorce rate has been
breaking up and scattering the next rung down the ladder, the family.

And the status of the father is seriously eroding.

*Today's world society is an impending avalanche sliding toward
hell. Is your family caught in the slide? Or will you gather your
loved ones and make a drastic leap to solid ground?*

I said *drastic.*

Let me give you two "Drastic Don'ts" and ten "Drastic Do's"—to
save you and yours out of the roaring, hell-bent avalanche that is upon
us all.

After you've read them . . .

MAKE THE RIGHT DECISIONS BECAUSE THEN YOUR
DECISIONS WILL MAKE YOU.

A drastic leap is a scary thing.

To jump all the way clear of a cascading avalanche—with the fear you'd feel, and the sheer effort of it—would be a leap you'd never forget.

If any part of your family is very close to this world's avalanche, reshaping your family at this point might well be a scary, drastic leap.

But, come to think of it, not jumping would be scarier. . . .

So let me spell out, under God's direction, what your "leap" might involve—how your family life could be reshaped to get it to the solid ground of godliness, settledness, and security.

First . . .

TWO DRASTIC DON'TS

THE FIRST DRASTIC
DON'T: DON'T RETREAT

Don't try to go back to yesterday;
go back to the Bible

"May you have warmth in your igloo, oil in your lamp, and peace in your heart."
—Eskimo benediction

Portrait: Walt and Sherry

Sherry, our firstborn, and her husband Walt Harrah (it rhymes with "Sarah") aren't your typical baby boomers—they lead the pack. They're not even today's pacesetters—they're *tomorrow's* pacesetters.

Walt's hair is shingled close up the sides and back, and the top he mousses and then scrunches into curls with his fingers. (He's also the comedian of our clan.) Sherry wears earrings that either cover most of her ears or dangle to her shoulders. Of course they drive a van. Their home's decor, where they entertain constantly, is art-deco-mod in black, white, mauve, and lavender. They've decorated it themselves, and it looks great.

Mindy, seventeen, tints her hair a different red and likes to sing Christian rock—really well. Beth Anne, eleven, is a teenie bopper with braces, ponytail, and flouncy skirts. Andrew, five, is into Little League T-ball.

These people give up saying "cool" or "rad" almost before it starts.

And what's their passion? Jesus Christ. Walt sings and writes and produces Christian music. He leads worship at their church. He and Sherry, side by side, co-teach a large Sunday school class of young marrieds. Sherry teaches other Bible classes as well and speaks at women's retreats. Together they pour their lives and God's Word into all the others they can touch. Grandparents Joe and Betty Sweet would be proud—although, superficially, not just a little shocked.

Their uninhibited enthusiasm for following God has cost them. Even in Walt's seminary-student years, he painted houses and sang and put himself through school without Sherry's having to leave caring for home and baby Mindy. After graduation, in the years of struggle to get established freelancing in Christian music, Walt continued never to pressure Sherry to work outside the home. The cost has been great—especially in pricey Orange County—but the financial loss can't be compared to their deep satisfactions, their secure kids, and the influence of their lives on others.

What does the Bible have to say about the Harrah family's lifestyle? It certainly doesn't say women can't work. Lydia was a dealer in expensive purple fabric (Acts 16:14). Aquila and Priscilla were a married couple in business together (Acts 18:3). Dorcas was a dressmaker—although maybe not for salary (Acts 9:36, 39). The woman of Proverbs 31 bought and sold property and clothing and who knows what else (verses 13–27).

But the Bible has everything to say about seeking first God's kingdom. It has strong words about not letting concern for food and clothes get in the way of following His principles (Matt. 6:25–33).

Walt and Sherry are enthusiasts for God and for His Word. Whatever it costs doesn't matter. Their eyes are on Him, on His plans for their lives, and on the jolly good fun of carrying out those plans—hairdo's, outrageous earrings, T-ball, laughter, mauve and lavender, and all.

Henry Ford once said,

> *You can do anything if you have enthusiasm. Enthusiasm is the yeast that makes your hopes rise to the stars. Enthusiasm is the sparkle in your eyes, the swing in your gait, the grip of your hand, the irresistible surge of will and energy to execute your ideas.*
>
> *Enthusiasts are fighters. They have fortitude. They have staying qualities. Enthusiasm is at the bottom of all progress. With it, there is accomplishment. Without it, there are only alibis.*

Enthusiasts *are fighters*. They don't let their family life just go with the flow and surrender to the avalanche.

Enthusiasts *have fortitude*. They're willing to be separate from all that is cheap, vulgar, desensitizing, degrading.

Enthusiasts *have staying power*. They maintain godly habits which, over the long haul, build them into winners.

As we say, there's no return to Joe and Betty Sweet's pre-avalanche day. The way is permanently barricaded. The old line "When *I* was your age . . ." has always been obnoxious and it still is. Parent, you are out of an earlier world, and God wants you to prepare your children for still a different world to come, where you and I can't follow. But in the meantime, God's name is "I AM"! He is always "now," always relevant, always contemporary.

Enthusiasts for God and His Word are contemporary, too—though not necessarily like the Harrahs in style. But they don't occupy themselves with trying to maintain the trappings of "the good old days"—they're occupied with truth. And truth, when it is loved and sought after, has a way of transforming life from timidity and over-conservatism to reckless, radiant, radical obedience.

So here's the first Drastic Don't: *Don't try to shape your family to some former day. Don't go back to yesterday; go back to the Bible instead.* Go back to its strong, clear, makes-sense, ever-relevant teachings. Whatever is happening around you, go back to what God Himself tells you to do in His Word.

If you don't obey Him, your family can't win. If you obey Him, you can't lose.

As God helps me, I want to spell out eleven more *disciplines of the home* for the 1990s and beyond—this unprecedented era into which we've now come.

If you decide these disciplines are unbiblical, trash the book (Acts 17:11). But if you see that they square with the Word of God, then note how your family matches up with His truths.

And be prepared to make some important, thrilling changes. Get ready, under His direction and by His Spirit, before it's too late, to reshape the structure and focus and spirit of your family life.

THE SECOND DRASTIC
DON'T: DON'T DIVORCE

"FOR THIS REASON," said God when He made Adam and Eve, "a man will leave his father and mother and be united to his wife, and they will become one flesh" (Gen. 2:24).

The two marriage partners are one whether they produce many children or none at all. Children must always be on the periphery—loved, but periphery. The man and woman are the center. When the children leave they drop off the outside, and the center remains the same.

That's the precious focal point to be guarded and protected! That's the priceless centerpiece, which is the stability of society present and future.

Portrait: A Childless Marriage

Did Aquila and Priscilla ever have children? Not that we know of.

When the Apostle Paul first met them they were a couple in trauma. They were displaced persons, newly arrived in Greece after having been kicked out of Rome for being Jewish. In Corinth they set up business together as tent-makers. "Paul went to see them, and because he was a tentmaker as they were, he stayed and worked with them" (Acts 18:3).

For at least a year and a half Aquila and Priscilla listened to Paul's teaching, and it so grabbed their hearts that when he moved, they moved with him. From here on they're business partners second, and bright, enthusiastic Christians first. And best friends with Paul.

What a model for a childless couple! They're never separated from each other. They give themselves tirelessly, even risking their lives (Rom. 16:4). They open up their home—to teach the great Apollos

Some insights on Aquila and Priscilla were gleaned from a sermon I heard by Dr. Samuel Kamelesian at Ilo Ilo, Philippines, March 6, 1984.

(Acts 18:26) and to house a local church (1 Cor. 16:19). In four out of six references Priscilla is named first—here we have "Mrs. and Mr."! Priscilla was obviously enormously gifted. How can a man live in the shadow of someone like that?

I see three things about this couple that answer that question.

1. They were individually liberated by faith in Christ. Priscilla had dignity given her by Him. And Aquila also was a child of God, and because of this they liberated each other. They weren't threatened. They didn't bind each other. If theirs hadn't been a secure marriage, do you think Aquila would ever have allowed famous, charismatic Apollos to come live in their house with them? No way.

2. Together, love and discipline made them a liberated unit. Their life was one. Whatever they went through, they went through together. They rolled with the punches. Not "tit for tat" or "if you get me, I'll get you." They supported and complemented each other.

3. Together, they were free to liberate other people. Ministry was their joy. There was no sense of their criticizing Apollos; it seemed to be, "Brother, we have an extra room; would you like to stay with us?"

   This was risky: Apollos would see them up close. Well, that's exactly what they had in mind! There are so many young Christians who would love to watch this kind of model couple up close. Discipling means proximity and exposure.

That's the reason why I'm including lots of stories of couples, parents, and families in this book as models. Good relationships and enthusiasm for God spawn more good relationships and enthusiasm for God.

Portrait: The Golden Years of Marriage

Abram and Sarai were married before their story ever begins in Genesis 11. You just can't imagine them apart. Sarai couldn't get pregnant, either—for much of their married life—and, like Priscilla, she simply gave herself to being a loyal, faithful wife. First Peter 3 calls her a "holy woman" who was "beautiful" because she "obeyed Abraham and called him her master" (v. 6).

But Abram did some horrible things; why should she obey him? When he took her to live in Egypt he got nervous over her gorgeous good looks, for fear the Pharaoh of the land would kill him to take her for himself. So he said, "Tell everybody you're my sister." (Even good men, in times of panic, can temporarily turn into wimps.)

Sarai "obeyed Abraham." She held her head up. She did what was asked of her. And she kept in her heart her loyalty to her husband—even, indeed, in Pharaoh's palace, until the trauma was over and she was returned. *With*, add the Scriptures, "sheep and cattle, male and female donkeys, menservants, maidservants and camels"—all donated by an embarrassed Pharaoh. Not bad Egyptian souvenirs when you've been abroad on a trip!

Years pass. Their green years turn golden. Abram grows in stature, wealth, godliness. A good woman makes a good man better. She's got to be proud and happy: he loves her, he lives with her.

Then together they're rewarded with changed names. The Lord God Almighty appears and says to Abram, "No longer will you be called Abram [Exalted Father]; your name will be Abraham [Father of Multitudes]!" (Gen. 17:5).

What's the difference? Just one sound: the letter "H"—the sound of breath. God breathes into Abram's name: "Your name will be Abrah-h-h-ham."

A marvel! God had long ago breathed into Adam, and he became a living person (Gen. 2:7). Years later Jesus would breathe His Holy Spirit into His disciples (John 20:22). (Both the Hebrew and Greek words for "breath" and "spirit" are the same.)

God breathes into Sarai's name as well. He says to Abraham, "You are no longer to call her Sarai; her name will be Sarah-h-h-h."

An exquisite reward, a spiritual high point, a new beginning in their together-life. Everything should be coming up roses from here on, right? Wrong.

They move to Gerar, Sarah is still beautiful, Abraham eyes the king, and he says, "Say you're my sister."

Abraham!! You did that one years ago! Are you really basically just a wimp, and your good actions have just been flukes? To save his own skin he puts his precious Sarah out to be vulnerable a second time—all these years later when he's supposed to be "mature." And, sure enough, she's still so beautiful, she ends up in the palace of another king.

This sort of thing brings many golden-years marriages to divorce. They've had wonderful days together and stacked up countless memories. . . . Then at midlife, that fascinating-or-fearful time which is moving inevitably toward old age, the husband may panic. He sees quietly shutting doors. He feels the terror of all those possibilities slowly closing away from view.

One way or another he becomes a fool, and off goes his wife to a lawyer.

Not Sarah! She sees the crisis come, pass, and fade, and she remains loyal. That's what makes her a winner, a "holy woman." At one point God says to Abraham, "Listen to whatever Sarah tells you" (Gen. 21:12). Beautiful.

And Sarah watches God keep fulfilling the blessings of their married love and the blessings of their shared devotion to Him. And then—He gives them a miracle baby son.

Portrait: The Green Years of Marriage

Isaac was the son: the sheltered, protected, rich man's only son—and at forty he was still a bachelor. Well, why wouldn't those very old parents dote on him and cherish him? They probably had trouble even *thinking* about sharing him with a daughter-in-law.

Probably Sarah was actually the hold-out. When she finally breathed her last, then Abraham arranged for his son to get a proper wife.

This wife was Isaac's distant cousin Rebekah, whose father Bethuel seems to have been a wimp. (Notice in Genesis 24 who the family spokesman was, who made the decisions, and who got all the gifts and attention. Never Bethuel!) And because Bethuel had trouble being assertive and decisive, Rebekah's mother and brother Laban had learned, if necessary through politicking and deception, to overlook him and run the family affairs.

Isaac, somewhat of a wimp himself, is paired with Rebekah, who has grown up learning how you get around wimps. Was it God's will? Absolutely! God was looking down time's vast corridors at the race He was building and the Savior He was preparing:

> *"From the rocky peaks I see them,*
> *from the heights I view them. . . .*
> *Who can count the dust of Jacob*
> *or number the fourth part of Israel? . . ." (Num. 23:9, 10).*
> *"Like valleys they spread out,*
> *like gardens beside a river,*
> *like aloes planted by the Lord . . ." (Num. 24:6).*

"I see him, but not now;
I behold him, but not near.
A star will come out of Jacob;
A scepter will rise out of Israel" (Num. 24:17).

But in the short view of things, here are Isaac and Rebekah, two love birds thrown together in marriage. Will they "live happily ever after"? Not on your life.

Rebekah can't get pregnant (shades of Sarah). Probably they bicker and blame each other. Finally she does, and she hates the pregnancy— I'm feeling this baby kick so much, I must be black and blue inside. Isaac, don't just stand there, do something.

It's twin boys, no wonder. Oi vey. Isaac likes Esau, Rebekah likes Jacob. They polarize. Papa champions the firstborn; Rebekah shows him, she teaches her underdog twin to con away the birthright.

Is it possible that two people can truly fall in love, and then totally fall out of love again? Of course. Rebekah freefalls down so far out of love that at one point she says, "I'm disgusted with living" (Gen. 27:46).

The green years. For one couple they withered: for Isaac and Rebekah. Isaac could have put her away, as divorced. He never did. They lived together; they produced the son whose name became Israel, patriarch of the nation; and when they died they were buried together; you can see their tomb in Hebron to this day. And they are a mighty link in the miracle-continuum of God's eternal promises to Abraham and to his seed.

Looking back, they've got to be glad they stuck it out.

*   *   *   *   *

Marriage has to be an unconditional commitment to an imperfect person.

That sounds really heavy, doesn't it! What if . . . ? What if this person to whom you've promised your commitment turns out to be more imperfect than you bargained for? Let me quote from Ray's and my book *You Don't Have to Quit:*

As God looks down on the total human scene, He sees each indi-
vidual, of course. . . . But He sees more. He also sees the whole
human picture; He sees the connections, the mergings together,
the patterns and the oneness of the generations that . . . we can
barely envision. Without the limits of time . . . God sees how

you belong to your great-grandfather and how you affect your great-grandson and how, in every particular detail, you are part of the continuum of the human generations. . . .

God gives hints [in His Word] of a commingling together of the behavior of generations which is unthinkable to us little people with limited perception. . . . You and we are holding hands with a great host of unseen persons in unbroken chains.

What happens when you freak out and say, "Oh, heck, I quit"? When you kick over the traces?

When you flee, when you say "I've had it," when you give up?

What damage is that doing to the others—the whole chain of your ancestors and your descendants? What kind of permanent wound or scar are you making? What instability are you building into the line? How many will grieve? How many will be hurt? . . .

Ask God for staying power, for determination, for patience, for gutsy courage to survive and survive well. . . . Your fortitude could have larger ramifications than you now know.[1]

What is God's great reason for wanting marriages to stay together?

Has not the Lord made [marriage partners] one? In flesh and spirit they are his. And why one? Because he was seeking godly offspring. (Mal. 2:15)

It's the kids He's concerned about. They affect all His future people. And He yearns for each new generation to succeed—to be brought back into His love forever.

At last we have statistics to discover what God has known through the millennia: *divorce ruins too many kids.* No wonder, then, He says He hates divorce (Mal. 2:16).

Divorce is hell. Divorced people everywhere are lamenting their plight—on call-in radio, on "Oprah" and "Donahue." Magazines are rife with stories of latchkey kids, custody kidnappings, delinquent dads, single moms, and offspring in shelters for the homeless.[2]

---

[1] You may also want to read all of chapter 17 in *You Don't Have to Quit,* formerly published under the title *Staying Power* (Nashville: Thomas Nelson, 1986, 1988), 102–104.

[2] Diane Medved, *The Case against Divorce* (New York: Donald I. Fine, 1989).

It's only recently that we've begun to realize the damages. We've thought, "Kids are resilient; they're more mature than we give them credit for," or "It's tough for now, but eventually they'll be fine," or "Better they have one parent with peace than two with constant arguments."

A while back a daily radio talk show psychologist spent one week interviewing adults thirty and older whose parents had divorced years before, when they were children.

He found not one happily married. Either they had never married at all or they'd had a series of failed marriages—and the same reason came through over and over: they didn't have the courage to develop a close, trusting relationship with anyone for fear of being abandoned again.

This is not to say if you're the offspring of a divorce, or if you're raising the offsprings of divorce, that God can't give you the miracle of healed deficiencies; "Nothing is impossible with God" (Luke 1:37). This is to say, for the sake of those precious kids of yours or your spouse's, don't divorce any more in the future—presuming on God for another miracle; don't tempt Him!

First Corinthians 7:12–14 says that the salvaging of a marriage, even an "unyoked" marriage, is what makes the children turn out not bad but good.

Writes Elizabeth Achtemeier in her book *The Committed Marriage,*

> *I grew up in a home which, for a period, was marked by violent differences, arguments, and the threat of divorce. Through all the turbulence and heartache, my Christian mother refused to agree to the separation because she thought it was wrong for a Christian to do so.*
>
> *Some outside the family thought she was foolish, but personally I am deeply grateful to her. Contrary to the belief of some psychologists, she prevented psychic damage to her children far beyond what measure of it we suffered in a troubled home.*
>
> *She lived to enjoy a mellowed and loving relationship with Dad in their later years. He himself came to a simple but deep Christian faith, and the last words I heard Mother say to him before her death were, "You really love me, don't you?"*[3]

[3] Elizabeth Achtemeir, *The Committed Marriage* (Philadelphia: Westminster Press, 1976), 127.

If Elizabeth's mother hadn't stuck out that marriage, I wonder how Elizabeth would have turned out. I wonder if the world would ever have been blessed and helped by her wonderful book.

> All the flowers of all the tomorrows are in the seeds of today.

But what if you've already done it—you're divorced from previous marriages? Have you sufficiently grieved, mourned, repented?

Let me tell you what I mean with an illustration from the days of Nehemiah.

Backslidden Jews wept when they listened to the reading of God's Word. So Nehemiah said, in effect, "Buck up! This is your new-beginning time! Let the joy of the Lord be your strength." So the people dried their tears, and because it was that time of year, they celebrated the happy, week-long Feast of Tabernacles.

But for them it was like dabbling in superficial ocean waves of fun when underneath, an undertow of unfinished mourning was dragging their spirits the other way. So as soon as they were left to themselves, they all gathered for a public confession, weeping, fasting, and writing down a list of new resolutions to which they all signed their names (Neh. 8–10). Only then was the old chapter truly closed, and they could follow with a genuine, powerful celebration (Neh. 12).

Said someone:

When my dog died I was inconsolable. Finally I realized I hadn't grieved adequately when my father died when I was nine. And I'd lived all those years with a low-grade depression.

Have you sufficiently grieved and repented over previous marriage failures? Maybe you and your present partner should do it together. Schedule a time. Talk it out. Read the Bible together, perhaps Colossians 3:1–19. Pray together, out loud.

Then perhaps you need to say to each other and before God, with all your children as witnesses, "We promise never to divorce again." And celebrate it with punch and cookies!

Of course you'll still have bad times ahead. But understand that you're now committed to one another "for better or for worse, in sickness and in health, for as long as you both shall live."

*   *   *

Commitment means a willingness to sometimes be unhappy.

Remember what the angel of the Lord told Hagar when she ran away from home? "Return . . . and submit" (Gen. 16:9). Or think about the Apostle John. Did he feel stuck when he was exiled to the island of Patmos for life? Certainly he did. But *on that island*, not elsewhere, God met him and gave him the Book of Revelation!

> "The best way out is *through*."
> —Robert Frost

Now Work Into Your Life What You've Been Reading

Make a list of the sentences in this chapter that grabbed you, and write down why. Or in a group, take some silent time to write them down, and then read them and explain why.

For instance,

"The man and woman are the center of the family." If you're a single parent, or raising children not your own, think how God's Word gives exceptions to that situation to show that God can make up for atypical families.

Or *"divorce ruins too many kids"*—when your own children have divorced parents in their backgrounds. Think of God's powerful "exceptions to the rule":

1. Moses, taken from both parents: Exod. 1:22–2:10.

2. Samuel, taken from both parents: 1 Sam. 1:20–28; 2:11.

3. Esther, an orphan raised by a cousin: Est. 2:7.

4. Timothy, with an unbelieving father: Acts 16:1–3; 2 Tim. 1:5.

Can you think of others?

Or maybe this sentence grabbed you:

"Marriage has to be an unconditional commitment to an imperfect person."

Or,

"Commitment means a willingness to sometimes be unhappy."

Write down, or talk through with your group, how you can work the sentences that grabbed you into your own life. Then pray them in.

You're eyeing the avalanche, and you're eyeing the rock, the solid ground. Can you make it?

No, in your own strength you really can't.

But the Spirit of Almighty God can—within you. Then ask Him to help you, and to work strongly in each member of your family, as you consider . . .

TEN DRASTIC DO'S

If you'll make the leap, God is willing to start you in a new place.

THE FIRST DRASTIC DO:
SLOW DOWN

DO YOU WANT an elegant family life? Do you want an elegant marriage?

"Simplicity, carried to an extreme, becomes elegance."[1]
> —Jon Franklin

It will call for drastic action to achieve that simplicity. Too many of us find ourselves wishing our microwaves would hurry up. Or we get impatient mixing our instant coffee! Thomas Carlyle (1795–1881) said simply, "There is nothing more terrible than activity without insight." But reversing a frantic lifestyle will call for a drastic slowdown.

Read the typical advice given these days to rectify the situation. The headline will say something like, "THREE JOBS, TWO KIDS, ONE PROBLEM: NO TIME."

Then the first paragraph describes the situation: the stress of parents' coping with work all day, then coming home tired each evening and rushing around buying groceries, cooking dinner, trying to catch up on housework, etc., with no extra time or energy for the family.

Then this typical article gives "solutions." (Only every solution demands more time and energy—just what these two don't have!) Establish traditions. Once a week bake cookies together; another time play games. Play with the kids for five minutes each evening when you first get home: "Play and laughter will do wonders for your attitude."

Final paragraph: "Remember, life is for living, laughing, and loving, not for whining, worrying, and working."

* * *

[1] Reprinted with permission from the July 1988 *Reader's Digest*. From *Writing for Story* by Jon Franklin. Copyright © 1986 Jon Franklin. Reprinted with permission of Atheneum Publishers, an imprint of Macmillan Publishing Co.

Great! Let's goforit.

First night: We struggle through the door with the last traces of our strength and force a laugh: "Ha ha ha ho ho ho!"

The children don't even look up from the TV.

We try it closer and louder: "Let's play together. Ha ha ha ho ho ho!"

This doesn't work for well past the five minutes earmarked for play and laughter, but then at last they speak. Without moving their eyeballs they say, "When's dinner?"

We haven't cooked any; life is for living, laughing, and loving.

Finally we've gotten their full attention. "What-a-at?" We've made eye contact! Only the looks we're getting are something between hatred and war.

Still, we persist in the New Effort for a whole week—until there's not a clean piece of clothing in a single closet or drawer, we can't open the laundry-room door because of the dirty laundry packed behind it, and the used dishes have overflowed from kitchen to living room tables, sofas, and chairs, and we have to sit on the floor.

Then we go back to whining, worrying, and working.

*   *   *   *   *

The "successful" families today must be taking steroids. Here are excerpts from a Father's Day article I'm reading:

> Donald is absolutely more than anyone could expect. He is always available for the four kids, the laundry, the groceries, the house. [Donald also works sixty hours a week as an oil company executive.]

> Two adults, two careers, and two children can sometimes be too taxing. . . . I can bring home the bacon, and I can fry it in the pan.

> My wife works five days a week. I work four nights a week. I have complete responsibility for my two boys, ages 3½ and 20 months, from 7 A.M. to 5 P.M. . . .[2]

So when does father sleep?

Unless you're the Bionic Man, year after year of this could start to grind on you. "Trying to be 'Superdad' with 60-hour work weeks," says

[2] "The Involved Papa Is a Sign of Modern Times," USA Today, 16 June 1989.

the Bureau of National Affairs after intensive research, "creates stress and guilt."

An executive with a large labor union would confirm this. His wife is an attorney; they have two boys, ages three and two; and the dad spends about 70 percent of his time traveling. "Last week I was gone all week. I experience great guilt and pain as a result of my reduced parenting role. . . . I try to call my children once a day. When I'm away they associate me primarily with phones and airplanes."

Dr. Kyle D. Pruett says this:

Many [parents] are fragmented and frayed. The only way to avoid this is to think about it clearly: Am I willing to drop down a few rpms on the fast track to make a place in my heart for my children now when it matters?[3]

Portrait: A Quiet Family

Our son Ray, Jr., took his wife Jani and the kids to northern Scotland for four years, while Ray got his Ph.D. at the University of Aberdeen. They were four quiet years. Would it have been harder to live those years in America at the same pace? I'm sure of it.

(Ray, Sr., and I went with our Nels to live in Kabul, Afghanistan, for part of Nels' second-grade year, and the three of us played a lot more games and danced a lot more "Looby Loo." Maybe one family solution would be to trade jobs with somebody elsewhere for a while and get a true break.)

Anyway, those years Eric was ages five to nine, Krista was four to eight, Dane was three to seven, and Gavin was their "wee Scot" born in Aberdeen, who came home to the States when he was two.

Around the family table they memorized one verse from each book of the Bible. And they talked about what each book was about, and who the important people were in each one. Their dad put big sheets of paper on rings like a flip chart, to help remind them.

Over and over they played the Anything Game, which meant just acting out any person, place, thing, animal, idea—while the others guessed.

They took walks by the River Dee. They skipped stones. They saw salmon jump.

They walked together to church, they walked to shops, they walked! (They'd had to sell their car to make it.)

[3] "Dads Struggle to Juggle Kids and Jobs, Too," *USA Today*, 16 Jan. 1989.

They ate not two but three meals together every day. (The school let out all their little uniformed students to go home for lunch.)

They had snow fights. They walked in the rain.

When the electricity went off, which happened fairly often, they lit candles and told ghost stories. Otherwise in the evenings either Ray or Jani read to them out loud; they covered C. S. Lewis's *Chronicles of Narnia*, a child's version of *Pilgrim's Progress*, many things.

Sometimes Ray, Sr., and I would go visit them on our way to or from speaking overseas. What a delight to see Krista and her mother preparing a tea party for the dolls or doing each other's hair. To hear all the family sing Scottish songs together. To listen to Ray practice his bagpipe. To watch Jani and Krista dance the Highland Fling. To walk to a nearby stable where mother and daughter rode horses. . . .

When the children were in bed, the four of us adults would simply sit and talk, without turning on any lights, until we were talking almost in the dark. Then there was time to get beyond just what they or we were doing—to how we were feeling, thinking, dreaming.

*   *   *   *   *

"All I want when I come home from work after decisions and deadlines is a relatively quiet atmosphere," says a stressed-out thirty-six-year-old father of three. "Instead I get a harassed wife, fighting kids, and a rushed dinner because there's always a game or meeting to go to *right now*."

Dolores Curran writes,

> *If one member is under stress it affects the whole family. Familiar symptoms include a constant sense of urgency; underlying tension; a desire to escape—to one's room, workplace, away; a pervasive sense of guilt for not doing everything for all the people in one's life.*
>
> *I recall running into an acquaintance at the supermarket. Her eyes filled with tears as she confided how she had been berated by her child's scoutmaster for forgetting an important den meeting. On that day of the meeting, she had four after-school activities to which she chauffeured various children, had a sick child at home, and had unexpected house guests.*[4]

---

[4] Dolores Curran, *Stress and the Healthy Family* (New York: Harper and Row, 1985), 165.

Maybe the greatest gift you could give your children besides Jesus Christ would be the gift of time.

(This was seen in a church bulletin: "We thank Thee, Lord, for our instant coffee, ready-made cocoa, one-minute oatmeal, and pop-up waffles. In haste, Amen.")

Maybe if you all slowed down, a measure of this prayer by John Greenleaf Whittier would begin to come true:

> Drop Thy still dews of quietness
>   Till all our strivings cease;
> Take from our souls the strain and stress,
> And let our ordered lives confess
>   The beauty of Thy peace.

In your offsprings' memories, when their childhoods are over, it would be better than a new VCR or a new van in the garage.

Have you finally subscribed to the world's values? Is *doing* more important to you than *being*? Then you're pressured.

Is *what you're acquiring* more important to you than *what you're becoming*? Then you're pressured.

Are jobs more important to you than relationships? Then you're pressured.

Do you think busy-ness, speed, and efficiency rank near the top of the list of virtues? Then you're pressured.

And are you ambitious to expose your children to more than most kids get? You're probably pressuring them.

Do you have huge expectations for them to achieve in many areas at once? You're pressuring them.

Do you want them to do, to be marvelous extensions of yourself? You're pressuring them.

And, last, if you don't possess, deep in your soul, an assurance of God's acceptance of you and your family, and other people's acceptance of you and your family, then you're pressured and you're pressuring. Trying to justify yourselves, qualify yourselves, promote yourselves can take an awful lot of time.

But probably you won't change much—unless you get gripped by a realization of the destruction that your over-busy life is causing—to your family life, your spouse, your children, your friends, your relationship with God, your soul.

Says Steven Wright, "I think God's going to come down and pull civilization over for speeding."[5]

⁵ "Quotable Quotes," *Reader's Digest*, Sept. 1989, 34. Reprinted with permission from Steven Wright and *Reader's Digest*.

* * *

Family, listen: It's time to come to a screeching slowdown. It's time to make brave, radical cuts in everybody's schedules. If the children are old enough, have a family pow-wow to discuss what might happen.

1. Maybe father shouldn't work for a while.

Jack MacDonald, thirty-one, is an architectural designer who's taken a break. Angie, his wife, is a financial analyst. Recently they moved from a small town in Tennessee to a Richmond suburb so she could take a job that didn't require travel.

That's when they decided that two salaries weren't worth it, when they have Drew, four and a half, and Drinda, two. Jack does the home keeping, and he takes his children for walks in the park; they play in the creek; they hunt for tadpoles. When the time is right, Jack says some day he'll get a master's degree and go back to work.[6]

2. Maybe mother shouldn't work for a while.

> *Better a meal with vegetables where there is love than a fattened calf with hatred. (Prov. 15:17)*

Good Housekeeping magazine is launching a major campaign to promote the "New Traditionalist," saying she represents "the biggest social movement since the 1960s." They say their research is showing that many women may want a side job for earning a little extra, but there's a new desire these days to bypass the all-encompassing career and focus more on home, husband, and children—to "eliminate and concentrate"!

Is it a true trend? "You're going to see more 'cashing out' as men and women exchange high-paid jobs for lower-pressure, family-oriented life-styles," says Faith Popcorn of Brain-Reserve.[7]

Now there's a support group called "Mothers at Home" that has seen its membership mushroom from 648 members in 1984 to 8,000 in 1989 and a magazine called *Welcome Home*—"a publication in support of mothers who choose to stay at home."

3. Maybe the teenage children shouldn't work yet.

We laud their ambition; maybe our values are upside down. Should they be ambitious for more time, rather than for more money? Are their jobs draining their energies from their intellectual and spiritual preparations for life? "How much better to get wisdom than gold, to choose understanding rather than silver!" (Prov. 16:16).

---

[6] "Staying at Home Is a Full-Time Job," *USA Today*, 16 June 1989.
[7] "Return to Tradition?" *Los Angeles Times*, 26 Dec. 1988, IV.

4. Maybe everybody needs to cut down, for now, on classes, projects, involvements.

You probably can make do with less money, but you definitely need more time and exposure to each other.

These family years of yours are so precious, and they can never be reclaimed. Only *now* is when your children are being formed. There are no reruns, no instant replays. This is all you get.

A hardware store in Vashon, Washington, has a blackboard sign headed "Today's Special." For years, the chalked-on message has never been other than "So's tomorrow."

*   *   *   *   *

Slow Down for an Elegant Marriage

"Never yell at each other unless the house is on fire."

The home isn't only for the children, it's also for the grown-ups. If there are only two of you without children, or if there are still two of you with children (whether you're parents or step-parents)—you're both responsible to set the pace and the tone of your family life.

You need to be there for each other.

You need to check each other occasionally: "Are you in accord with me, as I am with you?" (2 Kings 10:15).

You need time together, small talk, consideration of one another.

You need, husband and wife, drastic new exposures to each other. With a true pioneering spirit that's excited, cautious, relentless, you need to push into each other's hearts where no one else has ever been before, and discover, all on your own, what has never before been fathomed in your partner by anyone but God: the dark places, the bright places, the agonies and the ecstasies. And the more you come upon, the more you gather it all up in your arms and say, "This is all mine, God's gift to me," and hold tightly this amazing, labyrinthine, dearest treasure who is your Other Self.

Are there things in your partner you don't like? Well, there are things in *yourself* you don't like. Your partner has to take those as part of the whole love-package, so you take your partner's as well.

Portrait: The Jensens

Roger and Mary Jensen, fifty-one and forty-five, have come success-fully into the middle years of marriage. Roger is six feet five and "190 pounds of smooth, coordinated muscle"—but then, I'm quoting him! He's had seventeen years of coaching high school varsity basketball and tennis, followed by seven more in public school administration. Mary is also tall, and exquisitely lovely. She used to teach P.E., too, but she's been a housewife since the children: six-foot-five Jeep, nineteen and on a college basketball scholarship; Jimmy, fourteen; and Jodi, thirteen.

This family looks like Successful America, but it has weathered two total traumas:

One, a terrible car accident which hurt them all but nearly took Jimmy's life. After his week in a coma and many months of slow recuperation, Jimmy was in "special ed" classes because of learning disabilities, but now he's back in regular classes again. He's got a supportive family, and Jimmy's a fighter.

Two (and Roger and Mary consider this one far more traumatic), their sixth and seventh years of marriage, when they became "deeply disenchanted" with each other. They wanted to divorce. They felt stuck.

Both of them took time. Instead of making a hasty decision which would have blown apart everything, separately they waited on the Lord. They cried to Him.

Says Mary, "We both went harder than ever after the Lord, and then He brought us back again to each other."

Says Roger, "I decided that I was going to treat Mary with the kindness of Christ because *He* deserved it, she didn't."

Echoes Mary, "I remember ironing Roger's shirt and praying, 'Lord, I can't stand him, but I iron this shirt for You.'"

Both hung in with their godly habits of many years, their prayer lives, their devotional lives. . . . They took time. They waited.

"It actually took several years," says Roger, "and it was the toughest thing either of us has ever been through. But eventually our love for each other bloomed again."

For a long time neither of them disclosed to anybody the agony they'd been through. Finally, after much hesitation, prayer, and embarrassment, they shared it with their weekly small group—their very best friends. And then the group broke open, and every other couple confessed that they were either going through the same thing or had in the past! And as a result of Roger and Mary's honest confession, several other marriages got healed.

Today they look so elegant and happy together—and ornamented by those three secure, happy young people! Mary and Roger have looked deeply into what each other truly is, and they have deliberately gathered it all up in their arms and said, "This person is all mine, God's gift to me, and I totally receive this, my life partner."

* * * * *

"Each one of you . . . must love his wife as he loves himself, and the wife must respect her husband" (Eph. 5:33). It's a command to be obeyed. It's a discipline to be accepted.

Don't be objecting, "But what if . . . ?" and start conjuring up extreme examples of someone's being married to the Devil himself. Most of us are just ordinary, self-centered, obnoxious sinners, and we marry other ordinary, self-centered, obnoxious sinners. The challenge is to "love" and "respect" *anyway*. To give each other time. To be patient. To be compassionate. To think the best, to view with hope. To deeply study that stranger to whom God has joined you (Matt. 19:6). And to seek to understand.

You need to come to *know* each other.

"Adam knew Eve his wife, and she conceived and bore Cain," says the King James Version of Genesis 4:1. Recent translations say "Adam lay with his wife"; *The Living Bible* says "Adam had sexual intercourse with his wife." But the 1959 Berkeley Version says it like the old King James, "Adam knew his wife"—with a footnote that reads, " 'Knew' is the correct translation; it suggests the most intimate relationship between man and woman."

And have you noticed 1 Peter 3:7 in the King James? It reads, "Husbands, dwell with [your wives] according to knowledge." It's a special call to every husband to become the world's foremost authority on his wife, getting to know her thoroughly, intimately, more and more; knowing secrets about her that are strictly exclusive with you; knowing, for instance, through perhaps years of trial and error, what are special ways to give her pleasure.

All this takes time. It takes more time. It takes high-priority time. It takes sacrificial time.

"Adam knew his wife. . . ."

Slow down.

Ray and I take frequent little "mini-vacations." We may be in Tiberias or Timbuktu, but for a couple of hours we quit. We take a walk. We play "Battleship" (only paper and pencils needed). We explore wherever we happen to be. We talk. We sleep!

Slow down.

You've had cups of tea on the couch in front of the fire, you've talked and cuddled and talked and fondled and talked . . . and then you know each other.

It's a holiday afternoon and the kids are at their cousins'. You've played checkers and shared some Scripture and lain on the floor with Diet Cokes and talked and stroked each other. . . . You know each other.

It's late at night but you're agitated over a problem between the two of you, and although you need sleep, you have to talk it out. Wrapped tight in each other's arms you spell out the issue, you seek to understand, you confess, you weep, you kiss, you comfort, you know each other.

To chronically race home from work, shove stuff into the oven and into the clothes washer, discuss the most pressing budget and schedule items, fall into bed for a wordless quickie to relieve tensions, and then race back to work again—that's grotesque. It's worse than a bad joke, it's just a pathetic, repulsive caricature of a marriage. And that kind of pattern results in living with a stranger, and it's certainly not natural to love a stranger.

> Do not wear yourself out to get rich;
>   have the wisdom to show restraint.
> (Prov. 23:4)

> Why spend . . . your labor on what does not satisfy?
> (Isa. 55:2)

> In vain you rise early
>   and stay up late,
> toiling for food to eat—
>   for [the Lord] grants sleep to those he loves.
> (Ps. 127:2)

> He provides food for those who fear him.
> (Ps. 111:5)

Give the sacrifice of time, in the home, for each other. You'll be saying by your very presence, "You're wanted. I'm here for you. You're my best friend! I enjoy being with you more than with anybody. I love you."

Slow down.

In today's culture that's a "Drastic Do."

Now Work Into Your
Life What You've
Been Reading

This chapter is in head-on collision with our current culture's life-style, isn't it! If these words seem drastic to you, determine not to form your way of life according to society around you but from the Word of God.

1. Prayerfully, thoughtfully, read and apply to your own family needs:
   Psalm 23:1
   Psalm 37:7; 46:10
   Psalm 131
   Proverbs 17:1
   Isaiah 30:15
   1 Thessalonians 4:11
   1 Timothy 2:1–2
   1 Peter 3:4
   Isaiah 32:17.

2. Make a list of the ways you yourself could shift down to a more reasonable pace of life, to lead the way for your family. If in a study group, discuss these together.

3. Pray for your family members to be unified—to reach shared decisions about meaningful changes in the family pace.

4. If you're a working single parent, a family supporter with unusual medical bills, or in some other desperate situation where you see no true solution, remember Hagar! Read Gen. 21:14–20. As you look to God and trust Him, expect Him to work miracles for you. Pray together in your group for this.

THE SECOND DRASTIC
DO: BE THERE

"Mankind owes to the child the best it has to give."
—U.N. Declaration

A REAL ESTATE BROKER asked a young woman if she was thinking about buying a house.

"Why would I need a house?" she answered. "I was born in a hospital, educated in a college, courted in a car, married in a church; I eat my meals in restaurants and spend my evenings at the movies. When I die I'll be buried from a mortuary.

"I don't need a house; all I need is a garage."

Oh, but a house can headquarter a home. And a home is an incubator for ideals and virtues and visions! Character craves a climate, a locale to spring from, and for that, only a home will do.

Money can build or buy or rent a house.

Add love to that and you have a home.

Add God to that and you have a temple. You have "a little colony of the Kingdom of Heaven."

A Christian home is a powerful show-and-tell. Through the years Christian homes have won more Christian converts than all preachers and teachers put together.

Writes Charles Colson,

Ordained by God as the basic unit of human organization, the family is not only necessary for propagating the race, but is the first school of human instruction. Parents take small, self-centered monsters . . . and teach them to share, to wait their turn, to respect others' property. These lessons translate into respect for

others, self-restraint, obedience to law—in short, into the virtues
of individual character that are vital to society's survival.[1]

Says Dr. John Perkins, who works so effectively with inner-city families, there are three basic human needs, and all three ought to be met in the home:

1. *Every human needs to be loved, to feel he belongs.* Over and over, even when your child seems most obnoxious, you need to be saying,

"Susie, I love you tons. I'm so glad you're my kid."

"Steve, I know sometimes you feel stuck with a lousy mother, but don't give up on me, and I'll never give up on you. We belong! We're both Joneses, and we're gonna hang in there together."

"Karen—'remember who loves ya, baby.' "

"Hey, Todd, we're the great Gruesome Twosome. I've got you, and you've got me."

All through the years, din those kinds of words into their ears. They must learn to understand grace: that your love for them isn't based on their works, that your acceptance of them isn't conditioned on their behavior.

And Dr. Perkins says,

2. *Every human needs his own space, a place which is no one else's, and a sense of assurance that nobody's going to take it away.*

Make sure each child has a sense of "territory," a room or part of a room where he can stake his claim, and possessions which are only his.

It can be tough. Our son Nels kept a pair of mice for a while. He had a deal with his best friend Mike who had a snake. Every time Nels' mice had babies, the snake had lunch.

Then Nels himself got a snake, only one spring it escaped. In the fall it came out of the heating vent into the living room, when I was entertaining ladies.

So much for the children's possessions.

And Dr. Perkins says,

3. *Every human needs to be affirmed, to be considered significant.* Tell your kids things like this all the time:

"Joey, you're going to be a winner in this world. I can see it coming. Look out, everybody—!"

"Debbie, I'm so proud of your drawing. Maybe you're going to grow up to be a wonderful artist."

[1] *Against the Night* (Ann Arbor, MI: Servant, 1989), 76–77.

"Mike, you're really smart. I think your study habits are starting to get better, and all those brains are going to pay off!"

And forever give them hugs, tweaks, lip-smacks on the cheek, pinches, love-punches, downright wrestling on the floor—whatever. It all says, "I'm aware of you, and I like you."[2]

Our wonderful Jewish neighbors are proud grandparents, with frequent pictures and reports. Stella says to me, "You know what a genius is? It's an ordinary kid with a Jewish grandmother!" It seems to me Jewish families do tend to root for each other, and maybe it's one reason why they often achieve in such extraordinary ways.

I know a son who told his dying father, "You gave me the most precious gift you could give me—the gift of delight. You've delighted in my presence and in all my doings. For all that you've done as a father I thank you; but most of all, I thank you for the gift of your delight."

On one of the first pages of His Book, our heavenly Parent assures us right away that when He made us He thought His creation was "very good." And throughout the rest of Scripture, in spite of His parental agonies over our sins, He keeps reaffirming that same delight:

> The Lord takes delight in his people.
> (Ps. 149:4)

> [The Lord] rescued me because he delighted in me.
> (Ps. 18:19)

> The Lord disciplines those he loves,
>   as a father the son he delights in.
> (Prov. 3:12)

> The Lord your God is with you,
>   he is mighty to save.
> He will take great delight in you,
>   he will quiet you with his love,
>   he will rejoice over you with singing.
> (Zeph. 3:17)

To feel loved, to belong, to have a place, and to hear one's dignity and worth often affirmed—these are to the soul what food is to the body. And as you provide these for your youngsters, you're confirming

---

[2] See my book *Children Are Wet Cement* (Old Tappan, NJ: Revell, 1978).

their dignity, their worth, and their projected place of value in tomorrow's world.

These basic needs cannot be fulfilled by many of the parents today who divorce, work, travel, or who simply are too busy or too distracted—at the children's lifestage when they're most impressionable, fragile, and vulnerable. Unfortunately, the substitutes for meeting these three needs are everywhere: alcohol, drugs, and illicit sex. So misery abounds, abortions multiply, and prisons overflow.

However you can manage it, *be there!* Be available in your home for all the children-years. And deliberately seek to meet these three basic needs, by words and actions, as fully as you can.

But you're saying, "Look, I have to face the practical realities of living in this world. This seems too drastic to be taken totally seriously!"

But you live in a time of drastic wickedness and danger, and to go against the trends means accepting drastic solutions.

Parent-child love itself should be passionate, ultimate, drastic: "If you take [him] from me . . . you will bring [me] down to the grave in misery" (Gen. 44:29).

It's how your heavenly Parent loves:

"How can I give you up, Ephraim?
How can I hand you over, Israel?"
(Hos. 11:8)

"While [the prodigal son] was still a long way off, the father saw him and was filled with compassion for him; he ran to his son, threw his arms around him and kissed him" (Luke 15:20).

The kids must know! They must hear loud and clear how loved and wanted they are in this world! What more powerful way can they learn this than for you to be saying by your very presence, "You're wanted. I'm here for you. I like to be with you. I enjoy you. I delight in you! I'm available."

The average American mother spends eleven minutes a day in focused conversation with her children—the average father, only eight minutes![3] Can you imagine the damage that's doing to our children?

Says Dr. William Koch, child and adolescent psychiatrist at Lenox Hill Hospital in New York, "You teach a child to be charitable, first of

[3] Blayne Cutler, *American Demographics* (Ithaca, NY), as cited in *Reader's Digest*, Sept. 1989, 189.

all, by giving enough of yourself to the child. If the child feels that he has enough, then he's able to give."[4]

Sherry and Margie were both born in the wintertime, which meant they could have started into kindergarten before the age of five and into first grade before six. But we chose to keep them home for one more year of close parent-association, and we explained often to people in their presence, "We're starting them a little late. We love having them home; they're such a joy to us."

Says the Lord in Deuteronomy 6:6, "These commandments that I give you today are to be upon your hearts. Impress them on your children. Talk about them when you sit at home and when you walk along the road, when you lie down and when you get up."

The making and shaping of a good human being is an awesome task.

Every family experience determines a child's adult character, the inner picture he'll harbor of himself, how he sees others and feels about them, his concept of right and wrong, his capacity to establish warm, sustained relationships necessary to have a family of his own, his attitude toward authority and toward the Ultimate Authority in his life, and the way he attempts to make sense out of his existence. No human interaction has greater influence on his life than his family experience.[5]

Portrait: The Mark Odum Family

I read in a magazine yesterday about Mark and Myrtle, ages thirty-four and thirty-five. Along with their five-year-old son Jared, they're a handsome black trio living in St. Louis. The three of them are practically always together, says the article, as Dad and Mom run a political consulting and public relations firm out of their home.

They make less money than if they had two incomes working separately elsewhere—but they have a lot more satisfaction, and they're financially "in the black." Besides, they say, the freedom to choose clients whose views are compatible with theirs makes up for the lower income.

"We feel better about making less money on political campaigns," says Myrtle, "than making more money by helping to promote cigarettes or liquor."

---

[4] *Childlife*, autumn 1989, 5.
[5] Armand M. Nicholi II, "The Fractured Family," *Christianity Today*, 25 May 1979, [909] 11.

I have a picture of them here on my desk, sitting on the front porch of their eighty-year-old home. Mark's behind a table full of papers, making a call on his cellular phone. Jared is curled up on his mother's lap as she participates in the phone conversation.[6]

Portrait: Dick and Mary Norris

I made a long-distance call yesterday to our friend Dick Norris. Dick and Mary these days are bursting with pride and joy.

"Six kids, eleven grandchildren," said Dick. "Five have married well; they're all church leaders with Christian families. Stephen is fifteen; he's the only one left at home, and he really loves the Lord, too. His course is set."

"Dick," I said, "you have one of the most 'family' families I've ever known; the sense of Norris identity among the eight of you is so strong. Why?"

"We literally did everything together, under one roof," said Dick. "You know the business [selling cookware] was out of our home. Mary and I were both right there all the time. And as the kids began to get bigger, they all learned work, and they all helped. Vickie joined her mother doing paper work. The boys got packages ready and stacked shelves with merchandise, and when they could drive they delivered sets.

"These kids could see before their very eyes that what we all did together paid the family bills; it put bread on their own family table and bought their clothes.

"And also, it meant Mary and I were both right there teaching and living values before them."

(Two little words were running through my head: "*Be there. . . .*")

"I'm a morning person," continued Dick, "but Mary's the night owl. Just yesterday Vickie was saying how much it meant to her that during her struggles as a young person, she knew her mother was always available for the two of them to sit on stools at the kitchen counter and talk into the night."

Added Dick, "She says it was harder to talk to her dad. I'm working on that."

Midstream in their family's life, the Norrises phased out selling cookware, left heavily populated Southern California, and moved to the coast of Oregon. And what did they do there? They bought a motel, a

[6] *Business Week*, 25 Sept. 1989, 44.

family venture, where everyone could work together on the spot! At the time of my phone call Stephen, fifteen, was painting it. . . .

☼   ☼   ☼   ☼   ☼

How can you "be there" for your family? What are the needs around you that could be met in your home—and bring you money without your leaving the kids?

Says *Business Week* Magazine, "[In the 1990s and beyond] there will be pressure on business to accommodate a little breathing space for people, especially talented ones."

It reports that already Pacific Bell, for instance, offers its 62,000 workers the option of staggered shifts. And its managers get more: if they want they can work at home by telecommuting with personal computers supplied by the company! On any given day, out of 17,000 managers a thousand may be working at home.

Or once the last child is in school full time, can you work elsewhere during school hours only?

Because Ray and I travel and minister together so constantly, there's a wonderful young woman who weekly cleans our house and feeds and waters the plants. Sometimes her thirteen-year-old son works side-by-side with her on school holidays, and he's about as good as she is! Nancy explains that he's learned because all four of them clean their own house together every week as a team: Dad, Mom, the son, and a ten-year-old daughter.

Nancy announced to me today that both children got straight A's on the past year's report cards; obviously their morale is high. And now she tells me that Russ, her husband, misses her at his present job, so he's quitting. In past years they worked together in a greenhouse nursery and then ran a small restaurant together, so now together they're going to clean houses.

That suits Ray and me fine. As far as we're concerned, all four of them can come clean our house, too—and be all together for a few more hours each week.

Now Work Into Your Life What You've Been Reading

1. Separately or in a study group, read Deuteronomy 6:4–9. Think about how obedience to this lifestyle shaped the early Israelite families, clans, tribes, nation.

2. Read 2 Kings 11:1–3, 12, 17–21; 12:1, 2 to see the difference the priest Jehoiada made because he was willing to be a surrogate "parent" and stay close to a newborn, Joash, and protect and raise him. Because of Jehoiada's closeness to Joash, how long did the nation Israel enjoy peace and righteousness?

    What might have been the difference without Jehoiada? (If you want to explore this further, see 2 Chron. 24:15 ff.)

3. Read in Proverbs 4:1–4 Solomon's description of his father David, Solomon, and Solomon's own children. Is this the pattern of your own family's generations? If not, think how the pattern could begin with you, to produce godly descendants.

    In a group, describe families you know who model godliness in several generations. What do you think are some keys to their success?

4. Read Psalm 78:1–7. Pray alone or in a study group for opportunities to influence others in your family line.

THE THIRD DRASTIC DO:
REDISCOVER
DISCIPLINE

"If one examines the secret behind a championship football team, a magnificent orchestra, or a successful business, the principal ingredient is invariably discipline."[1]

—James Dobson

I WANT TO GIVE you a principle for perhaps, under God, producing the kind of children you long to produce.

> Methods are many,
> Principles are few.
> Methods always change,
> Principles never do.[2]

Our second daughter Margie and her John are enthusiasts for God. Anybody who knows them knows their fervor, their delightful, contagious zeal for Him.

I remember when they'd come over to see us when their kids were three, two, and one. John and Margie would perch on the couch, so excited they were nearly falling off the cushions, exclaiming, "Dad and Mom, we've just got to tell you everything the Lord's been doing! Listen to this, this is so tremendous you won't believe it. . . ."

And Ray and I would be smiling weakly, trying to appreciate all the wonders of God's mighty acts when out of our eyes' corners we could see one youngster drooling chocolate over the wingback, another reaching to destroy the sheet music on the piano, and the third kid lost in heavy concentration as he filled up his pants. . . .

[1] James Dobson, *Dare to Discipline* (Wheaton, IL: Tyndale House—Regal Books, 1970), 94.
[2] Source unknown.

I had lunch with Lisa, their oldest, the other day. Lisa has finished two years at Biola University. She's gorgeous, and she and a wonderful, godly young man are in love. And Lisa was leaning across the table nearly falling off her chair exclaiming to me, "Grandmother, I've just got to tell you everything the Lord's been doing! Listen to this, this is so tremendous you won't believe it. . . ."

See what I mean?

The parenting thing isn't so much "Do what I say" as it is "Be what I am" and "Do what I do." Like it or not, what you are and do will speak so loudly they can't hear what you say. They will become like you. Scary, isn't it!

Then here's an important principle you must never forget:

Successful parenting means:

> *One, becoming what you should be.*
> *And two, staying close enough to the children for it to rub off.*

Said Gideon, a great inspirer and motivator, "Watch me. . . . Follow my lead. . . . Do exactly as I do" (Judg. 7:17). Wrote the great Apostle Paul,

> *Follow our example. . . . [We] make ourselves a model for you to follow. (2 Thess. 3:7, 9)*

> *Join with others in following my example, brothers. . . . Whatever you have learned or received or heard from me, or seen in me—put it into practice. (Phil. 3:17; 4:9)*

> *I plead with you, brothers, become like me. (Gal. 4:12)*

So first, whether there are one or two parents to do this, *become what you should be.*

There are two ways to get milk into a newborn. You can put formula into a bottle and stick the bottle in his mouth. In that case you can be there or not, go nightclubbing, eat garlic, do what you please.

Or you can breastfeed your baby, which means staying on schedule, staying rested, and eating the right things. The second way demands personal discipline, closeness, *being there.*

And when we talk about discipline in the home I don't mean first the child's; I mean your own.

We were gentle among you [wrote Paul to the Thessalonians], like a mother caring for her little children. We loved you so much that we were delighted to share with you not only the gospel of God but our lives as well, because you had become so dear to us. (1 Thess. 2:7, 8)

Don't stick your parenting formula into a bottle and turn it over to somebody else. Give your children not only rules for living but your own lives as well, because they are dear to you.

What will you become in order that your offspring may turn out to be great human beings for God?

When I began to tithe, I found that for several years I had to give up the purchase of an automobile. When I began starting my day with prayer, I found it meant giving up reading my morning newspaper. When I began to reach after Christian love, I found that I had to give up a multitude of prejudices against a multitude of people.[3]

You see, disciplining your children can't happen effectively until you've disciplined yourself.

"Disciplining" means channeling, focusing yourself. It means "eliminating and concentrating." A river can be spread out all over the place, sluggish and slow. It has little force that way, although it can do great damage. But if you channel it, narrow it down, limit it, then you increase its drive and force, and it can power a hydroelectric plant.

That's what discipline does. "It teaches us to say 'No' to ungodliness and worldly passions, and to live self-controlled, upright and godly lives in this present age" (Titus 2:12). Restraint on the one hand. Commitment on the other. "Eliminating and concentrating!"

Discipline is for the parents first. You can't lead your children over paths you yourself haven't trod.

You say to them, "Go to bed," and you expect them to get up and go. Is God saying to you, "Go to a prayer meeting"? Or, "Go to that prison ministry"?

You tell your kids to eat their food. Is God telling you to feed regularly on His Word?

[3] Frederick M. Meek, "Christian Discipline," *The Princeton Seminary Bulletin* (date unknown), 30.

You give your youngsters allowances, and you consider it your right to guide them in handling those monies. Do you let your heavenly Parent guide you in handling yours?

"Keep his decrees and commands . . . so that it may go well *with you and your children after you*" (Deut. 4:40, italics mine).

Here's the principle again:

Successful parenting means:

One, becoming what you should be.
And two, staying close enough to the children for it to rub off.

"Good, the more communicated, more abundant grows," said John Milton (1608–1674). Yogi Berra said it this way: "You can observe a lot just by watching."

Step two is as crucial as step one. Stay close enough!

In you they must *see good,* over and over through the years until hopefully they've copied it.

In you, when they see bad—which they certainly will—they must also see *sorrow for the bad,* confessions, apologies, humility. Hopefully, through years of close association, they'll copy that humility, too.

But good must be good, and bad must be bad.

Our day is a growing mixture of unhealth, tolerance, lack of discernment, confusion. God says,

Woe to those who call evil good and good evil, who put darkness for light and light for darkness. (Isa. 5:20)

And He tells us,

Hate what is evil; cling to what is good. (Rom. 12:9)

This sounds so easy, so black and white. But it's tough, isn't it! It's hard to know what sins are bad enough to be worth "blood." In the battle against your kids' waywardness, you can't die on every hill. The big question is when to be tough? When to be tender?

George Washington's father: "George, did you chop down the cherry tree?"

George: "Yes, father, I cannot tell a lie. I did it with my little hatchet."

George's father gives George a big hug.

> *George's father to George's brother: "Did you push over the*
> *outhouse?"*
> *George's brother: "Yes, father, I cannot tell a lie. I did it with*
> *one big push."*
> *George's father gives George's brother a thrashing.*
> *George's brother: "Father! Why did you do that? When George*
> *confessed he chopped down the cherry tree, you gave him a hug!"*
> *George's father: "I wasn't sitting in the cherry tree."*

As I say, it's hard for fallible parents to figure out how to discipline with true justice. Sometimes any words at all are almost too much. I love Ring Lardner's line, " 'Shut up,' he explained."

But why does God say "hate evil, cling to good"? Because "sin, when it is full-grown, gives birth to death" (James 1:15). You don't kiss and hug somebody who has smallpox. Sin is destructive, powerful, terrifying.

So when we reach out to touch it—God says, "Whom I love [whom I really care about and want to have the happiest possible life] I rebuke and discipline" (Rev. 3:19). He disciplines us because He loves us so much—and more: it's how He proves we're really His children.

If your neighbor's kid has bad manners at your table, you don't correct him. On the other hand, your very correction of Junior proves he's yours, and you care about his behavior and you're responsible for it.

Then,

> *Endure hardship as discipline; God is treating you as sons. . . .*
> *If you are not disciplined . . . then you are illegitimate children*
> *and not true sons. (Heb. 12:7, 8)*

And Hebrews 12 here infers that discipline is basically to occur between parents and their children ("fathers" and "sons"), not between child-tenders and their charges. Why? Because the parents alone are responsible to God for their children's behavior, and their standards of behavior are unique. Before Him, they don't answer to anybody else's standards of behavior.

And the pattern starts with the parents first: As you submit to the discipline of your heavenly Parent, you have every right to expect that your own children will submit to yours.

When they don't? Then sin and pain must early be linked together in their minds. During the two's and following, if "no no" is deliberately ignored, a short, quick spanking comes. (Is there anything else as immediate and as eloquent?) When they knowingly, willfully sin, then there must be pain—your pain, of course, but theirs, too. Punishing is the deliberate infliction of hurt.

Of course we're not talking about child abuse. Still, it's crucially important that children grow up convinced that sin and hurt go together. That's how they learn to fear and hate sin!

But when they submit? Reward them lavishly; commend them, make over them! When children learn that good and pleasure go together, that's how they learn to go after the good.

Our heavenly Parent said it first: "Hate what is evil; cling to what is good" (Rom. 12:9).

And I mean, really openly commend them and make over them and enjoy them! If during their preschool years you were faithfully linking their disobediences with pain and their obediences with pleasure and fun and good things—you'll have started to win the battle.

Sin, thanks to the "old nature," will always be there, as it is with you and me—but it will be the unusual, the aberration. The direction of their life will be toward obedience—which means, turn on the charm and make their childhood fun! They're beginning to learn that the righteous life is the good life!

Portrait: The McClures

Daughter Margie McClure said to me today, "Somehow, parents need permission to brag about their kids. They need to know that if their youngsters are basically, generally, on track, it's okay to be wildly enthusiastic about them!"

John and Margie are wildly enthusiastic about their kids.

It's football season now—and their Bud is playing for his high school with all his heart. At the game last Friday night I counted twelve of us there just to root for Bud: his four grandparents, his parents, his sisters Lisa and Laurie with their boyfriends, and his Uncle Nels with his girlfriend.

And did we hoot and holler for him—especially Friday because it was Bud's seventeenth birthday. He got the works! We had a huge paper banner with "HAPPY BIRTHDAY JOHN McCLURE" for the whole stadium to read. Even his teachers teased him about it on Monday and asked, "Who were all those people?"

"Oh, just my family," said Bud, embarrassed but proud. (We take every chance we can in the family to say "That's our boy" or "That's our girl.")

After the game of course we all charged down onto the field with our banner wildly flopping, and Bud kissed every one of us—me, twice, I think by mistake.

Bud is a kisser. Everybody kisses everybody in our family. It's what you do to say hello or goodbye.

Let me illustrate. Last year Bud worked as a towel man at the athletic club in town where Ray, his grandfather, is a member and works out. Like any typical athletic club, most of its members are macho, body-conscious, egocentric, foul-mouthed, and "cool"—above all, you gotta be cool.

Picture this, then: Ray comes into the club, spots Bud across the way, and calls out "Hey, Buddy!" Bud drops everything and rushes over for bearhugs. And a bunch of cool cats act as if it's "unreal"—but they look a little wistful.

Or one more picture. Big, tough, modest, nice, kinda-bashful Bud frequently brings a bunch of his big, tough, nice friends to his house, just hanging around. Then they'll all decide to go out—so Bud kisses his mom and dad and goes.

The guys pick up on it. Not a word . . . no kidding about it, no goofing around . . . but the last few months when they go out they all kiss Bud's mom goodbye. It's what you're supposed to do at the Mc-Clures' house.

Last week was especially touching. One of the fellows has a rather harsh, difficult father. The "swarm" is heading out; Bud kisses his dad goodbye, and the friend kisses Bud's dad goodbye, too.

*　　*　　*　　*　　*

So here's the principle once more.

Successful parenting means:

> *One, becoming what you should be.*
> *And two, staying close enough to the children for it to rub off.*

We went to a wedding Saturday. Along the way in the ceremony the bride and groom lighted a "unity candle." Separately, they each took a candle burning alone, and then together, they held the two candles close to the third candle. And neither of them moved away until they were sure that the third candle had "caught," that it was burning, too, that it was producing a flame all on its own.

Remember—when the parents are becoming what God wants them to be, and the parents and children are spending a lot of time in their house together being family, then the house becomes a home, and the home becomes an incubator for ideals, virtues, and visions.

It's the way the fire is "caught."

Portrait: Myron and Gale Salisian

Our friend Myron Salisian is tall, dark, and enthusiastic. He's a forty-five-year-old Armenian American, married to tiny, blond Gale. Their children are Matt, ten, and Robin, seven.

Matt and Robin are real kids; they can make faces and punch each other like any kids if the occasion demands. But your overriding impression of them—and it's the obvious, correct impression—is that they're secure, obedient, happy kids.

Last night over spaghetti for the six of us, Ray and I asked how come.

Myron said, "When these kids of ours arrived, Gale and I were committed to making them our number-one project, seriously giving them our time. From their births on to this day, they get about two and a half hours of both of us each evening, from dinner until their bedtimes, in addition to other times of the day."

"What happens during those two and a half hours?" we asked.

"About four in the afternoon I phone Gale, and we talk fifteen or twenty minutes if we need to. That's so when I get home we won't be bursting with things to tell each other, but we can give ourselves fully to the kids.

"Then the time includes dinner, family devotions, games, stories, winding down, and tucking into bed."

"Baths?" I asked.

"Earlier we bathed them and stayed with them while they played a little in the water. Now, of course, for that they're on their own."

"How long does tucking into bed take?" I asked.

"Oh, about an hour," said Gale. "Our kids both take a long time to relax and go to sleep. Myron spends almost all of that time with Matt, and I'm with Robin. At the very end we switch just to give goodnight hugs and kisses."

"Has this routine meant very much sacrificing of other things?" we asked.

"Oh, yes," said Myron. "The first few years it meant no community service (I knew I'd have the rest of my life to make that up) and saying no to a lot of extra church activities as well."

"But being together as a family more than made up for all that, right?"

"Oh, come on, gimme a break," they said. "Most nights got pretty routine. I mean, how challenging is it for a six-foot, forty-year-old man to play games with toddlers? And sometimes at the end of the day, we were just plain tired, and/or more eager to be with each other."

Gale said, "Sometimes we'd look at each other at dinner and sing 'It's a long time to "nighty, darling" ' —you know, to the tune of 'It's a Long Road to Tipperary.' 'Nighty darling' was kind of our sign-off expression with the kids. . . . No—one-, two-, and three-year-olds aren't usually all that thrilling.

"Of course now," she added, "at ten and seven they've come into the fun years. It seems as if the more their minds and personalities develop, the more we really enjoy them."

A year ago this January, Ray and I took Myron and Gale as our team when we ministered to missionaries in Italy. Myron had been overseas only once and Gale, not for fifteen years. And they'd never been two weeks away from the children.

These two poured their wisdom and love into those missionaries, and came home forever changed. This summer, five months later, they took the kids with them back to Italy to encourage and minister further to some of the same missionaries. And Matt and Robin played with missionary children and got close to them.

Now this fall these fun people have formed the "Encouragement International, Especially Italy, Organization," or, in short, "Ee Eye Ee Eye Oh"! The four of them hope to go once a year to Italy to have a continuing ministry to that particular mission field. And we're not talking tourist-vacationing; Myron and Gale have true "Barnabas" gifts of prayer concern and encouragement in the Lord.

Soon Matt and Robin will, too.

Now Work Into Your
Life What You've
Been Reading

1. There's a crucially important concept in the first half of this chapter: "Become what you should be." How do you react to that? Does it sound discouraging, out of reach?

   Read *Disciplines of the Heart* chapters 4 to 7: "Dare to believe your life could be wonderful" and "Learn to let God work in you." When your theology is right, you'll be full of optimism, hope, and expectations for yourself.

   If you're in a study group, let that reading be a homework assignment; but for now read together, discuss, and take seriously—deeply believe—the following:

   Philippians 1:10, 11; 2:15
   Romans 6:6, 17, 18, 22.

2. Memorize Isaiah 33:6.

3. Think about a time in your life when you sinned and God inflicted pain! You discovered the hard way that the two go together. In a study group share your experiences.

   Discuss types of punishment you've found effective to curb sin in your children at different age levels. Take notes, to listen and learn.

4. How can you become truly enthusiastic over your children, and how can you let them know it? (Resource: Anne Ortlund: *Children Are Wet Cement*, Fleming H. Revell, 1981.)

5. Pray for your family to experience regularly the "pleasure" of righteousness.

THE FOURTH DRASTIC DO: SLASH THE TV WATCHING

"I find television very educating. Every time somebody turns on the set I go into the other room and read a book."

—Groucho Marx

THE PSALMIST DAVID didn't like television any better than Groucho. Listen to what he wrote about it:

> I will walk in my house
> with blameless heart.
> I will set before my eyes
> no vile thing.
> (Ps. 101:2b, 3a)

Maybe he allowed Christian programs:

> *My eyes will be on the faithful in the land,*
> *that they may dwell with me. (v. 6a)*

But not just any Christian televangelists; David was choosy:

> *He whose walk is blameless will minister to me. (v. 6b)*

I think it was one of his first duties as soon as the kids were up to get the tube turned off:

> Every morning I will put to silence
> all the wicked of the land;
> I will cut off every evildoer.
> (v. 8)

I'm kidding, of course.

But, seriously, you can't be too careful. You can't shield the family's eyes from garbage too much. Not even the news, much of the time, is childproof. Think about how a little one hears these items:

"Fifty-one people were killed in a plane crash this afternoon."

"Some condoms have proved more effective than others."

"Last evening was fatal for a local woman and her son. Their mutilated bodies were found in the trunk of their car. There was evidence of sexual foul play."

Turn it off! "The world is too much with us." Even some cartoons can be hyper and trashy.

Says Dr. Armand Nicholi,

Most damage comes not from programs that directly attack the Christian faith or standards, but from those that make anti-Christian assumptions and whose attack is subtle and indirect.[1]

Dr. Saul Kapel says, "In recent seasons . . . we were offered hilariously funny episodes involving abortion, divorce, extramarital relationships, rape, and the ever-popular theme, 'Father is an idiot.' "[2]

And yet by the time the average American reaches age eighteen, he has spent 11,000 hours at school and 17,000 hours watching TV—the latter, the equivalent of nearly two years of his life![3]

Turn it off!

What kind of young person do you want to deploy into this needy world from *your* home? Somebody who's just like the world? If not, then get him off the diet of television, which is this world-system's chief mind-shaper and voice of propaganda, and feed him better things.

> "I want you to be wise about what is good, and innocent about what is evil" (Rom. 16:19).

---

[1] Armand M. Nicholi III, "The Fractured Family," *Christianity Today*, 25 May 1979, [909] 11.
[2] Quoted by Dr. James Dobson in *Focus on the Family* Magazine, Nov. 1988.
[3] USA "Snapshots," *USA Today*.

Norman Corwin speaks of America as "a nation [that] has known greatness and stood as an exemplar to the world; . . . it has bred giants and accomplished prodigies." But trivializing influences have turned it away from all this, he writes, and gradually made it "indifferent, complacent, greedy, bored, hungry for kicks, amenable to getting-along-by-going-along, comfortable with mediocrity. . . ."

Trivializing causes damage in untold ways. It lowers sight; it crowds; it whittles away at our capacity to discriminate, to make choices, to have feelings.[4]

Through movies and television, children's senses get exposed to so much—the extremely dangerous, the totally shocking, the outrageously sleazy—that gradually they lose their ability to react. They get old too soon; they "know" too much: "toughly, smartly, sadly, wisely, agedly unenthralled"[5]—with jaded eyes still glued to the screen hoping the next joke will be funnier, the next behavior more bizarre. This is addiction: needing more and more input to produce the same kick.

And all their TV watching is damaging them physically as well. A just-released, ten-year study of 9.7 million kids from age six to seventeen says that their sedentary lifestyle is making them "fatter, not fitter":

- The number of physically "satisfactory" according to the test (which included sprints, sit-ups, push-ups, and long jumps) dropped from 43 percent ten years ago to 32 percent in 1989.

- Girls 12–17 take one minute longer to run a mile.

- The children average 14 pounds heavier, but they've lost cardiovascular endurance.

"The findings are ominous," says Dr. Wynn F. Updyke, director of the testing.[6]

Parent, understand what an enemy too much television is to much of what you're trying to accomplish in the home. It's an enemy of your children's bodies. It's an enemy of communication within the family. It's an enemy of play. It's an enemy of creativity. It's an enemy of time

[4] Norman Corwin, *Trivializing America* (Lyle Stewart Publ.) as cited in *Los Angeles Times*, 16 May 1984, V1.

[5] Joyce Maynard, *Looking Back: A Chronicle of Growing Up Old in the Sixties*, as cited in the Corwin article, *Los Angeles Times*, 16 May 1984, V16.

[6] *USA Today*, 15 Sept. 1989, 1A.

just to dream, to dillydally, to think one's own thoughts—so important for any child, to give his soul time to catch up to his body.

James Dobson shares a good idea in his book *Dr. Dobson Answers Your Questions:*

> *I read about a system recently. . . . First it was suggested that parents sit down with the children and select a list of approved programs that are appropriate for each age level. Then type that list (or at least write it clearly) and enclose it in clear plastic so it can be referred to throughout the week.*
>
> *Second, either buy or make a roll of tickets. Issue each child ten tickets per week, and let him use them to "buy" the privilege of watching the programs on the approved lists. When his tickets are gone, then his television viewing is over for that week. . . . Ten hours a week is perhaps a good target to shoot at. . . .*
>
> *This system can be modified to fit individual home situations or circumstances. If there's a special program that all the children want to see, such as a Charlie Brown feature or a holiday program during Christmas and Thanksgiving, you can issue more tickets. You might also give extra tickets as rewards for achievement or some other laudable behavior.*

Immediately, of course, you've got a problem. It's going to take plenty of emotional energy to fill in the gap left by vacated television. The pained cry day after day will be, "But, Mamma, what can I *do?*"

Well, there's dolls, tree climbing, jacks, books, hide-and-go-seek, "I spy," jump rope, dress-up, coloring and painting, building blocks, clay modeling, hopscotch, making up stories, putting on plays, biking, doll houses, stringing popcorn or paper strips, playing house, making doll clothes, touch football, sandlot baseball, playing with the garden hose in bathing suits, playing in the snow, baking cookies, recording on a cassette tape player, tricycles, wagons, trucks, paper dolls, making up an "amateur hour," selling lemonade, roller skating, walking the dog, organizing a secret club, mud pies, naps, or just sitting there staring. Just for starts.

Portrait: More About the Norrises

I was telling you about Dick and Mary Norris.

The Norrises picked with care the location in California where they wanted to raise their kids; the zoning laws had to be right.

The street where they lived looked like a typical suburban street, with big trees and one-story ranch homes. And theirs was a typical house on the block. It had a fairly small formal living room, a kitchen that opened onto a larger family room facing a pool outside, and side wings to the house that stretched a ways—including bedrooms for the parents and six kids plus working space for the family cookware business.

The pool area was typical, too. It looked like thousands of other California pools: no grass, just patio cement around it, and enclosed by a high fence.

Only one thing, if you were really alert, looked atypical: the fence had a little gate in the middle of the back of it. . . . What was this? You lifted the latch, pushed it open, and—

Rabbit hutches. Fat, sleek rabbits hunkered down inside.

Bantam chicken coops. Squawks, clucks, feathers—and a mild, not unpleasant, chicken smell.

Stretches of pasture.

Quackless ducks waddling around. Pheasants picking their way.

Two ponies tethered to posts!

One sheep!

Then you learned that Dick supervised the outdoor chores and Mary, the indoor. And you can bet, with all those pots and pans besides, there wasn't much time for television.

*   *   *   *   *

"The new American hearth, a center for family activities, conversation and companionship," announces *TIME* Magazine with irony and maybe sarcasm, "is the TV."[7]

Drastically change that! Drastically slash the television watching!

As Mark Twain said, "Whenever you find yourself on the side of the majority, it is time to pause and reflect."

---

[7] *Time*, 27 Dec. 1982, 70.

Now Work Into Your Life What You've Been Reading

The latest polling has just ascertained that the average American now watches television 7.02 hours daily, and as long as television has been in existence the hours graph has steadily climbed. To reverse this will indeed be drastic, and if there are two parents in your home, any new rules will call for shared decisions.

1. Thousands of wives feel lonely and cut off from communication because of their husbands' TV watching. Are you one of those?
   How can you—
   a. Be sensitive to his truly favorite programs and maybe share these with him?
   b. Stay cheerful and positive—in the remote possibility that you're not as fun as television?
   c. Plan activities together that you know he enjoys, to lure him away from his habit?
   d. Determine to be gentle, realizing you at least know where he is, and things could be worse?
2. A generation of children has grown up not knowing the skills for play that children developed in pre-TV days. How can you help them learn? Would parties and group projects help?
3. Brainstorm with your friends, brainstorm in your study group, and pray!

THE FIFTH DRASTIC DO: RECOUP MALE AND FEMALE

"And here's the happy, bounding flea.
You cannot tell the he from she.
But *she* can tell, and so can he!"
—Roland Young

MAYBE YOU'VE SEEN pictures of the sculpted crucifix in a major cathedral where the Christ sagging on the cross has male genitalia and female breasts. How sick, how pathetic.

Too many humans are wandering around these days having lost a strong sense of what all God's animals understand very well: the difference between male and female. Even lowly little fleas can make the distinction.

What happens when we humans start to blur the lines? Society goes bonkers. It's crucial today, in your very home, for father to "act father," mother to "act mother," and the boys to know they're future men, and the girls to know they're future women.

Of course God created the sexes equal, as Galatians 3:28 explains. And they're to receive equal consideration, equal respect, equal pay for equal work, and all the rest.

But they're different. And the differences must be clearly understood and followed.

Portrait: The Brainards

Our friends Chuck and Sher have been married for a lot of years, and their two boys and one girl are now grown and out of the nest. Here's what Chuck and Sher are like.

Chuck likes to arrange flowers. Whenever they have company, Chuck does the table centerpiece. He also does all the home decorating at Christmas time, at Thanksgiving, and any other time he can think up an excuse. He picks out the wallpapers. He arranges and rearranges the furniture.

And then there's Sher. A while back Sher had a problem with the refrigerator, so she took it apart and put it back together again. All by herself she blacktopped their driveway. And when rains threatened a hillside in back of their home, guess who built a retaining wall? You got it: Sher.

But hey—like those happy, bounding fleas, Chuck and Sher both know very well that he's a he and she's a she. Chuck is a take-charge person—whether it's running the Presbyterian church where he's senior pastor, or arranging to lead Holy Land tours, or deciding which night light best fits the decor of the guest bathroom. And he took an active, firm hand in helping bring up the kids.

Sher is soft-spoken and pretty, hard-working and serene. She's no drudge, and she's no bore! She has a mind of her own and a lot of emotional strength to keep going their lovely home and social life and her first-lady duties at the church.

Chuck's a he; Sher's a she; they fit together fine. Just don't compare their biceps.

What God Says Men Are

The Bible reveals the rich heritage we have in the traditional behavior of good men. How much we owe them! The "faith of our fathers" is the strong underpinning of the whole Judeo-Christian social structure. Men whom we never saw were obedient to God's plans for them, and thereby established a godly precedent for succeeding generations of men, and their lingering influence is still our good foundation.

The Psalmist says, "In [God] our fathers put their trust" (Ps. 22:4). How did they express that trust?

Let's go back to Israel. Within that nation were tribes. Within the tribes were clans. Within the clans were families. And within each family was one man, the husband-father who stood in front of his family when the Israelites were called together—representing his family's rights and needs (Josh. 21:1, 2) and answering for their sins (Josh. 7:14, 15).

You see, God's idea of a good man isn't one who wears sweats and talks sports. Our friend Chuck would never qualify! God asks men— generally speaking, because there are exceptions—to assume leadership, and leadership is basically assuming responsibilities and jobs.

1. Salvation at Passover came as the dad of each household took his stand of obedience and faith for those under his roof (Exod. 12:3, 4). We can be grateful thousands did.

2. When God wanted a census taken, He ordered leading men from each tribe to supervise the headcount. The fellows obeyed and worked hard until the job was done (Num. 1:1–19).

3. It was the men who, by their organization, leadership, and labor, literally established the communities in the new Promised Land, as Moses said to them, "Build cities for your women and children, and pens for your flocks" (Num. 32:17).

4. It was the men whom God designated to do the dirty job of fighting for and protecting their families from all enemies (Num. 32:17).

5. And here's a tender word: When David had been away out of town he came home to "bless his household" (2 Sam. 6:20). (For many years, as Ray drove home from his duties through the streets of Pasadena, when he came to a certain lamppost, in his imagination he would hang all his problems on that post, and then drive into the garage and walk into the house praying that he would be a blessing that evening to his household.)

Men are chosen by God to be men. Their manhood is a gift from Him, with all the rights, privileges, and responsibilities attached thereto. And God expects His men, under Himself, to love, protect, defend, and provide for the rest of His children.

God our heavenly Father created maleness, and He affirms it—just as any human father must affirm the maleness of his boys, teaching them manners, respect for women and girls, and care and defense of them at all costs. (His treatment of their mother will model all that.)

(I remember how thrilled I was in the third grade when two boys teased me, and my seventh-grade brother came along and discovered it, chased them, sat on them, and punched them good.)

Yes, in the beginning God our Father created maleness and also femaleness, and He pronounced them "very good." "Male and female he created them" (Gen. 1:27).

* * *

Two sexes provided for:

Procreation;

Interest, romance, and thrill;

Separate contributions to society's functioning;

And ever-new challenges to complement and encourage one another.

Three cheers, then, for all the good men who, under God, have sought to assume their responsibilities of leadership!

It ain't easy. "He that thinketh he leadeth, and hath no one following him—he is only out for a walk."

All leaders get their leadership tested—not only initially but periodically throughout their leadership.

I remember when Ray was burdened with the heavy duties of pastoring, and feeling a great need for the attention and encouragement of his family, and he drove home one night and walked into the house and nobody really noticed. Nels was doing homework, I was busy studying. . . .

Ray said, "Hi, Nels." Nels said, "Hmmph."

Ray said, "Hi, Anne." I said, "Hmmph." (This is his version of the story.)

And Ray thought to himself, "This household doesn't need me. They're humming along just fine. If I didn't walk through the door some night, they'd never know the difference."

Ray took the reins of leadership; he called me to a Summit Meeting. And when he told me how lonely he felt and how unnecessary, I cried. I mean, I cried buckets! His impressions were 180 degrees from the truth, but I'd been insensitive and I hadn't realized his need.

And when I cried, Ray was thrilled! He had only been seeing me in my strengths—Mrs. C.E.O. of the Home, efficiently running a tight ship and keeping everything under control. But he hadn't seen me for too long a time in my weakness, my dependency on him (which was genuine), my need of him, my joy in him.

At our Summit Meeting we made some changes. I canceled some conferences and cut out some other obligations; I took new steps in giving my husband more time, more attention, more support. And it was interesting: when we both unburdened ourselves in our weaknesses, we experienced a closeness we'd never known before, and we fell in love all over again.

Our physical love began to take on new liberty and new excitement; we started to find new dimensions of delight in each other, and I believe I'm now more and more conscious of his needs—as he has always been of mine.

How important it was that night when Ray saw something wrong, for him not to back off or surrender to it but to roll up his sleeves and seek to make it right! Fifteen years later we're still reaping the benefits of that Summit Meeting.

Three cheers, too, for all the good men over the centuries who have loved their wives!

Larry Christensen writes,

The love I have for my wife does not originate with me. It originates with God, and comes to me in the form of a command: "Husband, love your wife."[1]

We know a fellow who, when he was young and idealistic, married a girl with emotional problems. He knew he loved her, and he figured his love would nurture her back to health. On the contrary, her problems turned out to be so serious, she's spent most of her adult life in a famous psychiatric hospital. Rick has faithfully visited her over the years, gently taken her out for drives or overnights or occasionally longer little stints, prayed for her, been true to her, and fixed his eyes on the Lord in the hope of her eventual release to live with him. His house stands ready. Rick's hair is going from brown to grey. He still waits and loves.

Says Dietrich Bonnhoeffer, "It is not your love that sustains marriage, but from now on it is your marriage that will sustain your love." When lifelong commitment has been sealed before God, then, as G. K. Chesterton says, "that Thing marches on—that great, four-footed Thing, that quadruped of the home!"

And three cheers for all the good men who have commanded their children!

Now, if your family doesn't have that kind of father, all is not lost. Timothy had a dad who was apparently "out of it" spiritually (Acts 16:1). But his godly mother and grandmother made up the difference

---

[1] "The Christian Couple," *Bethany Fellowship Magazine*, 1977, 91.

(2 Tim. 1:5), and Timothy came to pastor with distinction the great Christian church at Ephesus.

But God's normal way is for a man to command his children. Said the Lord about Abraham,

> I have chosen him, so that he will direct his children and his household after him, to keep the way of the Lord by doing what is right and just, so that the Lord will bring about for Abraham what he has promised him. (Gen. 18:19)

A good father is

> Temperate, self-controlled, respectable, hospitable, able to teach, not given to much wine, not violent but gentle, not quarrelsome, not a lover of money. He must manage his own family well and see that his children obey him with proper respect. (1 Tim. 3:2–4)

"Able to teach . . . gentle. . . ." He's gracious, he's accessible, he's available.

Bill Cosby says,

> The father . . . must never say, "Get these kids out of here, I'm trying to watch TV." If he ever does start saying this, he is liable to see one of his kids on the six o'clock news.[2]

(Now, there's a threat for you.)

Almost any man can be a father, but it takes someone special to be a daddy.

A good man is available. And he stoops. He's translatable to his children's terms, on their level.

What a father God is! He has stooped through Jesus Christ to our level and become translatable on our terms. "As a father has compassion on his children, so the Lord has compassion" (Ps. 103:13). The awesome Tetragrammaton, that "Name" in Old Testament days which could not even be pronounced, has now become for us "Abba"—Papa, Daddy—so pronounceable that any little one can say it even before he has teeth! How tender! And how tenderizing!

[2] *Fatherhood* (New York: Doubleday, 1986), 158.

* * *

I watched a daddy in a restaurant the other day who had taken his little bouncy-haired moppet out to lunch. He leaned across the table and listened very seriously as she showed him her doll and explained something I couldn't hear but which took a very long time. He was meeting her on her terms.

That is, all but once when she had to meet him on his. In the middle of lunch she made another comment, and he gravely picked her up and carried her off to the men's room. . . .

To recap, *all honor and thanks to the good men who've been willing to shoulder leadership responsibility, who have loved their wives, and who have commanded their children.*

> Blessed is the man
> To whom his work is a pleasure,
> By whom his friends are encouraged,
> With whom all are comfortable,
> In whom a clear conscience abides,
> And through whom his children see God.[3]

What God Says Women Are

And *three cheers for mother!* Over the centuries she's worked as hard as father, and for very different reasons.

He has built the houses; she's added the colors, the smells, the music.

He has shaped constitutions to make citizens protected; she has sewn flags to make them weep and cheer.

He has mustered armies and police forces to put down oppression; she has prayed for them and patted them on the back and sent them off with their heads up.

He has shaped decisions; she has added morale.

The first man kept a garden, and the first woman was made to be a help "meet"—suitable—for him (Gen. 2:18, KJV). (Does the word "help" sound demeaning? Our God Himself is often called the same word—our help—as in Psalm 33:20.)

The woman in Proverbs 31 got up while it was still dark. She kept everybody fed and clothed. She bought fields. She planted vineyards.

[3] Source unknown.

She brought in income. She cared for the poor. She was wise. She was busy. She was fun. She was a *help*, and everybody loved her for it.

What did her husband do? He sat at the city gates. Don't laugh. That was the heavy-duty place, the hot spot, the place of governmental and legal and administrative affairs.

Celebrate the mother! She, too, no less than the father, has, under God, shaped a magnificent human tradition.

God's first command to people was to "be fruitful and increase in number" (Gen. 1:28). She's been participating in the reproduction process ever since, through the pain of it and the pleasure. She's been obedient.

She was told to be a help suitable for the man, and for millennia she's been obedient to that, too—meeting spiritual needs and physical needs either by her own hands or by overseeing servants.

Even when Jesus walked this earth, it was women who ministered to His practical needs (Mark 15:40; Luke 8:1–3).

And in the early church, who was the woman most loved and honored? Dorcas, who "was always doing good and helping the poor" (Acts 9:36). And for two thousand years women have been living out 1 Timothy 5:10:

Bringing up children,

Showing hospitality,

Washing the feet of the saints (that is, caring for believers' practical needs),

Helping those in trouble,

And devoting themselves to all kinds of good deeds.

Good work, mothers! What would society have done without you need-meeters? Men have produced the machinery; women have put in the oil to keep it smooth-running. Hooray for you!

Napoleon was once asked what France most needed. His answer: "Mothers."

Said Abraham Lincoln, "All that I am or ever hope to be, I owe to my angel mother."

Amnon, Absalom, and Solomon all had the same father, David. Amnon and Absalom had heathen mothers; they turned out wicked. Solomon had a good mother; he turned out wise and wonderful.

*   *   *

Writes Gary Allen Sledge,

It's difficult to know what counts in this world. Most of us count credits, honors, dollars. But at the bulging center of midlife, I am beginning to see that the things that really matter take place not in the board rooms, but in the kitchens of the world.[4]

Three cheers for women! Their contributions have been priceless.

But suddenly—really since World War II—our role as women is drastically changing. I see our greatest danger not in the new things we're stepping out and doing, but in the areas which as a consequence we're neglecting.

Titus 2:3–5 commands the younger women:

To love their husbands and children,

To be self-controlled and pure,

To be busy at home,

To be kind, and

To be subject to their husbands.

In these darkening "last days,"
Too many husbands and children are not loved.
Too many women are no longer "self-controlled and pure, . . . busy at home, . . . kind, . . . subject to their husbands."
And, remembering 1 Timothy 5:10,
Children are often not being truly "brought up."
Hospitality has dwindled.
Practical needs are not always being met.
Those in trouble are often neglected.
"All kinds of good deeds" frequently don't get done.
And citizens put more and more pressure on the government to meet these needs—because so many women have shifted to paying jobs and are no longer taking care of them.

Such a drastic change demands a drastic rethinking.
We must remember our original calling to be women.

[4] Excerpted with permission from "The Woman in the Kitchen" by Gary Sledge *Reader's Digest*, September 1989. Copyright © 1989 by the Reader's Digest Assn., Inc.

Whatever the sacrifice, we must get back to the basics, to what God has called us to be and do as women—which only we, and nobody else, can be and do.

It's crucial today, in your very own home, for father to "act father," mother to "act mother," and the boys to know they're future men, and the girls to know they're future women.

Now Work Into Your Life What You've Been Reading

Either on your own or in a group—

1. Notice descriptions of what God wants women to be and not be, do and not do. Make lists under those four categories:

   Proverbs 11:16; 12:4; 14:1; 19:14; 21:9, 19; 31:10–31

   Matthew 15:28

   1 Corinthians 7:39

   1 Corinthians 7:1–5

   1 Corinthians 11:3; Eph. 5:22

   1 Peter 3:1–4

   Titus 2:3–5

2. How do you react to Ray's Summit Meeting, pages 297–298? If you're a woman and married, do you tend, as I did, to be a functioning, insensitive, efficient "Mrs. C.E.O. of the Home"? How could that change?

3. Make a list of adjectives describing "what God says women are," pages 300–303. Rate yourself, on a scale of 1 to 10, against each of those adjectives. Have you a close friend who could pray for you concerning needy areas?

4. Society is desperately hurting these days from the blurring of male-female lines. Why don't you get on your knees about this, and intercede for society, and pray about what you can do to make a difference?

TAKE A BREAK

AN IMAGINARY SESSION—
SOME QUESTIONS TO ANNE
AND POSSIBLE ANSWERS

Question One: Should we have children or not?

Answer: Well, to repeat what Clarence Day once said, "If your parents didn't have any children, there's a good chance that you won't have any."

But seriously, I hope I can convince you of the privilege and wonder of producing and raising kids!

> Sons are a heritage from the Lord,
>   children are a reward from him.
> (Ps. 127:3)

> Our sons in their youth
>   will be like well-nurtured plants
> and our daughters will be like pillars
>   carved to adorn a palace. . . .
> Blessed are the people of whom this is true.
> (Ps. 144:12, 15)

Bruce Shelley has said this:

A person has something in him that wants to continue after he's gone. And if it doesn't, he feels cheated, shortchanged, outraged, defiled, corrupted, fragmented, injured.

Strong words! Maybe you don't feel like that now at all, if you're young and both pulling in good salaries or getting degrees and loving all the independence and the freedom.

But deeply, from the perspective of a long, full, human life—when God created people He made them "in His image." And as *He* is fulfilled in producing offspring (Eph. 1:23), so He made us to be the same.

Having children initiates you into an awesome circle. You join those who've become partners with God in creation.

> *Your child has three parents: a mother, a father, and a heavenly Father (by creation if not by redemption). The three of you, together, created the precious package that was delivered into your arms on the day of your child's birth.*[1]

You're saying, "But I see so much agony around me in raising kids."

"Making a decision to have a child," says Elizabeth Stone, "is momentous. It is to decide forever to have your heart go walking around outside your body."

But remember *these children are His*, and He cares even more than earthly parents care, and He shares the burden they are bearing. Again, when you parent, you join God in His very own occupation—parenting! And in a special way you enter into the recesses of the heart of God, when you suffer for sins not your own and rejoice in achievements and victories in which you only cooperated.

Is there any more important purpose for living in this world?

Q. But what right do we have to use up any more of nature's resources and pollute this world even more?

A. What if your own parents had asked that—?

Let's respect and enjoy this wonderful planet to the fullest, living as cleanly and thriftily and responsibly as we can while we do. ("Every litter bit hurts.") Train your children to do the same.

But may we never be horrified to discover that another precious human life has been conceived. China's one-child-per-family mandate is a tragic non-solution. God is populating heaven! Earth is only His vestibule, where He's getting His future citizens ready.

Q. But we just can't *afford* kids. We can barely pay the bills without them.

A. Back to Genesis 1. The command: "Be fruitful and increase in number" (v. 28).

The assurance in the very next verse:

[1] R. A. Scott, *Relief for Hurting Parents* (Nashville, TN: Oliver-Nelson), 62.

*I give you every seed-bearing plant on the face of the whole earth
and every tree that has fruit with seed in it. They will be yours for
food. (v. 29)*

Incidentally, later when the flood was over, God expanded that with
"you've been vegetarians long enough":

*Everything that lives and moves will be food for you. Just as I gave
you the green plants, I now give you everything. (Gen. 9:3)*

Does that sound generous enough? Are you saying, "Still, that's just a
worldwide principle. I'm talking about Cheryl and me. . . ."

Can you imagine an embarrassed God up there wringing His hands
and saying, "I didn't mean *you*, Gus and Cheryl! I just meant all those
other people!" If you wonder, check out Psalm 37:25, 26 and Psalm
145:15, 16 and many more of His promises to take care of His children.

Here's a principle you can count on:

> Whatever God asks you to do, He'll supply every resource with
> which to do it.

And on that you can bet your last dollar.

(We're talking about reproduction, and I can't resist throwing in this
little gem:

> They say a single oyster
> Lays a million eggs or two.
> Can you possibly imagine
> What a married one might do?
> —Agnes W. Thomas)

Question Two: What shall I do with my impossible teenagers?
Answer: Here's what a typical teenager is like:

A teenager is . . .
   *A person who can't remember to walk the dog but never forgets
a phone number.*
   *A weight watcher who goes on a diet by giving up candy bars
before breakfast.*

Someone who can hear a song by Madonna played three blocks away but not his mother calling from the next room.

A whiz who can operate the latest computer without a lesson but can't make a bed.

A student who will spend twelve minutes studying for her history exam and twelve hours for her driver's license.

A connoisseur of two kinds of fine music, loud and very loud.[2]

But there are reasons why our teenagers are the way they are.

Teenagers are people in transition. You and I have made enough transitions, even in our adult lives, to know how unstable they are, and how confused and depressed losses and gains can make us. Expect these kids to be restless, temperamental, critical of their present situation, and experimental—wanting to push outward and flex their muscles, and yet inside, scared to death to do it.

It's normal for them to go through stages of not liking you. Well, sometimes *you* go through stages of "not liking you," too! Tell them so. Marriages go through the same ebb and flow. You all just hang in there together because you're the *Joneses* or whoever—and no matter what others may do, the Joneses stick together.

When the feelings of closeness are there between spouse and spouse, between parents and children, between children and children—great! Enjoy them. If the "feelings" go for a while, you're still on the same territory and nobody's going to bolt. Say so—over and over. You're building in stability every time you do. And affirm the fact that the good feelings will later return; then you're also building in hope.

They don't have to like you, they only have to function as kids in the home and cooperate. You don't have to like *them* sometimes, either—but you have to go right on functioning as a parent and cooperating. That's the Joneses' style. You've all got staying power for the long haul, because it's gonna get *good*. Really good. Tell them so! Spell it out frequently, with words and hugs.

Be sympathetic to their scholastic struggles.

Aaron Schmidt, as a high school senior, did some pretty heavy research and wrote an essay with real insights about his age:

There are four levels of thinking, and, to make it brief, kids my age are treated as if we are on the highest level of thinking, which

[2] *What Is a Teenager?* (Bill Adler Books, 1986).

is the "formal" level. On this level you should be able to figure out all kinds of things. The problem is that most kids my age and even a lot of adults are only in the third stage, which is the "concrete" stage! Guess what level most of the school materials are on? Right! The "formal" level! No wonder we can get so bogged down.

A man named Dr. Epstein has also figured out some facts about us. He has discovered that our brain grows at different times! That is really awesome! During the years from two to four, six to eight, ten to twelve, and fifteen to seventeen, our brain is growing and it makes it easier to learn.

Notice that around thirteen and fourteen it isn't growing? Well, this is the time that most work is given to us in junior high and usually on that "formal" level! That's two strikes against us. I don't even have to tell you what grades in school most kids fail.[3]

It makes you begin to understand a conversation like the one I once read in the *New Yorker:*

Teenager: "Is Paris in England?"
Friend: "No, Paris is in France."
Teenager: "Oh, well, I never was very good at geometry."

You laugh. Would you want to go back to school with them and try to pass all their tests?

Half of all high school students have trouble with basic math. That means that out of fourteen million students . . . uh . . . uh. . . .[4]

Question Three: If our kids rebel, will they eventually return to our values?

Answer: Dr. James Dobson surveyed 853 parents and found, at the time of the polling, 85 percent success. Fifty-three percent of the young people had come back "home" to the values of their folks, and 32 percent more now somewhat accept their values. Of the 15 percent holdouts? Well, there's still time. The last chapter of their lives hasn't been written yet. Let that encourage you.

Our own four children, all out of the nest and all four in ministry, are close and enthusiastically going in the same direction as their par-

[3] Aaron Schmidt, "The 'Range of the Strange,' " *Stillpoint* Magazine, summer 1988, 19, 20.
[4] Sue Sebesta in *Quote Magazine.*

ents. Just the same, each has his own quirk of theological differences. Ray's comment: "We taught our kids to think for themselves, and dog-gone if they didn't go and do it!"

Question Four: Let's talk about the whole process of our kids' finding marriage partners.

Answer: Don't be too eager to get rid of them. Put from your mind the little thought, "Oh, boy, a guest room." Whom they marry means everything, in shaping the continuum of your family life and family contribution to the world. You want to pass your families' values on to the next generation.

> From everlasting to everlasting.
> the Lord's love is with those who fear him,
> and his righteousness with their children's children.
> (Ps. 103:17)

> We your people, the sheep of your pasture,
> will praise you forever;
> from generation to generation
> we will recount your praise.
> (Ps. 79:13)

(Wouldn't it be exciting to work this last verse, Psalm 79:13, into a family crest with your family name, to be placed over your fireplace mantel for the kids to grow up under? If you have more than one child, some day you might have to have duplicates made, to put over each of their mantels! "Let this be written for a future generation, that a people not yet created may praise the Lord" [Ps. 102:18].)

Ray and I believe that God has a specific mate He's preparing—if they marry at all—for each of your children. Otherwise, why would He spend all of Genesis 24 detailing the specifics of procuring a very partic-ular wife for Isaac? In each marriage He's choosing to put certain genes together, certain ministries together. He knows His ongoing plans.

In your young people's dating years, encourage Christian friends and Christian dates. Depending on the stability of your kids right then, maybe you can't insist. But hopefully as they approach serious-dating years you're getting closer again, and you can talk things over. Let them know it makes a big long-range difference whether the parents really approve or not of their in-law children.

Esau . . . married Judith, daughter of Beeri the Hittite, and also Basemath, daughter of Elon the Hittite. They were a source of grief to Isaac and Rebekah. (Gen. 26:34, 35)

Painful years passed. . . .

Then Rebekah said to Isaac, "I'm disgusted with living because of these Hittite women." (Gen. 27:46)
    Esau then realized how displeasing the Canaanite women were to his father Isaac. . . . (Gen. 28:8)

A family is a *family*. It's a unit. It has personality. It has structure. Additions have to fit. But finding those new additions is often a tricky thing. Thumbs-up or thumbs-down decisions on your part shouldn't come too fast. Ray and I have been known to get convinced and change our minds, and the kids' choices turned out to be exactly right.

I also remember my own parents weren't exactly thrilled over Ray. Poor boy! I think no man would ever really have been good enough for their precious firstborn daughter. And although I had graduated from college, and Ray was older yet and in the Navy and able to support me, still we postponed our marriage for a whole very long year until my parents knew we really meant it.

They, too, got thoroughly persuaded in succeeding years. They couldn't have been prouder as their son-in-law, at age thirty-five, was called to pastor a large church. But we've been glad, in the long run, that we moved slowly and received their blessing.

Q. What are the criteria for mates for our kids?
A. There seem to be only two thoroughly spelled out in the Bible.
One, believers are to marry believers (2 Cor. 6:14, 15).

Two—and this one's more complicated—they shouldn't marry divorced people (Rom. 7:2, 3). There could be two exceptions here, and sincere Bible students have differing opinions about them.

First Corinthians 7:12–15 seems to allow room for divorce from an unbeliever who walked out because of the spouse's faith. Matthew 5:32 seems to permit it if there was "marital unfaithfulness." You'd have to ask, "Has this person's church investigated and approved the reason for the divorce, and do they give full permission for the remarriage?" The opinions of the pastor and godly elders of the church should make a difference.

Beyond that, marrying within your race, whatever your race may be, can make adjustments easier (Gen. 24:1–4). Just practically, the closer the two are culturally, the easier the fitting together. . . .

But give them space. It's no time to "hover." That can discourage them from ever finding anybody at all.

Question Five: You apparently approve of birth control. Then how did your own children get spaced the way they did? I've heard you say that Sherry was born ten months after you were married, and Margie eleven months after that, and Ray, Jr., seventeen months later, and then fifteen years later you had Nels. Is that a little weird?

Answer: Sorry, we've just run out of time. Thank you very much.

TAKE A BREAK II

Izzy's wife died. They'd been married for many years. It was a big funeral.

The next day the rabbi thought he'd pay Izzy a call at his home to console him. When he pushed open the door, there was Izzy on his couch kissing a gorgeous redhead!

"Izzy!" cried the rabbi. "What are you thinking, with your beloved wife of so many years barely cold in her grave?"

Izzy cried, "In grief should I know what I'm doing?"

*   *   *   *   *

"Sweetheart," cried the enthusiastic honeymooner, "I couldn't live without you. If you ever leave me, I'm coming along!"

*   *   *   *   *

A fellow told his doctor he just couldn't do all the things around the house that he used to do. When the examination was finished he said,

"Now, Doc, I can take it. In plain English, what's wrong with me?"

"There's nothing wrong," said the doctor. "In plain English, you're lazy."

"Okay, Doc," said the fellow. "Now give it to me in medical terms so I can tell my wife."

*   *   *   *   *

"We have found the secret of a happy marriage. It's dinner out twice a week by candlelight and soft music. This is followed by a nice, slow walk home.

"She eats out on Tuesdays, and I eat out on Fridays."[1]

POST SCRIPT

If you're studying this book in a group, why don't you "take a break" with this chapter and have a party, or at least loosen up for a more fun time together?
Read "Take a Break" on the spot, if you like, or just assign it for homework.
Definitely read "Take a Break II" together, and add all the other family jokes you can think of. Hey, if they're really good, send them to me so I can laugh, too.
My address is at the end of this book.

---

[1] Bob Phillips in the Foreword to *If Mr. Clean Calls, Tell Him I'm Not In* by Martha Bolton (Ventura, Calif.: Regal, 1989), 8.

THE SIXTH DRASTIC DO:
TEACH RESPECT

"A man's children and his garden both reflect the amount of weeding done during growing season."

EVERYBODY'S CONCERNED ABOUT the eroding influence of authority figures: the police, the military, the church Catholic or Protestant, the courts, the schools.

But basic to them all, behind them all, *whose clout is really being challenged? The man's clout.*

And I see the woman as the key to rectifying that.

What's the current Dad fad? Television gives some clues:

Roseanne: "You may marry the man of your dreams, ladies, but fifteen years later you're married to a reclining chair that burps."

Or to her TV son: "You're not stupid. You're just clumsy like your daddy."

Cereal commercial: Husband and wife are playing tennis. She never misses a shot. Mr. Dork, though, lets a ball hit him right on the head. Presumably because he didn't eat the right cereal.

Airline commercial: Two reporters from competing newspapers are chatting. He: "I read your story this morning. You scooped me again." She: "I didn't know you could read."

Razor commercial: A gal dressed in a formal literally smacks a guy in a tuxedo across the face. If he were a member of any

*minority group—woman, black, gay, retarded, senior citizen—
can you imagine the outrage, the hullabaloo, the lawsuits? But a
man is fair game.*[1]

Says Dr. James Dobson,

*Respect for leadership is the glue that holds social organization
together. Without it there is chaos, violence, and insecurity for
everyone.*[2]

"Respect for leadership!" He's right.

And perhaps the initiator of it all, the one from whose respect all the
rest of respect emanates, is the wife in the home. God gives in Ephesians 5:33 this crucial instruction:

The wife must respect her husband.

What is God saying to the wife? He's saying,
Back off. Down, girl!

Don't be forever challenging him, criticizing him, contradicting
him, interrupting him, deriding him, competing with him, negating
him, scolding him, doubting him, overriding him.

In the Amplified Bible Ephesians 5:33 reads like this:

*And let the wife see that she respects and reverences her hus-
band—that she notices him, regards him, honors him, prefers
him, venerates and esteems him; and that she defers to him,
praises him, and loves and admires him exceedingly.*

Ephesians 5:33 ought to be a conscious, daily discipline. And it
ought to be physical as well as verbal! A marriage can get delicious
when the wife begins to enjoy every part of her husband's body—and
then begins to remind him over and over of all his parts and all his
qualities in which she delights!

(For wonderful models, go back to the conversations between the
lovers in Song of Solomon.)

She's choosing to ignore his weaknesses and admire his strengths.
(Of course he has plenty of both.) She's training herself to put him up,
not down. It's a key "discipline of the home."

[1] Bernard R. Goldberg, "Television Insults Men, Too," the *New York Times*, 14 March 1989.
[2] James Dobson, *Dare to Discipline* (Wheaton, IL: Tyndale House—Regal Books, 1970), 88.

*   *   *

Shirley Scott says, "I was visiting friends who'd just celebrated their 54th wedding anniversary. The husband tramped in from work leaving clods of dirt on the carpet. I said, 'His boots certainly bring the dirt in.' 'Yes,' she smiled, and went for the vacuum, 'but they bring him in, too.' "[3]

With this kind of mindset a wife is obeying Ephesians 5:33, and she's strengthening her own personal happiness, her marriage, her family life, her kids, and ultimately society.

You see, the wife who challenges, contradicts, doubts, overrides, and negates her husband will probably produce offspring who later challenge teachers, contradict government, doubt laws, override police, negate courts, and in general produce a hassled, ineffective, exhausted society. If father has no clout, eventually neither does anyone else.

On the other hand, when the wife, by an act of her will and in obedience to Ephesians 5:33, decides to continually and enthusiastically respect and support her husband, a whole chain reaction goes into place:

The children learn to respect Dad and Mom, too. They "honor father and mother."

Dad grows in stature; he changes; he may well *become what they're claiming him to be.*

He also begins to respect and praise Mom (Prov. 31:28).

And the children are on the road to respecting all government authorities, as Romans 13:1 commands.

The respectful woman is eventually an important key to the success of all society.

I love being a woman right now to say these things. When men teach the same thing, somebody's apt to call them power-hungry chauvinists. (And some of them are, but maybe they've become like that because of aggressive women in their lives who've challenged their every toehold of leadership.)

Says our heavenly Father in statements that are blatantly sexist,

Adam was formed first, and then Eve. (1 Tim. 2:18)

The head of the woman is man. (1 Cor. 11:3)

---

[3] From an old quote I received years ago. Source unknown.

To praise, enjoy, be comfortable with, and yes, follow these guys in our lives has got to be a voluntary thing. "You first, honey. . . . You first, my brother." Easy or not, it must initiate with us women.

Will this attitude produce insipid doormats? Yes, it will and often does—in vast areas of the world where it's merely a cultural tradition. And then enormous reservoirs of brains and gifts are wasted and lost.

But if a woman's "you first" is a spiritual decision, then it's simply saying that God calls the shots. In that case, one of two things will happen.

One, she'll learn to follow with grace and poise. And, generally speaking, she'll be honored and elevated and her gifts fulfilled in every way, because her unthreatening, encouraging attitude will evoke a similar response in the male.

Or two, the Lord may sovereignly choose to set aside the rules and appoint her a judge like Deborah, or a prophetess like one of Philip's daughters, or a corporation president, or who knows what. She'll be ready for whatever God plans.

Portrait: Curt and Lori

Lori is tall and angular and coordinated. She strides like the athlete she is, and she runs her fingers through her fashionably short haircut, and she laughs a lot. Lori was a straight-A student at a tough private college, and her round, blue eyes look right at you with no apology when she carries on a very sharp conversation. And in no time you see that she's strongly opinioned and precisely directional.

Lori is a leader if ever you saw one.

But Lori is also married to a leader—one who is also big and strongly opinioned and precisely directional. Curt could have had his pick of lots of girls in our church; he was a full-time pastor on staff and definitely our most eligible bachelor. Curt didn't pick a little petunia; he picked Lori.

She could have clashed with him at every turn; maybe she has. But anyone who knows Lori knows how affirming and encouraging she's become. Maybe this side of her was forged on the anvil of real agonies behind the scenes—I don't know. Any great marriage calls for all the tough disciplines we can muster.

I only know that Curt and Lori have a great marriage. She tells him over and over how wonderful he is, and she tells everybody else the same thing. And Curt is wonderful.

Curt's response? He tells Lori over and over how wonderful she is, and he tells everybody else how wonderful Lori is! And he's right; she's wonderful.

A little sickening, you say? Listen, it's worse than that: they have two tall, handsome teenagers who are proud of how wonderful their parents are.

A Portrait for the Birds

Sand hill cranes are very special. They can fly in their formations for longer distances and over longer periods of time than any other crane known.

Apparently there are three reasons why.

First, they rotate their leadership so that no single crane gets too tired. Second, they choose only their strongest cranes for leadership, to buffet those fierce wind currents.

And third, all the time the leader is leading, all the other cranes behind him are continually and noisily honking, honking their enthusiasm and admiration and approval!

Now Work Into Your
Life What You've
Been Reading

1. God considered Leviticus 19:3a so important for the Israelites that He built in the ultimate punishment for violators: Leviticus 29:9! Why do you think God thought this respect was so crucial?

    Notice how He coupled this respect with respect for Himself: Leviticus 19:32. Incidentally, do you teach this respect to your children?

    And notice whom else your children must respect:

    1 Timothy 3:4

    1 Thessalonians 5:12, 13

    1 Peter 2:17

    God also says whom the father must respect:

    1 Peter 3:7

2. If you're a wife, on a scale of 1 to 10, how do you rate your obedience to Ephesians 5:33b? In your notebook write measurable ways you can improve, and begin today!

In a group discuss these new intentions—and be accountable to report next time how you're doing.

THE SEVENTH DRASTIC DO: TEACH VALUES

"As the twig is bent, the tree inclines."
—Virgil, 70–19 B.C.

"Without God, we cannot. Without us, He will not."
—St. Augustine of Hippo, A.D. 354–430

WHAT DO WE DO with these fascinating, intimidating offspring? We put values into them as faithfully as we put in vitamins and food and sleep. We're fighting off death, and values are life-giving.

Said Romain Roland, "France fell because there was corruption without indignation."
And King Solomon wrote,

> My son, pay close attention to what I say;
>   listen closely to my words.
> Do not let them out of your sight,
>   keep them within your heart. . . .
>
> When you walk, they will guide you;
>   when you sleep, they will watch over you;
>   when you awake, they will speak to you.
> For these commands are a lamp,
> this teaching is a light,
> and the corrections of discipline are the way to life.
> (Prov. 4:20; 6:22, 23)

Teaching values means saying, "This is bad, this is good. Hate the bad, cling to the good." (See Rom. 12:9.) By word and by example, you set the bad on the left, you set the good on the right, and you say, "See that bad? Don't touch it with a ten-foot pole. See that good? Go after it!"

At every state of their development, over and over and over.

Look how love is defined in 1 Corinthians 13, and you get an insight into values.

Good	Bad

Love . . .

1. is patient, "waits on the Lord"

2. is kind, compassionate
3. does not envy, has a spirit of gratitude and contentment
4. does not boast, is modest, possesses true humility
5. is not proud, takes his place, acknowledges authority
6. is not rude but courteous

7. is not self-seeking but is fulfilled in helping others

8. is not easily angered but is self-controlled, temperate
9. keeps no record of wrongs, has a forgiving spirit

10. does not delight in evil but rejoices with the truth; is discerning, sees the difference, has deliberately chosen good
11. always protects, tries to shield the vulnerable

Its opposite . . .

1. is impatient, self-willed, demands instant gratification

2. is abusive, vengeful
3. wants what others have

4. brags, showcases himself

5. considers himself autonomous, demands all his rights

6. is ungracious, indifferent to others' needs

7. loves to improve himself, do good to himself, accumulate

8. has a hot temper, is easily frustrated
9. has a long memory of others' faults, tends to seek to "pay back"

10. is naive, permissive, accepts both good and bad, has a weak sense of values

11. looks out only for himself

12. always trusts, considers someone "innocent until proven guilty," gives the benefit of the doubt

12. has a suspicious nature, concludes the worst, is gossipy, adversarial

13. always hopes, is optimistic

13. tends to worry, be faithless, pessimistic

14. always perseveres, is willing to suffer to see things through

14. tries to avoid pain at all cost, quits and starts easily

Live and teach good values, constantly and consistently—

> *so that you, your children and their children after them may fear the Lord your God as long as you live . . . so that you may enjoy long life, . . . so that it may go well with you and that you may increase greatly. . . .*
>
> *Impress them on your children. Talk about them when you sit at home and when you walk along the road, when you lie down and when you get up. (Deut. 6:2, 3, 7)*

"I have now disposed of all my property to my family," wrote Patrick Henry. "There is one thing more I wish I could give them, and that is the Christian religion."

Think about these virtues of 1 Corinthians 13.
1. "Love is patient."

Becka and Frank and their three children were squeezed into a second-floor condo, and they couldn't afford to move until Frank got a promotion at work. Frank's company was full of rivalry and politics, and Frank refused to enter in to all that. He just held his head up and did his job, and the two of them waited on God. Most of the time they really didn't fret; they figured God's schedule was better than theirs.

Let me tell you something about Becka. She was a first-born baby who arrived when feeding on demand was the "in" thing; but Becka's parents philosophized that they didn't want to give Baby the impression that she was the center of the universe, and that humans would always drop everything to meet her needs. So when Becka cried off schedule her mother made sure that she was okay, and then let her cry. Becka learned early to "fit in"; she learned contentment; she enjoyed the rhythms of regular living.

Maybe this contributed to her patience regarding Frank's job—trusting that God's timing was better than her own.

I have stilled and quieted my soul;
  like a weaned child with its mother,
  like a weaned child is my soul within me.
(Ps. 131:2)

My soul waits for the Lord
  more than watchmen wait for the morning,
  more than watchmen wait for the morning.
(Ps. 130:6)

Eventually God gave Frank a remarkable promotion, at close to twice the salary. They've moved into a home, with room for entertaining and for the children to play.

Blessed are all who wait for him! (Isa. 30:18)

"Love is patient."

4. *"Love does not boast."* It's modest; it possesses true humility.

A hawk came swooping low over the jungle boasting, "I'm invincible! Nobody can touch me!"

A lion was roused by this and roared, "No, *I'm* invincible! Nobody can touch me!"

A skunk heard the roar and raised its head and said, "I think *I'm* invincible! Nobody can touch me!"

But then along came a cobra and swallowed them all up—hawk, lion, and stinker. Oh-oh. Bad joke.

Boasting never pays.

We parents need to learn this. We're in a competitive world that uses every phony trick to capture others' imagination, even their jealousy. Love is what they really want most, but they're often totally ignorant of how to get it.

Puff yourself, and you get admiration—or maybe envy. Deflate yourself and you get love. You can enjoy ever-deepening friendships all your life if you'll expose yourself, be vulnerable, be willing to let your weaknesses show.

The same is true in handling each other as a married couple, and in handling the children.[1]

*   *   *

[1] See Anne Ortlund's books *Children Are Wet Cement* (Old Tappan, NJ: Revell, 1978) and *Building a Great Marriage* (Old Tappan, NJ: Revell, 1985).

Last night Nels came down from Pasadena where he lives and works, to stay with us overnight. He and his friend and I went to see that fascinating movie *The Dead Poets' Society*. It reminded Nels of all his schooling years, and he said he felt we'd put him in the wrong elementary schools. I defended what we did. And so we went to bed.

I couldn't sleep.

This morning I had to say it to him: "Nels, my big mouth did it again! You were expressing some legitimate hurts last night, and it was time for me just to listen to your feelings. It wasn't the time for me to justify myself."

I went on to say, "I goofed a lot in raising you, and I'm still at it, and I apologize. You've turned out wonderfully well—not because of me but in spite of me!"

There were hugs, kind words, and all was well.

"All have sinned and fall short of the glory of God" (Rom. 3:23)— every member of the family. "All we like sheep have gone astray" (Isa. 53:6). We're all in this together.

We need to say so. Humility is more caught than taught.

"Love does not boast."

5. *"Love is not proud."* It takes its place; it acknowledges authority.

If a child gets no authority and no love, he may turn into a monster.

If he gets authority but no love, he may turn into a cringer.

If he gets love but no authority, he may turn into a tyrant.

But if he gets both love and authority, he may well become whole. When he learns to embrace both, over the long haul he'll learn to love his parents. He'll sing his alma mater with gusto. He'll salute the flag, maybe sometimes with tears in his eyes. He'll love God!

What if his country asks him to go to war? Well, he did difficult things his parents asked of him. He got used to *authority plus love*, and it put nerve and grit into him.

What if God asks him to die for his faith? Said Job, "Though he slay me, yet will I trust him" (Job 13:15).

Authority with love, when a child is small, sows the seeds of a great patriot, a great world-citizen, a great Christian.

Then point out policemen as his friends. Speak well of city officials ("don't they keep our streets clean?"). Pray together for state and national leaders (1 Tim. 2:1, 2).

When your youngster has a run-in with a teacher, a youth sponsor, the pastor—easy does it. Point out they have a tough job. Read together 1 Thessalonians 5:12, 13.

Don't ever have "roast preacher" for Sunday dinner. From his lips your child hears the Word of God. Don't spoil that!

And as your young person becomes a citizen of this world, teach him—

To obey government leaders: Romans 13:1, 2.

To pay whatever taxes they ask: Romans 13:7.

Not to speak against them: Titus 3:1, 2.

To obey even bad governments under normal conditions: 1 Peter 2:13–20 (remembering the Caesars under whom these words were written).

Show your older children what unbelievers will be like in the last days before Christ returns: 2 Timothy 3:1–5 (disobedient to parents) and 2 Peter 2:10–12 (despising authorities).

Gradually over his teen years, be weaning him from your authority to God's, from exterior to interior. When you're finally done with him, he'll be inner-directed; his first love and his first authority will both be God.

"Love is not proud." It takes its place. It acknowledges authority.

7. *"Love is not self-seeking."* It's fulfilled in helping others.

I sat in a Bible conference once listening to a missionary doctor from Africa. He told of driving a jeep all one night to take a woman back from the hospital to the village where she lived. There didn't seem to be anyone else to do it, and she had to go home, so he took her. The rain never let up once during that long, dark night, during that entire round trip, and part of the way the roads were almost impossible.

By the time he got back it was dawn. He was soaked, muddied, exhausted. He showered and went to work. Nobody at the hospital all day thanked him, nobody commended him, and this doctor simply had to pray, "Lord, that trip was for You. I'm glad the woman could get home, but I really did it for You, and Your commendation is enough."

When we go to our daily round of tasks in the home, together as a family, we go as servants. We don't protect ourselves. And for us parents God's commendation is enough. The children need their parents' praises—often and enthusiastically—until they're grown up and their heavenly Parent's approval will be enough.

Here's a Drastic Do for you: *teach your children to work.* When they're little, give them little jobs around the house. When they're bigger, give them bigger ones.

Maybe put a sign on their wall, "You can't have bread and loaf!"

Launch them into the world expecting to serve, not to be served—to please others, not just to please themselves.

"Love is not self-seeking."

10. *"Love does not delight in evil but rejoices with the truth."* It discerns, it sees clearly the difference between evil and truth, and then deliberately chooses truth.

Discernment is picking your way carefully along that coveted goal of godliness. Having examined the alternatives, it sees what will get you where you want to go.

Said Joshua to the children of Israel,

> *Now fear the Lord and serve him with all faithfulness. . . . But if serving the Lord seems undesirable to you, then choose for yourselves this day whom you will serve. . . .*
>
> *But as for me and my household, we will serve the Lord. (Josh. 24:14, 15)*

Discernment isn't having a seeing-eye dog, it's having a seeing eye. Make it your goal to bring your young people to the point where they're no longer dependent on the guidance of others; they can see for themselves the right thing to do.

This last attribute of love really sums up all the others. It says, "Look at right values, look at wrong values, and choose the right."

The choosing is the tough part, the part that takes courage. Tell your kids how teenager Daniel, under great pressure, "resolved not to defile himself" (Dan. 1:8).

Tell them what Paul wrote to young Timothy:

> *Don't let anyone look down on you because you are young, but set an example for the believers in speech, in life, in love, in faith and in purity. (1 Tim. 4:12)*

Paul was teaching values!

At every stage of your offspring's life—the baby, the toddler, the pre-teen, the teenager, the young adult—you do the same.

No adult or child ever got lost on a straight and narrow road.

Now Work Into Your Life What You've Been Reading

1. Chapter 11 of Hebrews is a series of stories of people who by faith turned their backs on poor values and chose worthy ones.

   From verses 4 to 12 you have five illustrations of making right choices over wrong. Who were they, and what did they turn from, and what did they choose?

   Verses 13 to 16 summarize what they were doing in making right value choices.

   Verses 23 and following give more illustrations. What are they?

2. Now Hebrews 12:1, 2 tells you to turn from bad values and choose good ones. What are you to repudiate? What are you to embrace?

3. What can you do to teach your children to do the same?

4. We're discussing here a life-and-death matter. Spend a good time in prayer about your own choices of God's values, and your influence on your children and others.

THE EIGHTH DRASTIC
DO: BELIEVE GOD

I. Faith for the Parents

"We have nothing to fear but fear itself."
—Franklin D. Roosevelt

IF YOU'RE A TYPICAL Christian today, with a typical Christian family, you're standing at a crossroads with a choice between fears and faith.

Do you want a family life that's distinguished by joy? Do you want an atmosphere of well-being and rest of heart and confidence and fun? Do you want a lot of laughter at your house? And doesn't it seem as if that's really the way a good Christian home ought to be?

If you sense yours isn't like that, you could have caught the disease that's rampant these days in Christian households—the disease of fear.

God never intends your house to be fearful. There are 365 "fear nots" in the Bible—one for every single day of the year.

Let me suggest three fears that commonly plague believers these days.

1. Christian parents may have an unhealthy fear of the school system. Everywhere Ray and I go we see them—mostly mothers—absolutely exhausted from home schooling, parents who aren't educationally or emotionally equipped to take over this huge, important task. Or we see them tense from debt because they've put their kids into Christian schools when financially they had no business doing it.

This is not a plea for public schools. God will lead you to the best schooling for each of your children, and the answer may be different

Some insights in this chapter were gleaned from sermons I heard—one each by Dr. Stanley Mooneyham (re. wheat and tares) at Palm Desert Community Church, Palm Desert, CA, June 12, 1989, and Dr. John R. Claypool (re. Joseph) at Princeton Theological Seminary, June 27, 1988.

for each. Certainly home schooling is a good opportunity for far more togetherness, influence, and bonding, and Christian schools are a way of exposing your children to the reinforcement of Christian values.

This isn't a plea for public schools, it's a plea for you to examine your heart to see if you're making decisions based on your fears or based on your faith.

Studies have shown that the home is by far the greatest influence on children, and if they're active in a good church, the church influence comes in strongly second. (I personally had only the first; my family seldom lived where there was a good church. But I had strongly godly parents, and all four of us children turned out totally the Lord's.)

What children do *not* need put into their heads is a spirit of unhealthy suspicion and fright.

> For God did not give us a spirit of timidity, but a spirit of love
> and of self-discipline. (2 Tim. 1:7)

It will take their whole childhoods to complete the job of encouraging them (and you'll temporarily back off when they're temporarily fragile), but as a general rule teach your children to go into the world strongly, as a confident minority, with their heads up.

Let them walk into it as Daniel's three friends walked into the fiery furnace (and they were probably teenagers themselves, or not much more). When the king peered into the fire he saw not three people but four—halleluia for the fourth, "Immanuel"! There they were, walking around in the fire "unbound and unharmed" (Dan. 3:25).

Tell your children over and over that One walks with them through all this world's judgment fires, and that this "one who is in [them] is greater than the one who is in the world" (1 John 4:4). They are to be free and unscathed, "unbound and unharmed."

Christian parents, give thanks every morning with your children for the privilege of school (so many children in the world never get to learn to read and write and have knowledge opened up to them!). Pray for His protection over them, pray that they'll be good witnesses that day for Jesus, and send them off with hearts full of trust in the Lord.

Security is not the absence of danger but the presence of God

2. *Christian parents may have an unhealthy fear of foods.* This is another fear currently nearing epidemic stage. Believers as well as others can be absolutely paranoid over what they might put into their mouths.

Wrote Jack Sharkey,

> Jack Sprat could eat no fat,
> His wife could eat no lean.
> A real sweet pair of neurotics!

Recently the Washington *Post* said it like this:

Americans are engulfed in an epidemic—not of cancer but of fear. However, many scientists say obsessive reliance on bottled water and organic products is foolish. Instead, Americans should devote more concern to three things that cause the vast majority of premature deaths: alcohol, tobacco and over-consumption of saturated fats.

"Driving a car is pretty risky compared with, say, drinking apple juice with a trace of Alar in it," says Prof. Richard Wilson of Harvard University and an expert in comparing risks. The average American is thousands of times more likely to die in a car wreck than of cancer from pesticides. But in interviews with 25 shoppers buying organic produce at a local supermarket, nearly half said they had not worn their seat belts on the way to the store.

"People have an inappropriate sense of what is dangerous," says former Surgeon General C. Everett Koop. The truth is, Americans have never been healthier. Average life expectancy has risen steadily for decades, and most cancer death rates have remained stable or actually dropped.[1]

A while back an entire grape harvest was snatched off American grocery shelves because two single grapes in an East Coast market had been found to contain cyanide. The two grapes made headline news, and from coast to coast went up a mighty roar of indignation. I never heard what hardships resulted for the South American grape growers. I only know that recently a tiny newspaper article commented that in the

[1] Reprinted from "News from the World of Medicine," *Reader's Digest*, November 1989, 26. An adaptation from © *The Washington Post* (7 May 1989, A1), "Seeing Risk Everywhere" by Michael Spector. Used by permission.

smoke of any single cigarette there is a hundred times more cyanide than there was in those two grapes.

Of course growers must be responsible to the public in their use of insecticides. And of course all parents must be responsible to their children to give them nourishing food. But so must Christian families be responsible to God for their attitude of restful faith in Him.

God says that He created foods

> to be received with thanksgiving by those who believe and know the truth. For everything God created is good, and nothing is to be rejected if it is received with thanksgiving, because it is consecrated by the word of God and prayer. (1 Tim. 4:3–5)

Christian family, give thanks for your food, and eat it together with happy hearts.

(The voices of fear are so loud everywhere around us, we can resist giving up our most familiar, ensconced fears! Romans 11 talks about *persisting* in unbelief.

A man went to a psychiatrist moaning, "Doctor, I'm dead."

"What?" said the doctor. "Listen, when you shave, sometimes you nick yourself and you bleed, right? Well, dead men don't bleed."

To prove his point the doctor picked up a scalpel and gently gave the man's chin a tiny nick and it bled.

"See, doc?" the fellow exclaimed, "dead men *do* bleed!")

3. *Christian parents may have an exaggerated, unhealthy fear of the world and the devil.* And it's true, your little family is tented smack in the middle of a huge battlefield! C. S. Lewis said, "There is no neutral ground in the universe. Every square inch, every second of time is claimed by God and counterclaimed by the devil."

But to get a good perspective on what the Christian's attitude about the world and the devil should be, take a look at Matthew 13:24–30, Jesus' story about the wheat and the weeds (tares).

The "tares," here, today we call darnel. It's a weed that looks very much like wheat but it's very toxic. Of course our natural instinct is to try to pull it out, but Jesus said no, you might pull out some wheat, too. Leave it alone until the harvest time.

But doesn't Jesus realize this stuff is poison? Shouldn't Christians organize a big slash-and-burn party and try to completely stamp all this stuff out?

Look, the time hasn't come. You try and eliminate the darnel, and the same vandal who sneaked in and planted it in the first place is still on the loose, and he'll just do it again.

Christian parent, understand the nature of evil. Like any weed, it's alive, it's multiplying, it's maturing. It has its own dynamic; it tends not to wither but to grow toward full maturity. From one sin planted in Genesis, chapter 3, came a huge harvest by chapter 6: "The Lord saw how great man's wickedness on the earth had become, and that every inclination of the thoughts of his heart was only evil all the time" (6:5).

That's sin for you. One seed can produce a terrible crop. It's true today, as well: evil is getting worse, it's maturing, it's on its way to its full bumper crop of the last days (2 Timothy 3).

But so is the wheat! "Satan is alive and well on planet earth"—but so is God! Don't get any fixation on Satan; don't let him become some kind of hero in your children's eyes. Really, he's just a poor loser. And sin is actually stale, trite, dull.

On the other hand, think about the wheat. Righteousness doesn't seek to be noticed; it doesn't pay for many full-page ads; and yet its quiet influence is incredible.

"Jesus went about doing good"—and there was profound power in that. Goodness is dynamic, too! It's on the move; it, too, is growing toward its full bumper crop. Let your children know that sin is getting worse, but goodness is getting better.

Don't spend your time, then, clucking your tongue like some kind of grain inspector; often we're not smart enough, anyway, to discern motives and intents. God will take care of all that later.

But celebrate righteousness! Celebrate God, who will win! Let your kids know that as Christians they're victors! And deeply believe it yourself—in all your personal trials and in the worst of your family situations. Your trust in God will color everything.

Jacob's paternal favoritism of Joseph was not good. Joseph's brothers' schemes were not good. Potiphar was not good, prison was not good, famine was not good. But for Joseph and his family, God took a whole string of not-goods and turned them into good (Gen. 50:20; Rom. 8:28). And that is His consistent eternal way.

Then as you guide your family through all the traumas, *calmly trust Him.* Keep daily nourished in Scripture and prayer, and *calmly trust Him.* Fix your eyes on Jesus, and *calmly trust Him.*

"Our Lord God Almighty reigns" (Rev. 19:6).

"The Lord God is a sun and shield" (Ps. 84:11).

"Those who are with us are more than those who are with them" (2 Kings 6:16).

"Don't be afraid; just believe" (Mark 5:36).

Faith justifies the soul (Rom. 5:1). It purifies the heart (Acts 15:9). It overcomes the world (1 John 5:4).

In every family problem, as a gathered unit—hopefully including everyone—spell out your problems and needs to Jesus, and ask for help. And then—"Stop doubting and believe," as Jesus said (John 20:27). Hope in God for your situations! "Be of good cheer"—because you have Him!

Let me say it strongly: A doubting, worrying mother is a bad mother. She's modeling fear, not faith; and she'll produce worrying, anxious kids who have no idea that "God is our refuge and strength, an ever present help in trouble" (Ps. 46:1). This is of top importance, because "without faith it is impossible to please God" (Heb. 11:6). Your kids must get firmly planted in lives of trust.

How, then, parent, do you quit worrying? *You give up control.*

I can fuss and stew when I don't feel a sense of control over somebody or something. Then, again and again, I have to turn the control over to God—and immediately peace comes, and I rest.

Therapists tend to want to get you in control of a situation; that very need to control is the root of all paranoia. Give it up. Open your hands. Release it all to God. When you see your helplessness and ask God to help—only then is invisible machinery set in motion to start solving your problems.

I remember when Nels was just beginning to walk, one morning he stumbled into our swimming pool. Unfortunately, I was in the middle of a long phone conversation—and I never turned and saw him until he was floating, face down, unconscious, on the top of the water, like a quiet lily.

I ran for him, grabbed him out, got the water to start gushing out of him, saw him choke, vomit, revive and cry, bundled him in a blanket and rushed him to his doctor, held him in my arms as he got a penicillin shot, and brought him home for a long, long sleep in his crib with lots of blankets and a hot water bottle, to thaw his little body from marble blue-white to pink again.

By evening he was fine, and Ray babysat while I drove across town to teach a Bible class. Alone in the car for the first time, all my tensions and fears had an opportunity to surface. Oh, how long and loudly I bawled! I had to drive around a while and arrive late at the class to get it all out of my system. How physical the emotion of fear can become!

I remember at that time literally cupping my hands, as in my imagination I placed Nels in them and offered him to God. Ray has told me sometimes he's done the same thing with each of our children. We've released our fears and put our precious ones into His tender hands.

And would you believe it: Nels earned college money as a *lifeguard* and even ran his own little lifeguarding company for two summers!

Years ago Ginny and her eight-year-old Anna arrived as our new next-door neighbors. Ginny was in the process of divorcing, and she was panicky with fears that Scott would kidnap away their daughter. Only Psalm 91, repeated to Anna over and over every bedtime, restored Ginny's emotions enough for her to receive Christ as her Savior:

> . . . I will say of the Lord, "He is my refuge and my
>   fortress,
>   my God, in whom I will trust." . . .
> He will cover you with his feathers,
>   and under his wings you will find refuge. . . .
> You will not fear the terror of the night,
>   nor the arrow that flies by day. . . .
> No harm will befall you,
>   no disaster will come near your tent.

And it never did.

Do not be anxious about anything, but in everything, by prayer and petition, with thanksgiving, present your requests to God. And the peace of God, which transcends all understanding, will guard your hearts and your minds in Christ Jesus. (Phil. 4:6, 7)

> Worry is unnecessary.
>   The Lord is looking out for you and yours.
> Worry is futile.
>   It never solves the problem.
> Worry is harmful.
>   Doctors agree it causes many health problems.

Worry is sin.
It doubts the wisdom and love and power of God.

Tony Melendez is a young Nicaraguan who was born with no arms and one club foot. His story from poverty and despair to concert tours and acclaim is told in his moving book *A Gift of Hope*. The hope was given by his mother:

> *She believed that God had created me with something wonderful in mind, and she never let me forget it. When I grew discouraged, she said, "Trust God, Tony. He made you. He will take care of you. . . ."*

> *"Don't worry, Tony," Mom would reassure me again and again. "God has something wonderful in mind for you. Don't get impatient. . . . Trust Him and He will take care of you. You will see.[2]*

Today, singing in concerts and playing his guitar with his agile bare feet, Tony Melendez has received numerous awards and honors, including a special commendation from President Ronald Reagan. He has played for Pope John Paul II. He has completed his first album, "Never Be the Same," and his story is being featured on NBC television.

One mother's gift to her son!

Give your family the same gift—unswerving trust in God.

Do you believe in the sun even when it isn't shining? Then believe in God even when He seems silent.

Faith in God
sees the invisible,
believes the incredible,
and receives the impossible.

For your family life . . .

> "Grace, mercy and peace from God the Father
> and Christ Jesus our Lord"
> (2 Tim. 1:2).

[2] Tony Melendez, *A Gift of Hope* (New York: Harper and Row, 1989).

> Grace for every step,
> Mercy for every stumble,
> Peace for every situation.

Think about it once more: Your little family is tented smack in the middle of a huge battlefield! How are you going to react? How are you going to lead your children to react?

With Almighty God protecting you and planning for you and providing for you and loving you, you have nothing to fear but fear itself.

YOUR HOME HAS A MAGNIFICENT VIEW—IF YOU LOOK STRAIGHT UP

II. Faith for the Child

"Any parent knows that a newborn is just a loud voice at one end and no sense of responsibility at the other."

—Dr. Roy Fairchild

You have roughly twenty years to turn your new baby into a civilized human being, to lead him from immaturity to maturity, from fears to faith.

It's a big assignment.

Here comes a newborn into the world; talk about trauma! The womb was wonderful. It was an incredible all-provisional environment; this babe led an effortless existence. Stuart Emery has said it would take thousands of dollars a month to have an apartment in New York City comparable to the womb. It has twenty-four-hour security and twenty-four-hour room service. It has a constant level of temperature; it has peace, comfort, and safety.

Suddenly the tenant receives an eviction notice, and it wasn't his idea at all. Like it or not, he's bodily dumped out, even experiencing a drop in temperature of about 26 degrees. Talk about a "cold, cruel world"!

And he can't ever go back. No wonder he comes into the world crying—he's lost so much! It will be a long time before he may sense gains that really make up for his losses, opportunities which in the womb weren't possible.

Maybe as long as he lives, immaturity will keep him, even subconsciously, looking back with nostalgia—dreaming, fantasizing, trying to create for himself another womb. Or maybe he'll actually grow up, and he'll find the courage to look forward, be realistic, adjust, suffer, and achieve. He'll move from fears to faith!

Portrait: Joseph: A Young Man We'd All Like to Have Raised

Joseph got off to a shaky start. He came into the world after his father Jacob had had ten sons by three other women who couldn't stand each other, and his own mother Rachel couldn't get pregnant all those years and was almost hysterical with jealousy.

So when baby Joseph finally arrived he was the proof of Rachel's triumph, the adored extension of her own ego, hated by the other three women and all ten of their sons, and as obnoxious as the baby of the family can ever be.

(The fact that much later number twelve son would arrive didn't change Joseph's own status.)

Dr. Kevin Leman in The Birth Order Book talks about family "babies":

> Last borns carry the curse of not being taken very seriously, first by their families and then by the world. In fact, your typical last borns have a "burning desire to make an important contribution to the world." . . .
> Last borns are treated with ambivalence—coddled, cuddled and spoiled one minute, put down and made fun of the next. . . . We babies of the family grow up with an independent cockiness that helps cover all our self-doubt and confusion. We say to ourselves, "They wrote me off when I was little. . . . I'll show them!"[3]

But who could have ever pictured The Brat as someday prime minister of a world empire?

"Coddled, cuddled, spoiled":

> Israel loved Joseph more than any of his other sons, because he had been born to him in his old age, and he made a richly ornamented robe for him. (Gen. 37:3)

[3] Kevin Leman, The Birth Order Book (Old Tappan, NJ: Revell, 1985), 135, 149.

"Put down and made fun of":

When his brothers saw that their father loved him more than any
of them, they hated him and could not speak a kind word to him.
(v. 4)

Joseph's response to his brothers was tattling on them (v. 2) and bragging in front of them (vv. 5–11). No wonder they wanted to get rid of him!

When Joseph was lifted out of the cistern that day to be sold to passing traders, all his fantasy-world had to be left behind. Suddenly he was nobody's hothouse plant, the apple of nobody's eye. The essence of maturing, I think, must be a willingness to live with how things are, rather than how we wish they were. For the first time in his life, Joseph could no longer dream and fantasize and take full advantage of his little womblike world. It was time to choose reality: to look forward, be realistic, adjust, suffer, and achieve.

Little Last Born may have been thinking, "They wrote me off: *I'll show them.*"

Even being sold to Potiphar, and into a second dysfunctional family, didn't stop the process. Joseph's growing trust in God (Gen. 39:9) matured his sense of reality; he understood his limits: "God has given me this, this, and this—but not this. I can't take what He hasn't given" (Gen. 39:8, 9). He had moved from fears to faith.

In prison as a result, he didn't look back, he didn't whimper over reduced status, he didn't ask why bad things happen to good people, he just went to work. As he had served Potiphar, now he served the prison warden.

Joseph was grown up. He had once been parented; now he did the parenting: he listened to the dreams and problems of others. It was the idea of, "Ask not what your country can do for you; ask what you can do for your country!"

And in time, this attitude put him in a position to do exactly that, serve his entire country.

Joseph is a beautiful model of the maturing young person. Looking at him, you see what's needed between the womb and adulthood: to train your kids to look not back but forward, to lead them away from fantasizing to realism; to help them emerge from being cared for to caring, from being parented to parenting; to assist them in gaining the courage to be realistic, to adjust, suffer, and achieve.

In other words, *to lead them from fears to faith.* In the end a mature, successful Joseph could see the Big Picture and discern through good and through bad the quiet, persistent actions of a loving God. So he could say with total compassion to his chagrined older brothers,

> *You intended to harm me, but God intended it for good, to accomplish what is now being done, the saving of many lives. (Gen. 50:20)*

Joseph had come to see eternal truth—that God's reality is infinitely better than all our fantasies, that the losses from leaving the womb really do open up enormous opportunities for gain, that forward is truly better than back, that with God the best wine is always last.

What a joy, then—for you to learn to walk strongly forward with your Abba Father, your Lord God Almighty, the great Jehovah who guides you! And as your fears dissolve into faith, keep your children close by you—so that before long theirs will do the same.

Now Work Into Your
Life What You've
Been Reading

I. FAITH FOR THE PARENTS

1. Don't rush on to the next chapter until you've answered a crucial question:

   Are you basically living by fears or by faith?

   Write down things you're afraid of. (In a group, allow some quiet time for this, and then overcome some momentary fears enough to read your lists to each other!)

2. Joshua 1:6–9 says that *faithful Bible reading* can produce a certain result. What is it (vv. 6, 7, 9)? How does the rest of the book of Joshua indicate that Israelite history profited from the obedience of one man, Joshua?

3. Second Chronicles 15:1–15 says that in a wicked society, *Spirit-filled preaching* can produce a certain result. What is it (v. 8)? And what was the effect here on all the Israelites because of the obedience of one man, Asa?

4. How can it make a difference in your own world if you're a person of faith and courage?

5. Memorize 1 Corinthians 16:13.

6. Read 1 Samuel 29:6 to see that even if you're in a terrible situation, you can encourage your own heart in God. Tell Him in prayer that you will do this.

II. FAITH FOR THE CHILDREN

1. The Bible says that fearing the Lord is to be our one positive, happy, wholesome fear. What can you do to instill this one fear in your children?

   Read Proverbs 14:26. Can you think of specific ways to build your children's sense of security in God? See also Isaiah 54:13.

2. You long to establish (or else continue) a godly line of descendants, as described in Psalm 112:1, 2.

   Read verses 6–8, and pray that each of your children, by name, will become this. Don't rush your praying. Don't go on to the ninth Drastic Do until you feel you've made headway in your heart about this matter of your and your family's putting off fears and putting on faith.

   And as you wait before Him, envision each of your children, one at a time, becoming strong, faithful men and women of God. Starting today, begin a daily prayer habit of seeking God's promises in His Word for your children, and then holding these promises back up to Him in continuous, persistent prayer. See Luke 11:5–10 and Luke 18:1–7.

THE NINTH DRASTIC DO:
LEARN TO COCOON

"He strengthens the bars of your gates and blesses your people within you"

—Psalm 147:13

"The best way to keep children home is to make the home atmosphere pleasant—and let the air out of the tires."

—Dorothy Parker[1]

COCOONING IS IN. It's the new term for an old occupation—being at home! Somewhere back in 1989 somebody was wandering the streets and couldn't think of anything to do, and he thought, "Hey, I could go home." It seemed like a really far-out, outrageous thing to do, but he tried it. And the idea's been catching on ever since.

I heard about a gal who said she didn't know where her husband was every night. Recently one night she stayed home—and there he was!

Colonel Sanders' business has never been so hot. In fact, suddenly at any fast food place they're hardly asking, "Here or to go?" The big thing is to go—home. In America, at least, restaurants mail out their menus, and they promise dinner delivered to your home within fifty-nine minutes. Movies are to rent and take home.

Well, as long as you're home you could play patty cake with the baby, or "so big," or peekaboo, or "This little piggy went to market."

With a little older one you could do "Here's a church, here's a steeple" with your fingers. Or make a cat's cradle with string. Or lie on your tummies on the floor and play Parcheesi or Old Maid or dominoes or jacksticks or marbles.

---

[1] *Peter's Quotations* (New York: Bantam, 1977), 77.

With older ones you could break out the card table and have a vicious game of Monopoly or Trivial Pursuit or Uno. If you got hungry you could pile sandwiches together and make cocoa.

You could mark the children's heights on a doorjamb with a book and a pencil.

You could get out the photo album and paste in 947 loose snapshots waiting in a shoe box. You could put up the projector and see slides or movies of the "old days," or see the videos. You could bring the baby books up to date.

You could make up stories, breaking them off at a high point, and the next person has to go on from there.

You could go outside and toss the football or throw the Frisbee or jump rope or play hopscotch or fly kites. Or make a snowman.

The possibilities are endless.

I read an article recently about summer camps. (Incidentally, "a lot of parents pack up their troubles and send them off to summer camp!") But this article exhorted, "Sending your children away to camp teaches them flexibility." I'm not opposed to camps, but I have yet to see a child who needs flexibility. *Old* people need flexibility. Kids need security! They need *a place*. They need *the same people*. They need to *do the same things over and over* in that place, not to be sent somewhere else. They need patterns, habits, rhythms that build the foundation of comfortableness and trust.

Said Robert Frost, "Home is the place where, when you have to go there, they have to take you in."

Better than that,

"The house of the righteous stands firm" (Prov. 12:7)

"The Lord's curse is on the house of the wicked, but he blesses the home of the righteous" (Prov. 3:32).

In all the little daily patterns of the home—the laundry going into the same hamper, the sweaters into the same drawer, the hair getting washed and the shoes polished on Saturday nights—God is at work. He delights to glorify Himself in the commonplace. He chooses the lowly things of this world, even the despised things, to prevail over the seemingly powerful (1 Cor. 1:28). He fills ordinary water containers with His mysterious wine. He fills clay jars with treasures. He makes our little daily chores channels of His grace.

And, says Gloria Gaither,

Children are learners. They learn everywhere. They learn sitting down and standing up. They learn wide awake and half asleep. They take in knowledge through their eyes, ears, noses, taste buds, fingers, feet, and skin. They learn while parents are teaching, and they learn while parents hope they're not teaching. Children learn from joy, they learn from pain. They learn from hot, cold, work, play, comfort and discomfort.

Sometimes we adults associate learning [only] with books. . . . But when the books are closed and the lessons are over, children go on learning. No knobs turn off their little minds. . . . They go on learning, watching me, seeing how I handle problems, sensing my unguarded reactions, picking up the "vibes" of our home.[2]

You can have endless variety in the way you put together your family life, but whatever you do, you can't omit two disciplines and thrive. These two are to be your bedrock, regular, ceaseless, foundational home activities of the drastic new lifestyle.

Two Drastic Disciplines for Your Cocooning

One: At least once a day sit down and eat together.

"Now when the even was come, [Jesus] sat down with the twelve" (Matt. 26:20, KJV).

No one was busier than Christ was—but this was His appointment, to which He was committed.

"The Lord Jesus, on the night he was betrayed, took bread . . ." (1 Cor. 11:23).

He sat down with Judas who would betray Him, and with Peter who would deny Him. . . . He sat down.

Eating together is a sacred thing, a ritual of commitment to each other. It says loud and clear, without any words, "We belong to each other." The family table should be a central spot of the home; you have many beds but only one board.

> Blessed are all who fear the Lord,
> who walk in his ways. . . .
> Your wife will be like a fruitful vine

[2] Gloria Gaither, "Those Teachable Moments," *Moody Monthly* Magazine, Sept. 1978, 91–92.

within your house;
your sons will be like olive shoots
around your table. (Ps. 128:1, 3)

The ritual of the table is to be faithfully observed.

Within an hour or two before, nobody microwaves a pizza. They must come hungry.

The TV is off. (Forty percent of American families watch television while they eat! Unless some history-changing world event is taking place, no. No. No, no, no. Never again until the children are out of the nest. Then the rules can change to suit yourselves—but even then, watch the need for communication.)

1. Everyone gathers promptly at the appointed hour. Hopefully Mother gets seated by a male member of the family. (I usually do at least Thanksgiving and Christmas.) (To this day John is never allowed to seat his sister-in-law Sherry. He'd land her on the floor.)

2. Then comes the blessing—hopefully by Father or whomever Father appoints. Otherwise Mother instigates it.

3. Mother always takes the first bite. (When our kids are home they have their forks poised, heads bent over for action, screaming at me, "Take a bite! Take a bite!")

4. You sit up. You look each other in the eye. You eat slowly. You talk. (This one's a toughie, because they have to be taught that meals are for fellowship as well as food. They'll want to just put their heads down and shovel it in. Even show them how to hold their knives and forks and to keep their free hand in their lap; it could make a difference in their careers. One time Ray didn't hire a man because his table manners were so bad; he figured they were an indication of the rest of his living.)

5. You pass what's in front of you. You offer seconds. Manners develop thoughtfulness, concern for others.

6. You wait between courses until all are through before you take off plates or begin a new course. If you're feeling fancy, no stacking at the table.

7. Hopefully you have fun! Food digests better with laughter.

8. No one leaves the table before Mother does. If they must, they ask her if they may be excused.

Sounds complicated? Look, any pig can go to a trough and satisfy himself. You're not raising pigs but people.

By the way, don't get too impressed with the Ortlunds' eating habits. My influence means so little that when we get together—even though we observe most of the above rules—the males, now in their maturity, often have raucous burping contests, or open wide their full mouths to display everything. Especially in front of the females. And they consistently get the same reaction—the females scream, "Oh, gross, gross!"

During Ray's twenty years at Lake Avenue Congregational Church when the children were all in the nest, his evenings got fuller and fuller. In those days, we realized that dinner was too rushed to be the central family meal.

So breakfast became traditionally the Big One, and we gave it over an hour. No matter what I threw together in the evening, breakfasts were a Big Deal. I might fix any of these:

Hot cereal

French toast

Baked corned beef hash with eggs

Other egg dishes

Waffles with different toppings

Broiled fish with broiled tomato halves

Toasted bacon sandwiches

Pancakes

Fried grits or cornmeal mush with syrup

Creamed chipped beef on biscuits

Ham and fried potatoes.

The fruits were varied: juices or melons or hot baked apples or broiled grapefruit halves with honey or either pineapple sticks or strawberries with powdered sugar. . . .

The breads were varied: toast or sweet rolls or muffins or hot biscuits or English muffins or rusks. . . .

The drinks were varied: coffee, cocoa, milk. . . .

It was then that we had family devotions and shared what was going on in our lives and got prayed for.

They told what things were done along the way, and . . . [Jesus] was known of them in breaking of bread. (Luke 24:35, KJV)

The Missouri Synod Lutherans have composed a wonderful litany which would be a great thing for a family to memorize and say together at the end of every dinner, holding hands:

> God made us a family.
> We need one another.
> We love one another.
> We forgive one another.
> We work together.
> We play together.
> We worship together.
> Together we use God's Word.
> Together we grow in Christ.
> Together we love all men.
> Together we serve our God.
> Together we hope for heaven.
> These are our hopes and ideals;
> Help us to attain them, O God;
>   Through Jesus Christ our Lord, Amen.[3]

I could see memorizing and saying in unison the first four lines when your children are very small, adding the next three lines to total seven when they get bigger, and adding the next four to total eleven still later. . . .

Before long it would certainly become pure routine, and yet it would be, even subconsciously, a powerful affirmation of your family's unity and specialness under God. And it would shape their ideals later for raising their own families.

[3] "The Christian Family Standard" adopted by the Family Life Committee of the Lutheran Church, Missouri Synod. Quoted by Oscar Feucht in *Helping Families through the Church* (Saint Louis, MO: Concordia, 1957).

* * * * *

The second drastic discipline for your cocooning:
Once a day have family worship.
You say your family is full of stepparents and stepchildren and cast-offs and misfits and also-rans? *"The family that prays together stays together."* Try it. Have patience—and yet before long the mellowing and meshing will begin to happen.

You only have one stretch of time—a very few years, really—to help them understand what in life is most important. *You're teaching values.*
When you reward your children for physical or intellectual or social accomplishments and not for Christian accomplishments, they're getting a system of false values. Again, if you feed them nourishing food for their bodies and you don't feed them the Word and prayer and fellowship for their spirits, they're getting a monstrously false impression.
But "once a day"? Doesn't that seem too drastic? Impossible?
They can't be fed spiritually just once a week in church any more than they could get fed physically only once a week. *You're teaching values*—what's important on a scale of one to ten—by what you don't do as well as by what you do.
Says the Lord,

> *Do not let this Book of the Law depart from your mouth; meditate on it day and night, so that you may be careful to do everything written in it. Then you will be prosperous and successful. (Josh. 1:8)*

> *Day after day . . . Ezra read from the Book of the Law of God [to the people]. (Neh. 8:18)*

> *The Bereans were of more noble character . . . for they . . . examined the Scriptures every day. (Acts 17:11)*

"Biblical truth," writes Dr. Carl Henry, "transcultural as it is, proclaims the gospel to a generation that is intellectually uncapped, morally unzipped, and volitionally uncurbed"![4]
Says Dr. Donald Bloesch,

[4] "The Road to Eternity," *Christianity Today*, July 17, 1981, 32.

If anything characterizes modern Protestantism, it is the absence of spiritual disciplines or spiritual exercises. Yet such disciplines form the core of the life of devotion. It is not an exaggeration to state that this is the lost dimension of modern Protestantism.[5]

Can you—for your family—recover the lost? Yes, you can, but you haven't a minute to lose. Start reading God's Word and praying with your kids every day. This may be so opposed to, and opposite from, their present culture that it would seem a truly drastic thing to do— especially if your children are getting bigger and this hasn't been their habit.

What can we say?

If this world's culture is an avalanche sliding toward hell, and it is; and you don't want your own precious children to go with it, and you don't—

Then apologize for your delay, roll up your sleeves, use all your strength, and literally snatch them out of the current mind-set and leap in the opposite direction—for that solid Rock!

Portrait: The Peters Family

Jon and Sallie Peters have three children, all in the wiggly, messy stage. They live in one of those comfy early-American homes with lots of baskets and braided rugs and rocking chairs. They're into health foods and aerobics and Scrabble after the kids are in bed.

Jon's job takes him traveling usually over two nights a week. When he's home he leads the family in devotions; when he's gone, Sallie takes over.

Jon's theory is "short children, short devotions; longer children, longer devotions." So theirs are still pretty short—maybe five to ten minutes.

Sometimes they read a little bit of Scripture from *The Living Bible.* (Recently some bits have been

Psalm 95:5, 6

Proverbs 20:11

Psalm 92:1, 2

[5] Donald G. Bloesch, *The Crisis of Piety* (Grand Rapids, MI: Eerdmans, 1968), 63.

1 John 4:11

Proverbs 20:12.)

Sometimes they tell a Bible story. Lately they've told about—but not read—Daniel eating good food (Dan. 1:3–16); Jesus loving to have little children around Him (Matt. 19:13–15); God making the earth and everything in it—people, too (Gen. 1); and Philip telling a man about Jesus (Acts 8:35).

Sometimes they memorize a verse together. Some of these have been—

"I will trust and not be afraid" (Isa. 12:2) and
"Children, obey your parents" (Eph. 6:1).

(Jeffrey, two, just sits and looks, wide-eyed, with his thumb in his mouth.)

Sometimes Jon asks for a "testimony"—how Jesus has helped one of them that day.

Almost always they sing at least one song together, often action songs that require standing up and sitting down. (Jeffrey just sits and looks, wide-eyed, with his thumb in his mouth.)

Then they have prayer. They fold their hands and bow their heads and shut their eyes, and sometimes Jon prays and sometimes Sallie prays and sometimes one of the older kiddies gets prodded into praying.

Jon says later he'll start shifting to the New International Version and read a little longer passages, stopping to explain words or ask questions. They'll do a little more memorizing. Eventually he hopes they'll memorize the names of the books of the Bible and have races looking up verses, with prizes.

He has also stashed away Kenneth Taylor's *Devotions for the Children's Hour* (Moody Press) and Donald Grey Barnhouse's *Teaching the Word of Truth*. The latter is a systematized study of doctrine with stick-men illustrations.

(We hope that when Jon does all these wonderful things, Jeffrey won't be sitting there, wide-eyed, with his thumb in his mouth.)

And all this isn't only for the children. It brings the two of you close in an important daily commitment together before the Lord.

What if one spouse isn't a believer, or simply can't or won't take part? Or what if you're on your own, raising your family as a single parent? Still you can gather together whomever you have, or whoever will come, daily before Him. In effect you'll be saying, "Here am I, and the children the Lord has given me" (Isa. 8:18).

Learn to cocoon: Eat together, worship together. In these days those practices are drastic!

Make a *family* out of your family.

Now Work Into Your
Life What You've
Been Reading

1. The smell of baked cookies permeating the house when Dad or the kids come home is probably mostly gone, but what *really* draws family members back to the nest?

   a. If your home has two parents, make a list of what draws — or would draw — *her* back.

      Then make a list of what draws — or would draw — *him* back.

      Now rate on a scale of one to ten whether those warm, nice things are strongly present, sometimes present, mostly lacking, totally absent. What can you do to correct or improve your home's drawing power for your spouse?

   b. List what draws, or would draw, the kids back. Do you see some drastic new plans for action?

2. Proverbs 27:8 is such a sad, pathetic verse! And straying children are just as tragic, even if they're just chronically roaming "mall orphans." God loves homes! He knows the stabilizing, securing effect it has on His people to have a *place*.

   Read carefully Isaiah 32:17, 18, a prophecy of what happens when the Holy Spirit comes upon His people. Pray that your home may become, or continue to be, this kind of center — a center for righteousness, peace, quiet, and confidence for every person under your roof.

THE TENTH DRASTIC DO: GET CONTROL OF YOUR FINANCES

> *Workers earn it,*
> *Spendthrifts burn it,*
> *Bankers lend it,*
> *Women spend it,*
> *Forgers fake it,*
> *Taxes take it,*
> *Dying leave it,*
> *Heirs receive it,*
> *Thrifty save it,*
> *Misers crave it,*
> *Robbers seize it,*
> *Rich increase it,*
> *Gamblers lose it. . . .*
>   *I could use it.*[1]

ARE YOU RELATING? If you're typical—even a typical Christian—you're in poor financial health. You've got get-rich-quick dreams in your head, you're into fudging (lying) in financial matters, or you have investment worries or overdue bills.

Eighty percent of all Christian families are either overspending now or are still suffering from past overspending! In that sense they're definitely "worldly": they've joined the mind-set and lifestyle of the society around them.

Says Martha Bolton,

> *Every family ought to have a budget—a list that shows exactly what you'll need to borrow from American Express to pay off your VISA card so you can use it to charge your MasterCard payment*

[1] Richard Armor, *Going Like Sixty: A Lighthearted Look at the Later Years* (New York: McGraw-Hill, 1974), 77–78.

so you'll be below limit and can use that to charge your Discovery and Dining Club payments."[2]

And that's about the way we operate!

If you're this average Christian family, you need to make some drastic revisions in your money handling. You need to take control again, to gather it together and channel it according to a good plan.

If you're typical you need drastic new ways to earn, spend, save, and give. Let's talk about each of those.

1. *Get drastic new wisdom for earning your money.*

Ralph Waldo Emerson said it right: "Money often costs too much!"

Jesus said, "Do not work for food that spoils, but for food that endures to eternal life" (John 6:27). And another time He said, "Look at the birds of the air; they do not sow or reap or store away in barns, and yet your heavenly Father feeds them. Are you not much more valuable than they?" (Matt. 6:26).

Is He saying, "Quit working and sit around"? No, 2 Thessalonians 3 says it's not good to be idle.

But *even as you work, understand where your supply comes from: your heavenly Father. And if you are not able to work, keep on understanding where your supply comes from: your heavenly Father.*

Your job is not your source of supply, your Father is. That's a drastic concept. Wash the world's concepts right out of your head, and believe the word of your Abba Father, Almighty God!

Then if you need *more* money, the answer isn't necessarily for more people in the family to work, or to work harder or longer; the need is to look to your Source: "Give us this day our daily bread."

Maybe He's created the shortfall to teach you dependence and prayer. What's He saying to you? What are you learning? . . . Keep your attention on the divine Distributor.

> The eyes of all look to you,
>   and you give them their food at the proper time.
> You open your hand
>   and satisfy the desires of every living thing.
> (Ps. 145:15, 16)

Never, never does He mean for you to exhaust yourself "like the heathen" (Matt. 6:32)—like all those orphans!

[2] Martha Bolton, *If Mr. Clean Calls, Tell Him I'm Not In* (Ventura, CA: 1989), 43.

Yuppies hyperaggressive to "be millionaires by thirty" are doing to themselves physiologically exactly what Columbia River salmon do, fighting their way upstream. The salmon, also, are "climbing the ladder," and they make it—and then die of cardiovascular exhaustion. Learning to be content (see Ps. 131) will literally heal your heart.

> *It is senseless for you to work so hard from early morning until late at night, fearing you will starve to death; for God wants his loved ones to get their proper rest. (Ps. 127:5, TLB)*

> He gives food to those who trust him; he never forgets his promises. (Ps. 111:5, TLB)

Ask Him, because He's trying to teach you to pray. But also *expect Him* to take care of you. If you truly believe that the Lord is your Shepherd, then you shall not want.

If you're in a situation where your job hurts your family and yet seems indispensable, and what I'm advising sounds too totally drastic— stop, look, and listen. Are there reservations in your heart? Are you saying, "Yes, I want to live God's way, but there's no way we could get along with less money"?

Jesus put it right to us when He said, "You cannot serve both God and Money" (Matt. 6:24). The bottom line is, you choose to depend on your money, or you choose to depend on Him.

Tottie Ellis, Vice President of Eagle Forum, guesting an editorial column recently for a secular newspaper, wrote this:

> Money may buy a house but it won't buy a home. It may buy acquaintances but it won't buy friendship. Money can hire somebody to watch the children, but it cannot buy nurturing.
>
> We worship at the altar of objects. The material is elevated to a place of absolute value, causing the family to lose vitality. *We've become more devoted to possessions than to the children!* [italics mine]
>
> . . . America is in danger of losing its way. . . . Materialism is a monster which is loose in our nation and attacking our families. . . . You can have the family without society, but not society without the family. . . .[3]

[3] *USA Today*, 30 August, 1989, 8A.

May God give you, reader, drastic new wisdom, clarity, insight for your earning money, and may He give you the courage, as well, to obey that wisdom.

Portrait: Bob and Brenda

Bob Ortlund is our nephew. Age thirty-eight, Bob is another typical Ortlund, with a blond, Swedish-American look; he could be one of our own kids. What you notice about him right away is that he's medium framed but incredibly muscular. As a child Bob was small, quiet, and asthmatic. Then through his high school and college days, the Lord "grew" him in every dimension. And he developed both a body and a spirit of solid steel.

All his adult life Bob has been a forest-fire fighter. He has watched America dry out: he used to be away from his home and family fighting fires three months of the year; now it averages six, but has been up to nine. He and his buddies get airlifted all over the western United States, to do what must be one of the world's dirtiest, most exhausting, and most dangerous jobs—and sometimes on little food and sleep for many days, and sometimes losing his friends. The pain of it all, especially being away from his family for long stretches, has caused a stomach ulcer.

"Still," his wife Brenda tells me, "the ulcer's much better now. The Lord wonderfully gave him a better job as a Fire Management Officer; he still does fire fighting but it's part administration, too, so even during fire season now he's not gone so constantly."

Brenda is like Bob: strong and quiet and unflappable. She stays at home in their small town in the mountains of Arizona with Sarah, nine; David, six; and Breanna, eighteen months. She feels a lot of pressure from other people to get a job and add to Bob's modest salary.

Brenda says to me, "The Lord is so wonderful. I pray that He'll honor our obedience in the lifestyle we've chosen, and He does: I find things on sale really often—like half price for the kids' things! The quality is great, but the price is way down. That's only the Lord."

And it will blow you away when I tell you how well they're doing in ownership of this world's goods—but I'll save that for later.

2. Get drastic new wisdom for spending your money.
The spirit of the world is discontent and greed. I'm all for free enterprise—but the fact is, the free enterprise system, overused, can keep you so dissatisfied that you buy and buy and buy.

Now there's nothing basically wrong with living comfortably and dressing well and driving a nice car. It depends on the price! If they came at the cost of too much debt, or disagreeing over whether to buy or not to buy, or simply out of spirit of discontent; or if desire for them makes us cut back on saving or giving, or makes us take on too many jobs to pay for them—then, for us, at this time, they're wrong.

> *Coveting is material inebriation. It's an addiction to things that don't last and a craving for things that don't really matter. It forces us to depend on tomorrow to bring us the happiness that today couldn't supply."*[4]

> *A greedy man brings trouble to his family. (Prov. 15:27)*

> *Keep your lives free from the love of money and be content with what you have. (Heb. 13:5)*

As parents, as a family, *discipline your desires.* Otherwise, four things will happen:

1. Your family life will have an atmosphere of being cheated, or being incomplete.

2. You'll place unbearable strain on your marriage. If either spouse is pressured by the other to supply more than he or she can supply, there will be a deep sense of inadequacy and failure.

3. You'll compound stress in your children. "Environment, where the best is always in the future," says Tim Kimmel, "breeds an attitude that makes the present look cheap."[5]

4. You will play into the hands of the powers of this world system that want to control you. Your chronic borrowing from them to "keep up" makes you their servant and makes them your lords.
   "The rich rule over the poor, and the borrower is servant to the lender" (Prov. 22:7).

---

[4] From *Little House on the Freeway* (Portland, OR: Multnomah Press, 1987) as quoted in *Focus on the Family* Magazine, Feb. 1988, 3.
[5] Ibid., 3.

Which brings us to your third need for wisdom:

3. *Get drastic new wisdom for saving your money.*

If you'll start today saving $10 a week at 8 percent interest, compounded daily, in five years you'll have $3,194. In ten years you'll have $7,960; in twenty, $25,673. And in thirty years of faithfully stashing away that modest little ten dollars a week, you'll have $65,092!

Says the Lord in Proverbs 13:11,

Dishonest money dwindles away,
  but he who gathers money little by little makes it grow.

When you buy something on credit you not only lose the price of the merchandise but the interest on the loan as well—and that interest can be very high.

When you save for it in advance and pay cash, you've been paying *yourself* as that money waited, accumulating in the bank. Then you have the purchase and a reward for yourself as well!

Long ago Ben Franklin said, "He that can have patience can have what he will."

So here is a drastic financial discipline (perhaps excluding your home and, in early years, your car) which will put you light years ahead: "Pay as you go, or don't go."

Portrait, Continued

I want to tell you more about Bob and Brenda Ortlund's money handling.

When they got married they had literally no money. Brenda was in the middle of her senior year of college, and they got married on her spring break. Bob had finished college and had his first full-time job—with the Forest Service, marking timber. They lived in Flagstaff, a good-sized city in the Arizona mountains, where Brenda's school was.

With her bachelor's degree in hand, Brenda's heart's desire was graduate work in the same university. Bob tried to find work in the city, but nothing opened up. Meanwhile the Forest Service offered him a firefighting job: he'd be stationed in Young—population 400!—which was quite a distance away from school and deeper into the mountains.

Should they live apart except for weekends? They both agreed it wouldn't be good for their marriage. So Brenda put away her graduate dreams, and they moved to Young. From there she often traveled on one-day trips to distant schools, either as a speech therapist or as a substitute teacher.

Both were working and saving. . . .

Eventually they could buy a small trailer and a little piece of ground. They rejoiced over getting a "toehold" in some equity! Other good things were happening, too. They got involved in the little local church and made dear friends, and baby Sarah was born. After that Brenda worked only occasionally, taking Sarah along. Now there was much less income, a third mouth to feed—and Bob and Brenda decided to start tithing!

Laughing, Brenda says that once they started, they kept tithing no matter what. All the bills kept getting paid, and they didn't know if they missed a month if that would change. . . .

Life had its tough times. Bob was offered a better firefighting job and a move to Payson, a larger town, but when they were ready to sell their trailer—imagine the irony—it caught fire and burned! Salvaging what money they could in selling "as is," with their drastically shrunken equity they bought a place in Payson.

It was a tiny house with two bedrooms. Bob often says he doesn't know how his income stretched in those years, but they kept adding an extra twenty-dollar payment to the principal whenever they could. They both were willing to sacrifice to whittle down their debt. And even with the arrival of baby David, eventually they owned their little home free and clear.

A friend showed them a piece of ground they could buy. "Why don't you build?" he said. Even owning the lot, they didn't know when they'd be able to put a house on it—but they were outgrowing the little one, so they kept saving. Bob gets a lot of overtime pay during fire season, so each fall they'd add a big lump.

In three years they were ready to build: a wonderful two-story home on a hillside, with large rooms and four bedrooms. They built it all at once, with Bob and Brenda, not knowledgeable in construction, contributing what labor they could.

"At least to us, our home is so beautiful," these two say, who are still only thirty-eight years old! "We've tried to be faithful, but it's really just the Lord. We feel so thankful. He's been so good to us."

4. Get drastic new wisdom for giving your money.

When you've restrained yourself from overspending and you've systematically saved, you will always have, to give. What a relief—to be on top of it instead of always under! To live financially on the offense, not the defense!

And what fun! Remember "the words the Lord Jesus himself said: 'It is more blessed to give than to receive'" (Acts 20:35).

Here's how God lays it out for you:

> *Do not show ill will toward your needy brother and give him nothing. He may then appeal to the Lord against you, and you will be found guilty of sin. Give generously to him and do so without a grudging heart; then because of this the Lord your God will bless you in all your work and in everything you put your hand to. (Deut. 15:9–10)*

> *There will always be poor in the land. Therefore I command you to be openhanded toward your brothers and toward the poor and needy in your land. (Deut. 15:11)*

This isn't being "liberal" or "conservative," this is God's Word. And my purpose here isn't to consider what part the government should play, but what you as a family should do.

In America, at least (and many places elsewhere), the Great Divide between rich and poor has been widening, in part because the rich have been close-fisted. Look what's been happening:

In 1969 the richest 5 percent of Americans owned 15.6 percent of America's wealth.

In 1979 they owned 15.8 percent of it.

In 1987 they owned 16.9 percent of it![6]

If you're in this category, here's what God says:

> *Command those who are rich in this present world not to be arrogant nor to put their hope in wealth, which is so uncertain, but to put their hope in God, who richly provides us with everything for our enjoyment.*
>
> *Command them to do good, to be rich in good deeds, and to be generous and willing to share. In this way they will lay up treasure for themselves as a firm foundation for the coming age, so that they may take hold of the life that is truly life. (1 Tim. 6:17–19)*

[6] *Business Week*, Sept. 1989, 178.

If you say you're just "middle class"—compared with much of the world you're truly rich, and these words apply also to you. If you feel you're struggling, it may be partly because you live in an area of the world where the standards and expectations are always rising, and it's easy to jump on the bandwagon of the discontented, the hyped, the Type A's, the greedy, the exhausted.

The world is full of people so busy stretching for the brass ring that they forget to enjoy the merry-go-round.

Says the Lord,

Good will come to him who is generous and lends freely.

. . .

He has scattered abroad his gifts to the poor,
his righteousness endures forever;
his horn will be lifted high in honor. (Ps. 112:5, 9)

But—"If a man shuts his ears to the cry of the poor," God says, "he too will cry out and not be answered" (Prov. 21:13).

Obviously we've been shutting our ears to their cry, because the poor have been getting poorer.

In America, in 1969 the poorest 20 percent of the people owned only 5.6 percent of the nation's wealth.

In 1979 they owned 5.2 percent of it.

In 1987 they owned only 4.6 percent of it![7]

Realistically, this translates into growing homelessness, disintegrating housing, more sickness without medical care, more dropping out of school, deeper loss of hope, and ever-stronger temptations to stealing and drugs.

And if this distresses you—in places of galloping inflation like Brazil and Argentina, or in famine areas like Sudan and Ethiopia, the misery of the poor is even greater.

Open your heart and your wallet! Part of repentance and renewal in the Christian family should be a drastic rebirth of a sense of responsibility toward the poor. One "discipline of the home" should be regular, ongoing giving to ease their suffering.

To paraphrase Proverbs 14:21—

[7] Ibid., 178.

The family which despises its neighbor sins,
  but blessed is the one which is kind to the needy.

And a similar paraphrase of Proverbs 22:9 —

A generous family will themselves be blessed,
  for they share their food with the poor.

One of your disciplines of the home should be planned giving. To your
church and other Christian efforts, of course.

But also, have a jar on the breakfast table where both adults and
children can drop in bills or coins for the poor. Take out of it when
people you know are legitimately hurting for money. And when it's full,
all together pray over that money and the poor people who will receive
it, and then send it on its way to rescue missions, Salvation Army,
World Vision, or wherever, and throw in a generous check besides.
Then start filling the jar again.

> He who is kind to the poor lends to the Lord,
> and he will reward him for what he has done.
> (Prov. 19:17)

Now Work Into Your Life What You've Been Reading

1. Jesus had much to say about money. Prayerfully read Matthew 6:19–34, and let Him teach you.

2. Assess where you're strong, where you're weak in
   a. Earning,
   b. Spending,
   c. Saving,
   d. Giving.

   Can you frankly guess why you're weak in any of these areas? Does it go back to fears versus faith? Is the bottom line a decision regarding Matthew 6:24?

   Maybe it's time to make a fresh, full commitment to the Lord. (On your knees?) If you're in a group, you may want to do this as well.

3. First comes decision, then action. Before you go on to the next chapter, take some drastic new steps to take back control of your money—"to gather it together and channel it according to a good plan." If you have a spouse, do this together; pray that your hearts will be agreed. If necessary make an appointment with a financial advisor—perhaps even a godly couple in your church with a good track record. Would it be good to be accountable to them for a while, to get off to a good start?

"[You can be] confident of this, that he who began a good work in you will carry it on to completion until the day of Christ Jesus."

—Philippians 1:6

EVEN WHAT HE has begun to work in your family!

He's very diligent about it. Said Jesus, "My Father is always at his work" (John 5:17).

The only thing is, He is spirit, and you can't literally watch Him do it, and you can't hear Him breathing hard. . . . But He is working.

And working.

And working.

God is at work in everything. In everything.

All the time.

When a couple, say, leaves home for the office on any given morning, they're probably only aware of their own work, and not conscious—or barely conscious—of God's. But He is very busy. . . .

When [they] rush outside, their shoes scuff through the outer layers of atoms in the carpet, like Dr. Zhivago and Lara trudging through snowdrifts, sending sheets of ions flying like powder. The couple receives a 400-volt electrical charge in the process, but that discharges the moment they touch the metal doorknob. The carpet, left behind, has no such outlet. For half an hour their electrostatic footprints will remain clearly in place. With special equipment that can photograph heat images, the path would show a dim blue-green.

The bustle of the humans' departure causes other changes, as well. On a cold day, some of the vapor from water that evaporated up from all the hand washing, teeth cleaning and showering— possibly five pounds of it on the average busy morning—will have to come down. Part of the water will soak into the wooden floor-boards and make them swell. Other water will cling to the walls.

The empty house does not sit still. For one thing, sunlight is banging against the window glass, and some rays are squishing through and piling up. They heat the dining-room table, splitting formaldehyde loose from the varnish, and also warm up the carpet fibers and the pockets of air between them, producing a slow-motion, Medusa-like writhing. This starts air currents rising.

Where the sunlight hits the walls, it causes color-giving parti-cles floating in the paint to vibrate like pinball flippers on the loose. Much of the radiation carries through to the underlying brick or wood or concrete. This stretches the material in all direc-tions, yanks it up, pulls on every nail and screw in the wall and pushes the roof upward. The whole house begins to stretch. By the time the couple comes home, the house will be several centimeters larger, but when night falls it will sag again.

Even in rooms where there is no direct sunlight, there are other curious goings-on. Sweaters stacked in drawers leach molecules into one another, while hangers in the closet, sagging from the weight of clothes, emit an ultra-low-frequency groan.[1]

Who would have thought it? Who could have imagined?

And all this physical activity is typical of a million other ways, as well, that God is silently working.

And your family—whatever the combination of humans under your roof—is a mystery, a marvel, a wonder. God has put you together, and things are happening in you and between you, from day to day, from moment to moment, of which you're totally unaware.

His movements are constant, but they're often subdued, delicate, even invisible. Mostly, you can only realize what He's been up to, in you and your family, in retrospect, as you look back. You have to read God's work in your life like Hebrew: backward.

But imperceptibly He's always at it. Don't draw conclusions too quickly about what He's doing. Michel de Montaigne (1533–1592) said, "We undo ourselves by impatience," and he was right. Or as Yogi Berra said, "It isn't over till it's over."

[1] From *The Secret House* copyright © 1986 by David Bodanis. Reprinted by permission of Simon & Schuster, Inc. Also reprinted with permission from the February 1987 *Reader's Digest.*

God is powerfully at work. Believe what you cannot see; His movements are simply imperceptible to your naked eye.

> *The Lord works everything for his own ends—even the wicked for the day of disaster. (Prov. 16:4)*

Sometimes Ray and I lead cruises. Each day aboard we get our shoes out of the same closet, our clothes out of the same drawers, and it looks as though nothing has changed. But we're not in the same place! The ship has moved, and we're in brand new waters.

In your family life you really never repeat anything. You may use the same words or motions, but you can't repeat an experience, because God has brought you to a new place. Behind the scenes, unnoticed, He's been moving you to where you've never been before. All things are new. Your family life isn't cyclical but linear.

Professor Albert Einstein used to clap his hands rapidly twice and say to his students, "Between those two claps, you and I moved thirty miles through space."

Every member of your family is changing, becoming—either better or worse. You must see your life together as a journey. Otherwise you tend to handle your spouse or children by repeating what worked yesterday—without noticing that it isn't yesterday anymore. Your partner has changed; so have the children. Everybody's in a new place. What shaped up Kevin when he was eight isn't going to work when he's thirteen.

(A pastor can think he's pastored a church five years when maybe he hasn't. Maybe in reality he's pastored it only one year, repeated five times over.)

In one marriage survey, a man married thirty years said it was almost like being married to a series of different women: "I have watched her grow and have shared with her both the pain and the exhilaration of her journey. I find her more fascinating now than when we were first married."[2]

God is at work in all the kaleidoscoping family transitions: not only in the high points but in the endings, beginnings, detours, dead ends, and in-between times. His powerful tools are not just the promotions and graduations but the failures and firings and losses and sicknesses

---

[2] Jeannette and Robert Lauer, "Marriages Made to Last," *Psychology Today*, June 1985, 24.

and shocks and periods of boredom. In them all He's silently, busily, unceasingly encouraging, punishing, shaping.

"The counselor talked to me, and I think I'll take algebra."
"I can't believe I'm pregnant! What went wrong?"
"I did it! I left teaching to go to seminary."
"I do believe I'm losing some hair, right there on top in back. I found it in the mirror."
"The doctor says it's cancer."

In them all, God is tenderly, strongly at work.
"In his heart a man plans his course, but the Lord determines his steps" (Prov. 16:9). And during all His working—all God's silent activity in the disappointments, surprises, delights, irritations—transformations are taking place. "Lord, Thou art the journey and the journey's end."
Do you feel as if nothing is happening in yourself, in your family?
I guess so does a lobster, encased in that ridiculous armor. As he grows it even gets crowded inside. But he sheds it fourteen times during his first year of life. Each shedding takes ten days, and each time in the period between shells—when he's naked, exposed, vulnerable—he grows about seven percent.

You feel stifled, unfulfilled? You don't know when you'll break out into change?
Wait for God.
Wait on God.
Wait in God.
Wait with God.
Life is not fixed. Let it happen; don't rush it. "It is God who works in you to will and to act according to his good purpose. Do everything without complaining or arguing" (Phil. 2:13, 14). Keep your eyes fixed on Him, live in obedience as you see it, and then just *be there*.

All you're doing is tending sheep, . . . binding up a scratch, . . . leading to a drink of water, . . .
Year after year after year. . . .

And then suddenly you notice nearby there's a bush on fire.

Now Work Into Your Life What You've Been Reading

Listen to these words from *Disciplines of the Heart*, and interpret them for your family life:

> God is at work in everything. *Do you believe that? You won't truly rest and trust if you believe He's only at work in some areas of your life, and the rest is up to you. . . . Are you believing practically at this moment how great He is . . . for you? It should begin to relax your muscles even as you read.*
> "Be still," says the psalm.
> "Let your hands hang down," says Hebrews. . . .
> Let God be God.

1. Assess the possibility that you've been working at this family thing too hard. Some parents get super-conscientious, hovering, over-directing, tense, driving, unpleasant.

   "Be honest in your estimate of yourselves" (Rom. 12:3, TLB).

   "On a scale of 1 to 10—10 being obnoxious in the intensity of my parenting as if it all depended on me; 5 being trust in God while I function in obedience as I see it; and 1 being out to lunch, off the scene, totally uninvolved—I rate myself _____."
   If you're from 6 to 10, how about reading (or re-reading) pages 182 to 184 of *Disciplines of the Heart?*

2. Have a time of worship and praise to such a God—whether alone or in a group. Read Psalm 86:8–13 in praise and prayer.

YOUR RESPONSE TO
WHAT YOU'VE READ

Though no one can go back and make
A brand new start, my friend,
Quite anyone can start from now
And make a brand new end.[1]

THE DECADE OF THE NINETIES and then the turn of the century are here. Signs everywhere point to Jesus Christ's soon return—both the ingathering of believers and the growing intensity of wickedness.

And what about you? Do you feel you're emerging into the new era spiritually mature, comfortable in God, coping?

Business Week, in September of 1989, assessed the Western world as "prosperous but edgy, and problems abound, from deficits to crack. . . ." And it announced that Baby Boomers, for all their affluence, are anxiety-ridden! It called them "a generation that carries the scars of its heritage":

"Even though they never experienced the Depression and have lived in prosperity, they were brought up in the shadow of the Holocaust, the Bomb, and the Cold War," says Richard Easterlin, University of Southern California professor.

"So they tend to worry more and to be more anxious about future security."

They worry, for instance, about losing their wealth:

49% are "very concerned" about inflation.

49% are "very concerned" about unemployment.

47% are "very concerned" about foreign competition.

[1] Source unknown.

42% are "very concerned" about a decline in economic growth.

31% are "very concerned" about the possibility of another stock market crash.[2]

And they're "very concerned" about threats to the environment, rising crime, the drug war, homelessness, the spread of AIDS, the threat of nuclear war—all real and legitimate concerns. But not many Boomers *act* on any of these concerns—which means the concerns simply degenerate into worry, into a general feeling of malaise, and into a sense of "eat, drink, and have another ski weekend, for tomorrow we die," a vague helplessness in the face of impending doom. They live in fear and not in faith!

Listen to this wistful, wishful "altar call" to the world from secular *Business Week:*

> *Emotions other than greed and self-interest—impulses such as altruism or a collective spirit of endeavor—still motivate. . . . There are hopeful glimmerings that people are beginning to respond . . . to some decidedly nonmarket incentives.*[3]

This book is an appeal to "nonmarket incentives"—
To restore godly families,
To recoup strong, loving marriages,
To produce again for tomorrow's world happy, hardworking, stable, courageous, God-fearing children,
To please our God and secure His blessings for us and our descendants,
To see repentance, reform, renewal, revival in the family through a return to His *disciplines of the home.*

It's high time.
The world may be in a free-fall avalanche to hell, but you've decided that you and your family aren't going along. As we said, *make the right decisions. Because then your decisions will make you.*

Maybe you've had great damage done already, with bitter memories and unerasable scars—but *start where you are.*

---

[2] Poll of 1,250 adults conducted 25–29 Aug. 1989, by Louis Harris and Associates, Inc. Results should be accurate to within three percentage points. *Business Week,* Sept. 1989, 175.

[3] *Business Week,* Sept. 1989, 175.

The journey of a thousand miles begins with a single step

Right now, alone before Him or with your group, why don't you sign your name to new commitments? If you have a marriage partner, hopefully sign together. Then bring your signed book to your final group session for report, dedication, and prayer.

Drastic Don'ts:

---

1. Lord, I'm not going to try to drag my family back to yesterday— that's impossible. But I want to go back to the Bible and courageously follow what You want us to do, together as a family.

_____
your signature

_____
your partner's signature

2. Lord, I'm not going to divorce, from here on, ever.
[If you now have a marriage partner] As I did when we married, I surrender my heart again to lifelong commitment, faithfulness, love.

_____
your signature

_____
your partner's signature

Drastic Do's:

---

1. Lord, give me the courage to slow down, to truly seek to capture the elegance, the grace, of a more simple life, as You desire for me. Work this in me as I surrender to Your Spirit's control.

_____
your signature

_____
your partner's signature

2. Lord, I'm going to seek as a lifestyle to stay close to my kids until they're out of the nest. Please make them great men and women of God.

_____

your signature

_____

your partner's signature

3. Lord, as a loving, faithful Father, please continue to discipline me, and help me to do the same with those You have given me.

_____

your signature

_____

your partner's signature

4. Lord, with the loving firmness of Your Holy Spirit, I'm going to slash the TV watching.

_____

your signature

_____

your partner's signature

5. Lord, I want to model and teach "male" and "female."

_____

your signature

_____

your partner's signature

6. Lord, I want to model and teach respect for authority.

_____

your signature

_____

your partner's signature

7. Lord, I want to seek after the values of Your Word, and model them and teach them to my children.

_____
your signature

_____
your partner's signature

8. Lord, I want to *believe You.* "Help me overcome my unbelief!" (Mark 9:24). I want to live not in unhealthy fears but in joyous trust in You.

_____
your signature

_____
your partner's signature

9. Lord, in these precious years, teach our family to "cocoon"—to love our home, our table, our family altar.

_____
your signature

_____
your partner's signature

10. Lord, please preside over my [our] finances. And as I [we] handle them in obedience to You, I trust You to care for all our needs.

_____
your signature

_____
your partner's signature

_____
Date

If you've made these new commitments to the Lord, would you write and tell me? I'd love to hear.

Your friend in Christ,

Anne Ortlund
c/o Renewal Ministries
4500 Campus Dr., Suite 662
Newport Beach, CA 92660